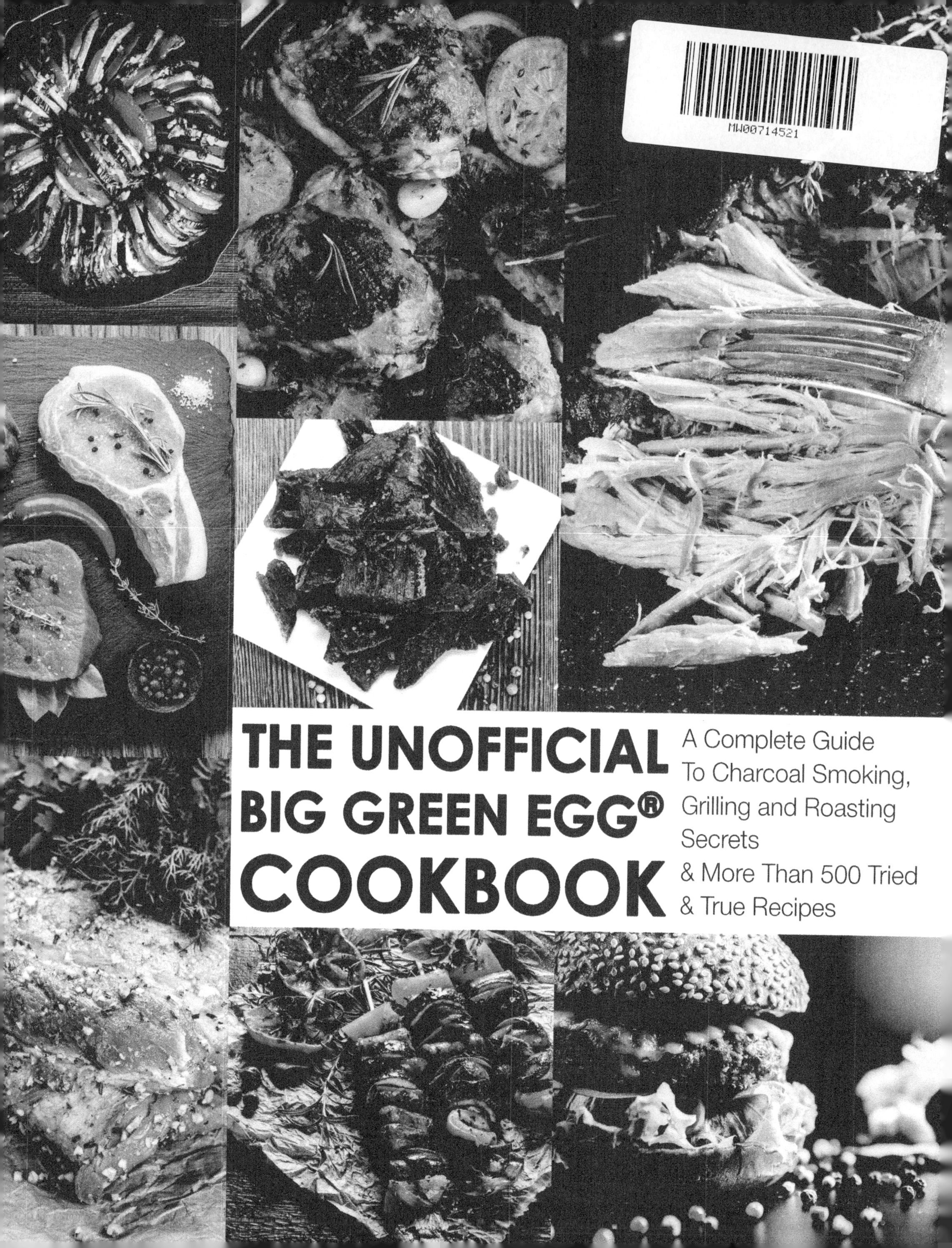

THE UNOFFICIAL BIG GREEN EGG® COOKBOOK

A Complete Guide To Charcoal Smoking, Grilling and Roasting Secrets & More Than 500 Tried & True Recipes

The Unofficial Big Green Egg® Cookbook: A Complete Guide To Charcoal Smoking, Grilling and Roasting Secrets & More Than 500 Tried & True Recipes

Cooking With A Foodie publishes its books in a variety of digital and print formats. Some content that appears in print may not be available in digital format, and vice versa.

ISBN: Print 978-1-944797-03-4 | Ebook

The following images are licensed by Shutterstock:
Cover:
(Front) Anna Shepulova, Dar1930, HandmadePictures, Valentyn Volkov, DronG, zi3000, martiapunts, GreenArt, Durch Goncharov_Artem

Interior:
Lena Ivanova: p. 4 | dbullock: p. 13, | Sophie James: p. 15 | Kichigin: p. 16 | margouillat photo : p. 19 | Valentyn Volkov: p. 21, 22, 23 | 7th Son Studio: p. 25, 29 | Alex Staroseltsev: p. 25 | goir: p. 25 | Binh Thanh Bui: p. 25 | DronG: p. 31, 32 | Warut Prathaksithorn: p. 32 | AnjelikaGr: p. 33 | Diana Taliun: p. 34, 37 | JIANG HONGYAN: p. 35 | Tiger Images: p. 35 | Levent Konuk: p. 39 | geniuscook_com: p. 41 | Enlightened Media: p. 41 | Kelvin Wong: p. 41 | Bon Appetit: p. 43 | siamionau pavel: p. 44 | Richard Griffin: p. 45 | Efired: p. 46 | farbled: p. 49 | James Stiles Photography: p. 50 | MaraZe: p. 51 | Jan Havlicek: p. 73, 85 | Picsfive: p. 113 | Ralf Beier: p. 120 | Picsfive: p. 208, 214 | Brent Hofacker: p. 233 | MSPhotographic: p. 244 | GreenArt: p. 253 | Amarita: p. 257 | minadezhda: p. 275

A PERSONAL INVITATION TO JOIN THE FIRESIDE PIT

Hi BBQ Friend,

Thank you for checking out my book. I think you'll love it.

I'm very grateful to have wonderful readers who support us, so I'm going to extend to you an invitation to join my exclusive club—**the Fireside Pit.**

This is a brand new oer I created to see whether folks would be interested in seeing more great products from me. It will be like a reside chat by the barbecue pit.

Once in a while, you will receive promotional offers on top-of-the-line products that either I sell or ones from companies I personally trust.

Membership is always free, even if you decide to leave and come back later.

What do Fireside Pit Members get?

1. Get recipes, secrets and techniques straight from the pros right to your inbox
2. Get printable BBQ information guides and charts
3. Incredible offers on popular bbq and kitchen products like the one featured below

Sign Up At fpclub.smokeandgrillmeat.com

Contents

THE ULTIMATE BIG GREEN EGG® GUIDE 5
THE SCIENCE OF GRILLING & BARBECUE 11
THE SCIENCE OF FLAVOR 13
CHARCOAL GUIDE 14
SMOKING ON THE BIG GREEN EGG® 15
FREQUENTLY ASKED BARBECUE QUESTIONS 18
MEAT BUYING GUIDE 20
BEEF 20
PORK 30
LAMB 38
POULTRY 42
TOOL GUIDE 46
IS IT DONE YET? 47
TEMPERATURE GUIDE BY CUT 48
A WORD ABOUT COOKING OUTDOORS 50
RECIPES 50
Rubs, Marinades, and Sauces 51
Beef 68
Roasts 69
Burgers 78
Steaks 84
Poultry 92
Whole Chicken 93
Wings & Things 98
Other Poultry 110
Pork 117
Roasts 118
Chops 129
Ribs 137
Seafood 142
Fish 144
Shellfish 154
Pizza 165
Sides & Salads 183
Desserts 205
GETTING THE MOST FROM YOUR BIG GREEN EGG® 221
BEGINNERS GUIDE TO USING A DUTCH OVEN 222
Dutch Oven Recipes 223
Chicken 224
Beef 231
Pork & Seafood 239
Casseroles 247
Sides 255
Desserts 263
Bread & Biscuits 273

The Ultimate Big Green Egg® Guide

Getting Started With Your Big Green Egg®

Congratulations on your purchase! You are well on your way to cooking delicious food over charcoal in one of the easiest pieces of equipment on the planet! Before you begin, there are a few things to remember.

1. Always use your Big Green Egg® (BGE®) on a flat, level surface away from structures or trees.
2. The EGG® is designed to be used with a metal nest so a gap below the EGG® can enhance airflow. DO NOT place the nest on a flammable surface. Ideally, your Big Green Egg's® nest should rest on a non-porous (preferably granite) tile that is sufficiently thick for heat protection of the surface below.
3. DO NOT leave the dome open. Remember, "if you're looking, you're not cooking". Furthermore, never leave your BGE® unattended in high winds.
4. The first time you light your BGE®, do not allow the temperature to exceed 350°F / 177°C. This will allow the gasket adhesive to cure and adhere to the EGG®.
5. NEVER use lighter fluid to light your charcoal. These chemicals alter the flavor of your food. Instead, use BGE® charcoal starters or the BGE® electric charcoal starter to light your coals.
6. When you are moving your BGE®, first make sure it has completely cooled. Never try to move a warm or hot BGE®. The EGG® is designed to be gently pulled, never pushed. Always move it with a partner over flat, level surfaces.
7. When cooking above 400°F / 204°C, be sure to lift the lid off the EGG® about 1-2 inches before opening the dome completely. This allows heat to escape the egg in a controlled manner while preventing injury. This process is called "Burping the EGG®".

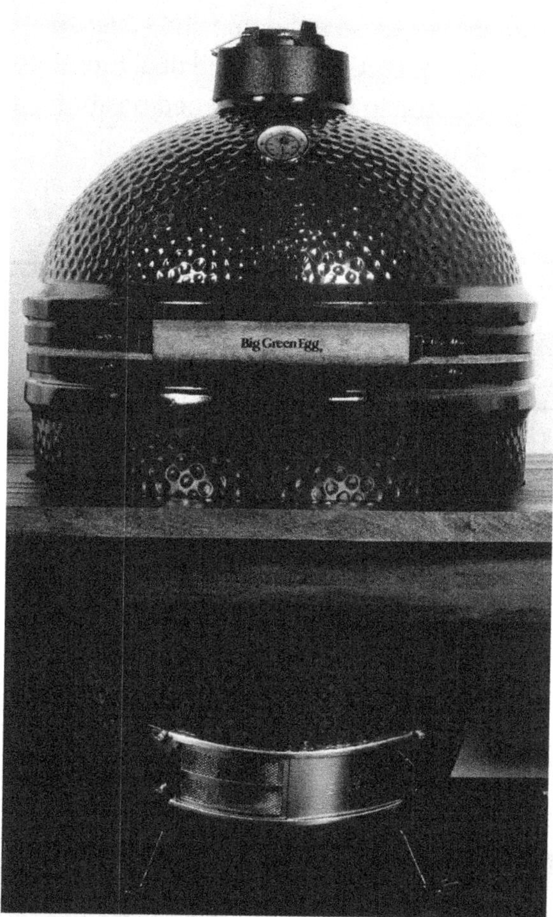

Lighting Your Big Green Egg®

The Big Green Egg® is easy to light and easy to use. By following these steps, you can be cooking over natural charcoal in minutes.

1. Rake out any ash from the firebox using an ash tool.
2. Remove the cap from the EGG® and slide open the stainless steel draft door.
3. Pour natural lump charcoal into the EGG® to the top line of the firebox.
4. Nestle your charcoal starter into the charcoal and light. If using an electric starter, nestle it beneath a layer of charcoal and plug the starter in.
5. Replace the cooking grill and after 7 minutes, close the dome and cover the top of the EGG® with the dual function metal top in the fully opened position. If you are using an electric starter, after 7 minutes, remove the electric starter and unplug it. Be sure to place the starter on a heat proof surface (cement, granite, or concrete are ideal) to allow it to cool before storage. Replace the cooking grill and close the dome with the metal top fully open.
6. When your desired temperature is reached, it's time to cook!
7. Once you have finished cooking, you will notice there is quite a bit of lump coal left in your EGG®. This can be reused for another cooking session. Simply close the Precision Flow Draft Door completely and replace the Dual Function Metal Top with the EGG®'s cap. This will extinguish the coals completely. To use them again, simply stir the remaining coal with an ash tool and add enough natural lump coal to fill the firebox. Start as you would a new batch of coal.

Cleaning Your Big Green Egg®

NEVER use water to clean the inside of your EGG®. Because the EGG® is made of ceramic, water can seep into its pores. If this water is then heated too quickly, it can cause the EGG® to crack or break.

Between cooking experiences, use an ash tool to rake through unused charcoal, paying special attention to the fire grate. Use the ash tool to dislodge any small pieces of charcoal or ash that are lodged in the air holes of the fire grate as this will prevent your EGG® from heating properly. Open the Precision Flow Draft Door and screen and use the ash tool to sweep any ash into an ash pan. Dispose of the ash in the garbage.

Storing Your Big Green Egg®

The Big Green Egg® can be used in all seasons, but it will remain cleaner if it is covered when not in use. In order to properly store the Big Green Egg® for an extended period of time, you must:

1. Clean the interior and dispose of all of the ash that is inside of the Egg. Make sure to clean the firebox holes, cooking grid, and fire grate and ensure everything is dry before storing the EGG®.
2. Cover the EGG® and store where it will not come in contact with rain or snow during winter months.
3. Before using again, be sure to check for condensation or other moisture build up inside of the EGG®. Light a small amount of charcoal and allow the EGG® to heat at no more than 350°F / 177°C in order to burn off any residue or moisture that may remain.
4. Do not leave an unused EGG® open or with the lid off. Rain or snow should NEVER be allowed inside the EGG®. Because ceramic is porous, water will seep into the EGG® causing it to be less effective when cooking. Should water get inside of the EGG®, light a small amount of charcoal and bring it to no more than 350°F / 177°C until the moisture has evaporated.

Big Green Egg® Accessories

To make the most of your Big Green Egg®, consider purchasing the following accessories:

- **convEGGtor®** - This ceramic plate is designed to provide a heat-directing barrier between your food and the fire. Use the convEGGtor® to transform your Big Green Egg® into and outdoor convection oven. The patented design allows heat to radiate within the dome to allow for effective baking, roasting, and barbecue.
- **Pizza and baking stones** - Your Big Green Egg® can be instantly transformed into a pizza oven by using the convEGGtor® in conjunction with the Big Green Egg® pizza stone. Cook pizzeria style pizzas, french breads, and calzones on this patented stoneware accessory.

- **Charcoal starter - electric** - Starting your Big Green Egg® is as simple as plugging in this easy-to-use electric starter. Simply bury the starter in the middle of your charcoal, plug it in, and in 7 minutes have lit charcoal ready for your cooking pleasure.

- **Charcoal starters** - By using Big Green Egg® charcoal starters, you are assured perfect coals in no time without lighter fluid or chemically soaked "ready light" briquettes. Simply nestle a starter in the natural lump charcoal, light it, and in 7 minutes you will have coals ready for cooking.

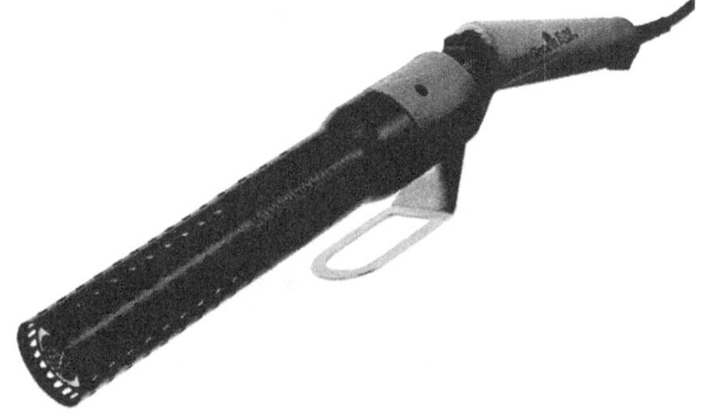

- **Ash tool & ash pan** - Make cleanup a breeze with the Big Green Egg® ash tool and ash pan. Because the BGE® is designed to be self-cleaning, a simple brush with the ash tool is all it takes to keep your EGG® cooking for years to come. The ash pan provides the perfect vehicle to carry any ash from your BGE® to the trash can.

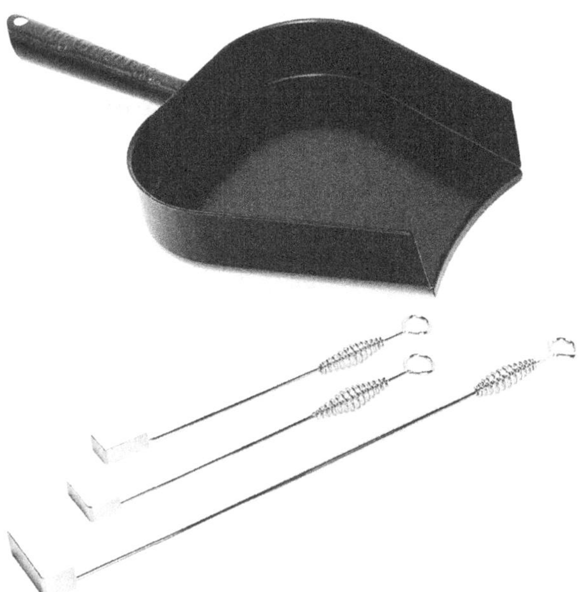

- **Cast iron Dutch oven** - The Big Green Egg® is marketed as an "outdoor oven". In order to get the most out of that claim, you need the proper tools to make slow braised dishes and casseroles. Enter the cast iron Dutch oven. When cared for properly, this piece of equipment can last a lifetime and be passed down to the next generation. It is easy to clean, retains heat well, and turns your Big Green Egg® into the outdoor oven it is meant to be.

Big Green Egg® Hacks

- **Baking -** In less time than what it takes your oven to preheat, your BGE® can be ready to melt cheese, bake, or finish a piece of chicken or fish you start on the stove. Simply prep the EGG® for indirect heat with the convEGGtor® and grate in place and place your heat-proof pan on top.
- **Steaming -** Want to turn your EGG® into a steamer? Simply set up the EGG® for indirect heat and add a heatproof pan of water to the grate. In 4-5 minutes your EGG® will become a steamy environment perfect for steaming vegetables or fish, or proofing bread.
- **Prevent fish from sticking to the grill -** When grilling fish, create a bed of lemons on the grate and place the fish on top. Not only will the fish come out lemony and delicious, it will prevent it from sticking to the grill.
- **Easily check the doneness of your steak -** Don't have a meat thermometer? (You really should get one.) Check the doneness of your steak by using your thumb. Simply place the tip of your thumb to the tip of your index finger and press the flesh of your thumb just below the bottom joint. This texture will resemble the texture of a rare steak. By pressing the tip of your thumb to the tip of your middle finger, your flesh will resemble a medium rare steak. The texture made by pressing the thumb to your ring finger will resemble a medium steak and the texture made by pressing your thumb to your pinky will resemble a medium well steak. If your steak is firmer than that, feed it to the dog. You don't need overcooked beef in your life.
- **Clean your grill with this natural alternative to chemicals -** Don't have a grill brush? Ball up a small piece of aluminum foil and rub it across the grate for easy, disposable clean up. If you're hesitant to use foil and you do not intend to cook fruit first, use a half of a

cut onion to clean your grill. Onions are natural disinfectants and are easier on the environment than harsh chemicals.

- **To make juicier burgers -** Shape the patty with an indentation in the middle and add a pat of butter into the indent during the last few minutes of cooking. The butter will keep the burger moist, juicy, and delicious.
- **Keep chunks of meat from falling through the grill grate -** When skewering meats or veggies, use two skewers instead of one to keep food steady.
- **Sides you didn't know you could grill -** Use your EGG® for epic grilled cheese sandwiches, quesadillas, or garlic bread.
- **A delicious trick to make evenly cooked sausages and hotdogs -** If you are using your EGG® for hot dogs, skewer the hot dog with a bamboo skewer and cut the hot dog on a diagonal down to the skewer. Roll the hot dog, continuing to slice at an angle until you reach the end of the hot dog. You will end up with a perfect spiral cut hot dog. Grill for more crispy goodness on the outside and more surface area for delicious toppings.
- **Use rosemary stems for kebabs -** Replace bamboo skewers with woody, sturdy herbs for kebabs with maximum flavor.
- **Use a Mason jar to easily coat your meats -** Shake dry rub onto meat pieces in a Mason jar! Simply add your dry rub to a wide-mouthed, quart sized canning jar along with pieces of meat. Shake to coat and repeat!
- **Use a muffin tin to keep your condiments organized -** Bonus points for placing the muffin tin inside of a 9x13 pan filled with ice to keep them cold.

Controlling the Temperature

The Big Green Egg® is designed with precise temperature control in mind. From its Precision Flow Draft Door to the Dual Function Metal Top, the Big Green Egg® maintains its heat within an air tight ceramic chamber and sealed fire box. Best of all, the EGG®'s temperature gauge provides precise readings up to 750°F/ 400°C, giving you a level of accuracy that is unmatched in competitor ovens.

1. Light your charcoal using a Big Green Egg® charcoal starter. Allow the coal to burn for 7 minutes with the dome open, or until several coals are lit.
2. Close the dome of the EGG®, leaving the Precision Flow Draft Door and Dual Function Metal Top open to allow the EGG® to come to the desired temperature.
3. When the desired temperature is reached, slightly close the Precision Flow Draft Door and Dual Function Metal Top in order to maintain the temperature inside the dome.
4. When you are finished cooking, close the Precision Flow Draft Door completely and replace the EGG®'s lid on the top. The coals will extinguish themselves and can be used again for another cooking session

The Science Of Grilling & Barbecue

Understanding the magic behind grilling and cooking irresistible barbecue is really just a matter of science. When heat is applied to meat, it starts breaking down physically and chemically - a process known as denaturation. If you learn how to control how the meat changes and when, you will master the process of creating flavorful and tender meat over and over again.

A Quick Breakdown Of What Meat Is Made Of

Depending on the animal you're looking at, most lean muscle tissue is generally 75% water, 20% protein, 5% fat, sugars, minerals and vitamins. Of course, different cuts will vary in these numbers, but it is important to have an overview of what meat is made of to be able to control the cooking process.

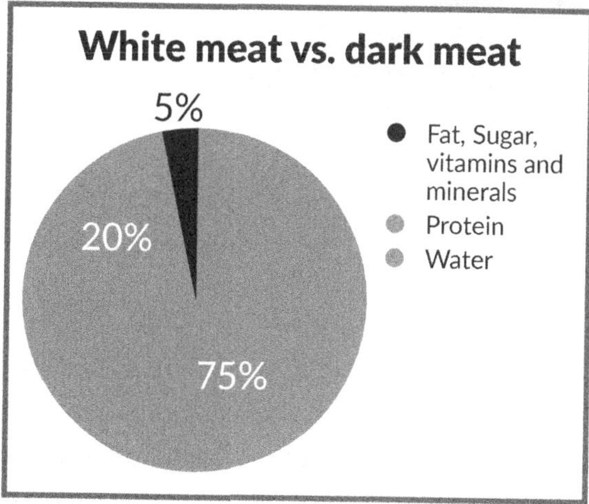

When an animal grazes a field, takes long walks, runs away from threats, and all the other wonderful things animals do, its muscles get tougher and need more oxygen. A compound called myoglobin accepts fuel from blood in the form of oxygen and iron, so the more active an animal is, the more myoglobin it needs. Myoglobin is what causes meat to turn darker and more flavorful. White meat, like the kind in chicken breasts, is only meant for fast bursts of explosive energy - not extended periods of exercise. This is why the lower part of the chicken tends to be darker, since the legs are constantly walking. Birds like ducks or geese tend to be dark all around because all their muscles are actively being used when walking, flying or swimming.

MUSCLE FIBERS

Muscle fibers are basically tubes of fiber that are called sheaths when bundled together. A whole bunch of sheaths bundled together are what make up the muscle. These fibers are like threads filled with water and different kinds of proteins - actin and myosin being the most important since they control the muscle's basic movements by either letting it contract or relax. When an animal grows as nature intended, it's muscle fibers get bigger and tougher from exercise.

CONNECTIVE TISSUE

Without connective tissue, the meat would just fall off the bone -- and no, not in the delicious barbecue way. Most people are familiar with tendons, which directly keep the muscles attached to the bone, but the shiny thin wrapping you see around muscles known as silverskin is also a type of connective tissue that is keeping different kinds of muscles attached together.

Collagen is a soft connective tissue that is found throughout the muscle, usually near fibers and sheaths by holding them together. This tissue melts into a liquid when heated, and covers the muscles in a silky coating that can also add moisture. Melting collagen takes time, so that's why tough cuts of meat are cooked low and slow over a long period of time.

Fats are a type of lipid that give the muscles energy. They can be found beneath the skin, between layers of muscle groups and even stitched inside the muscle fibers and sheaths. Fat is very important in the cooking process because it is absolutely delicious and absorbs much of the essential flavors of the food the animal consumes. Marbling is typically intramuscular fat, and can be seen as thin white or yellow lines in the surface of the meat.

Water content in meat is unfortunately underrated. Most of the liquid in meat is water! No, that red juice leaking out of your meat is not blood (blood is much darker and thicker). The water in the meat is important because it is the most basic source of nutrition for every living thing. We tend to take water quality for granted, but don't forget that everything the animal eats or drinks ends up in its muscles, and eventually in yours if you eat it.

What is the Difference Between Grilling and Barbecuing?

Often time we use the term "grilling" and "barbecue" interchangeably when, in fact, we are talking about two very different processes. Grilling is done over high heat (350-400° and up) where barbecue actually refers to the process of cooking food with smoke over a low, slow heat (350° and lower). Grilling is perfect for meat that is already tender, for lean cuts, and for vegetables and seafood that cannot stand up to low, slow cooking. Barbecue is ideal for cuts that are naturally less tender, less expensive, and in many cases more flavorful.

Direct vs Indirect Grilling

Barbecue and grilling aficionados will talk about "direct grilling" and "indirect grilling" with reference to their grills. Direct Grilling refers to cooking foot hot and fast directly over a heat source. This method is ideal for cuts of meat that are small and either already tender or tend to remain tender when cooked quickly. Indirect Grilling refers to cooking food away from the heat source. Large cuts of meat, or cuts that need to cook "low and slow" in order to achieve maximum flavor and texture are ideal for indirect grilling.

THE SCIENCE OF FLAVOR

On a normal charcoal grill, charcoal is deposited into half of the grill in order to create dual zone temperatures. This allows for both direct and indirect grilling on the same apparatus, at the same time. For instance, our "Beer Can Chicken" recipe would be started on the cooler section of the grill, then moved to the hotter section at the end in order to crisp the skin.

The Big Green Egg's ® patented design allows for indirect grilling without creating dual zone temperatures. The convEGGtor®, a ceramic plate, distributes the heat of the natural lump charcoal around the food. The convEGGtor® makes it possible to cook large pork roasts, whole chickens, and beef roasts without the guess work of indirect heat. Simply add the convEGGtor® once the charcoal has been lit, place the grate in place, and you are ready for indirect grilling.

The convEGGtor® is also an essential tool for getting the most out of your EGG®. Bake bread, cookies, cake, or casseroles with the convEGGtor® in place.

According to science, flavor is made up of three basic things:

1. Taste
2. Physical stimulation
3. Smell

We have tiny receptors in our taste buds that bind to specific compounds that tell us whether what we're eating is sweet, salty, bitter, or sour - the four basic tastes. But our tongues can taste more than just these four sensations by combining hundreds of compounds, all of which go through chemical and physical changes when cooked.

Physical stimulation comprises of all the physical qualities of biting, chewing and swallowing food. When you chomp on a chicken wing, you experience layers of different textures - crispy skin, juicy meat and a hard bone in the center. Even the sounds of biting into different foods affect the physical experience, just as their appearance would. When you eat spicy habanero wings, the burning sensation and pain in your mouth is also considered physical stimulation.

Smell is a complicated sense because it is so closely related to taste. It is believed that most of the flavor that comes from smoke is smell. Smoke consists of water vapor, gases and the tiny particles that result from combusting wood (cellulose and lignin, if you're curious). Smell is probably the most important sense because it is a very powerful stimulus, capable of triggering vivid personal memories unlike any other sense in our body.

Charcoal Guide

For the charcoal novice it would seem like all charcoal is created equal. This is simply untrue. All charcoal began at one time as wood, burned in an oxygen-poor environment until all that is left is lumps of carbon ready to be lit for your cooking pleasure. But that is where the similarity between natural lump charcoal and briquettes ends.

Charcoal Briquettes

While readily available, charcoal briquettes are not actually charcoal. Instead, they are a combination of charcoal and other ingredients molded into uniform, easy-to-burn lumps. Popular brands may include coal, starch, sawdust, and a host of chemicals to make them easy to light and easy to use. These may seem like a bargain, but briquettes actually burn faster than other types of charcoal and result in a lot of ash, making them incompatible with the Big Green Egg®. This bears repeating. NEVER use charcoal briquettes in the Big Green Egg®.

Natural Lump Charcoal

Whether labeled under the Big Green Egg® brand or another brand, natural lump charcoal, or hardwood lump coal is charcoal made from chunks of wood, without fillers or chemicals to enhance their lighting or burning power. This type of charcoal burns longer, with less ash, and can be reused when extinguished properly in your Big Green Egg®. As an added bonus, because Natural Lump Charcoal is made with real wood, it produces a smoky flavor often absent in charcoal briquettes. However, Natural Lump Charcoal is not uniform and therefore does not burn as evenly as its briquette counterpart. This is where the design of the Big Green Egg® comes in. With its airtight ceramic chamber, a single load of Hardwood Lump Charcoal can burn at the perfect smoking temperature (225 to 250 °C) in the EGG® for up to 18 hours without reloading the firebox.

Coconut Charcoal

There is another option that can be used in the Big Green Egg® if Hardwood Lump is unavailable. Charred coconut shells, pressed into a form and known as Coconut Charcoal, is a great option for a sweet smoke with very little ash. This sustainable form of charcoal is a popular, but more expensive option for those who are looking for an alternative to hardwoods. However, it is important to purchase coconut charcoal that does not contain fillers or chemicals or the ash will affect the performance of your EGG®. Bottom line, in order to maximize the performance of your Big Green Egg®, be sure to only use Natural Lump Coal or Coconut Charcoal with no fillers added. Not only will you be assured of using your EGG® for years to come, your food will have that smoke-enhanced flavor you are looking for.

Smoking On The Big Green Egg®

The Big Green Egg® is one of the most versatile outdoor ovens on the market. Not only is it fantastic for grilling a piece of chicken, it can be used to make succulent slow smoked barbecue. But before you begin your low and slow process, check out a few of our best tips for the tastiest barbecue this side of the Mississippi.

WOOD CHIP GUIDE

Wood chips are a wonderful way to enhance the flavor of the natural lump coal you will be using in your Big Green Egg®. Begin by soaking the wood chips for at least 30 minutes to reduce the likelihood of flare-ups. When the charcoal has been lit, add the drained woodchips and close the dome to allow the Big Green Egg® to come to temperature. Any non-resin wood chips can be used, but these are a few of our favorites.

Wood	Level of Smoke	Ideal For:
Alder	Light, sweet	Chicken and fish
Fruit Woods (Cherry, apple, peach, plum)	Light, sweet	Poultry, fish, and pork.
Pecan	Light to medium	Any meat, fish, poultry
Hickory	Medium, rich flavor	Any meat, fish, poultry
Maple	Medium, sweet	Vegetables, poultry, fish, or pork.
Oak	Medium to strong	Pork, beef, lamb
Walnut	Strong	Beef or lamb, but may overpower chicken or fish.
Mesquite	Strong	Beef or lamb, but may overpower chicken or fish.

BARK & SMOKE RINGS

There are indicators barbecue connoisseurs use to determine great barbecue - bark and smoke rings. No, we're not talking about cowboys and dogs, we're talking about the appearance of meat once it has been smoked.

Bark refers to the outer crust on a piece of smoked meat and it is caused by two chemical reactions - the Maillard reaction and polymerization. The process begins when meat is coated in a spice rub where parts are reactive with water and parts are reactive with fat. For instance, salt, a major component in our spice rub recipes, is reactive with water while spices are reactive with the fat from the meat. When the piece of meat is smoked at a low temperature, water vapor from the meat mixes with the water soluble components while the melting fat from the meat mixes with the fat soluble components making a thick slurry on the surface.

Once the water vapor begins to dry, the Maillard reaction kicks in and a crust begins to form on the surface of the meat, turning a dark mahogany. While it may look like your brisket is burned, if it is cooked correctly there is no burned carbon flavor. All you are left with is an intensely flavored crust of pure barbecue goodness.

The ***smoke ring*** refers to the pink ring on the inside of a cut of beef, pork, or chicken. The process is actually quite simple. All meat contains myoglobin, a compound that gives it a pink color when it is raw. Beef contains the most myoglobin, but even chicken thighs contain enough to give them a dark appearance when they are cooked, hence "dark meat". When myoglobin is exposed to nitrogen dioxide in smoke, it locks in the pink color on the edge of the meat giving it a definitive "smoke ring". But because nitrogen dioxide only penetrates the meat from the outside, adding moisture via a mopping sauce can help the gas to penetrate further into the meat giving you a more definitive ring.

THE TEXAS CRUTCH METHOD

Barbecue takes forever. That is a simple fact. It is impossible to start a pork shoulder half an hour before dinner and expect it to turn out the way you want it to. BUT, it is possible to hurry along a large piece of meat a little bit.

The Texas Crutch (also known as The Texas Cheat)

When cooking large piece of meat such as a pork shoulder or brisket, the internal temperature will rise quickly over the first two or three hours and then stop going up. This is called "The Stall Zone" and has been making beginner barbecuers panic for generations. Despite speculation about what causes this plateau in internal temperature, Dr. Greg Blonder, a physicist, recently discovered that it is actually caused by evaporation.

When large pieces of meat are cooked at a low temperature, water is released, evaporates, and cools on the surface of the meat, creating a stall in the internal temperature. The meat is, in effect, sweating the same way humans do.

How do you beat it? You could just wait. The stall zone can last up to six hours, so mow the lawn, watch the game, and come back to the brisket or pork shoulder later. Once the evaporative effect stops, the temperature in the meat will steadily increase again.

Or you can increase the cooking temperature of your meat. By raising the temperature to 275°, the stall doesn't last nearly as long as it would at lower temperatures.

But there is a better way- competition cooks refer to it as the "Texas Crutch". When the meat hits 150°, wrap it in foil with a splash bit of liquid (apple juice or beer are favorites) to finish cooking. Not only does this ensure the bark is a deep mahogany without being tough, the internal temperature cruises right through the stall zone and finishes in less time.

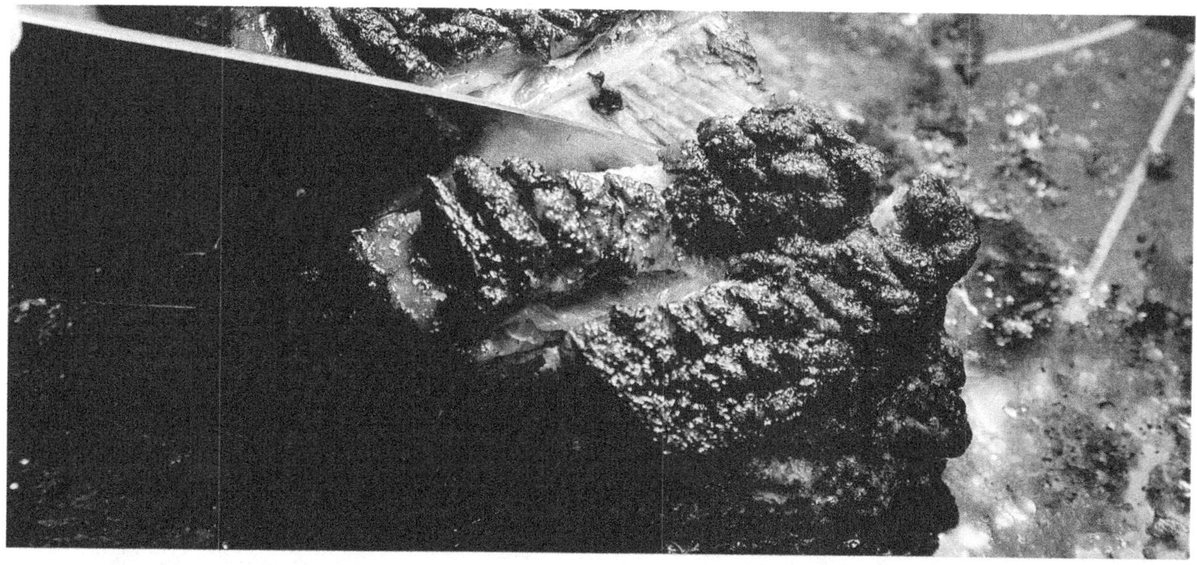

Frequently Asked Barbecue Questions

What is smoke?

Smoke is a complicated byproduct of combusting natural elements such as wood, charcoal or gas. It contains lots of microscopic compounds like creosote, ash, carbon dioxide, carbon monoxide, water vapor, and phenols to name a few. Depending on what you're combusting, the list of contents in the smoke will vary. If you cooked a pair of spare ribs with the same rub on two different grills -- one over a gas grill and the other over charcoal, you can actually see and taste the difference. They both will taste fantastic, but noticeably different. This is why some barbecue aficionados buy more than one kind of smoker.

What kind of smoke should I be looking for?

The nature of smoke depends on several factors ranging from the source of heat to the setup of the smoker. The type of smoke that is coveted by experts is thin, blue smoke; it won't actually be deep blue, but a bluish gray tint. The color is determined by the amount of particles present in the smoke and how well those particles are spreading out.

Black and gray smoke is a result of the fire being deprived of oxygen -- it can make your food taste bitter and nasty, kind of like an ashtray. Billowing white smoke appears as a thick cloud and is also not the kind of smoke you want to cook with. The best way to achieve thin blue smoke is to use natural wood as a heat source, keep the smoker clean of sticky grease and creosote and finally, make sure the fire is getting oxygen.

Why does poultry and pork sometimes stay pink inside when fully cooked?

The simple answer to this question is carbon monoxide, a gas that reacts with myoglobin in meat and turns it pink. Grilling or smoking with heat sources such as charcoal, wood or gas produce plenty of carbon monoxide. Some other causes could be presence of nitrites in the meat or in leafy vegetables that transfer to the meat during the cooking process.

This is why using a thermometer is always highly recommended. Checking for doneness can be deceiving because judging the meat just by its color is simply not reliable.

Should I soak my wood?

When using wood chips with the Big Green Egg, it is important to soak the wood first. Because the wood chips are added directly to the charcoal, soaking the wood first will allow smoke to develop instead of fire.

What is juiciness and how do I help my meat stay juicy?

Meat is made up of around 75% water. Not blood, water. But what cooks refer to as "juiciness" goes beyond the water content in the finished product.

Scientists have been able to measure tenderness with the amount of pressure it takes to cut a piece of meat, however juiciness can only be measured by human experience. In reality, a piece of pork shoulder that has been cooked way past "well done", reaching an internal temperature of 200°, is considered "juicy" where a piece of steak cooked to an internal temperature of 200° is considered inedible charcoal. The difference? Fat and connective tissue.

In order for a piece of meat to retain its juiciness, it must be cooked the appropriate length of time in order to reach the appropriate internal temperature for that cut of meat. Like we've said before, temperature matters more than time and the cut you are using matters almost as much as temperature. Later in this guide you will find a comprehensive meat buying guide to help you choose the appropriate cut of meat for your smoker.

That being said, beginner barbecuers tend to have a better barbecue experience when they choose a less expensive cut of meat with a lot of fat and connective tissue. These pieces are more forgiving of the "low and slow" process, only getting better the longer they are cooked. As the fat and connective tissue melt, they become juicier and more succulent than their leaner counterparts, yielding a delicious end product.

MEAT BUYING GUIDE

WHERE TO BUY MEAT

Do your best to source meat from places like farmer's markets, butchers, or local co-ops. There is a remarkable difference in the quality of local, organic, free-range meat and poultry.

BEEF

Shopping for beef can be incredibly confusing. Every beginning cook has walked into a supermarket to buy a steak and stood paralyzed in the meat case, staring at package after package of beautiful meat, asking themselves what a "chuck tender steak" is. And every beginning cook has, at some point, walked out of the supermarket with the wrong cut of meat for their preparation. Rather than continue to make costly mistakes, check out this handy beef-buying guide for your next barbecue.

BEEF CUTS AND OTHER BASIC BEEF TERMS

Before we start, let's get a few definitions out of the way.

- Primal cuts - In butchering, primal cuts are pieces of meat that are separated from the carcass during butchering.
- Subprimal cuts - Subprimal cuts are made by butchers to break down the larger cuts into more usable pieces. If the loin is the primal cut, the tenderloin would be a subprimal cut.
- Forequarter - Cuts of meat that come from the front of the cow
- Hindquarter - Cuts of meat that come from the back of the cow

PRIMAL CUTS OF BEEF

		Also Known As
Forequarter Cuts	Chuck or shoulder	Bone-in chuck steaks and roasts (arm or blade), and boneless clod steaks and roasts
	Rib	Short ribs, the prime rib and rib-eye steaks
	Brisket	Corned beef or pastrami
	Shank	Used primarily for stews and soups; also used in ground beef
	Plate	Short ribs, Pot roast, and Skirt steak. Also used in ground beef, as it is typically a tough and fatty meat.
Hindquarter cuts	Loin	• Short loin, from which the T-bone and porterhouse, or strip steaks are cut. • Sirloin, which is less tender than short loin, but more flavorful. This can be further divided into top sirloin and bottom sirloin (including tri-tip). • Tenderloin, which is the most tender. It can be removed as a separate subprimal, and cut into filet mignons, tournedos or tenderloin steaks, and roasts (such as for beef Wellington). They can also be cut bone-in to make parts of T-bone and porterhouse steaks.
	Round	Round steak, eye of round, top round, and bottom round steaks and roasts.
	Flank	Flank steak, London broil, and skirt steak.

CLASSIFICATION OF BEEF ACCORDING TO GRADE

Once upon a time, you had to rely on your butcher's word when examining the quality of your meat. Today, the U.S. Department of Agriculture (USDA) classifies quality into three categories: prime, choice, and select. This grading system not only applies to beef but for most meats such as pork and lamb.

Meat Grade According to the USDA	Characteristics	Availability	Cost
Prime	• Has several marble streaks (like "veins") • Tender • Flavorful	• High-end butcher shops • Specialty restaurants	• Twice the price of choice meats, but depends on the cut
Choice	• With some marble streaks on meat • Somewhat tender • Acceptable flavor	• Local meat shops and supermarkets	• Relatively affordable given the quality, but depends on the cut
Select	• With slight marble streaks on meat • Tough • More on the bland side	• Local meat shops and supermarkets	• Cheapest among the three grades of meat

LABELING BASICS AND OTHER TERMS EXPLAINED

Recently consumers have become more interested in where their meat comes from. In response, producers have begun labeling their products with terms such as "grain-fed" or "organic". However, the USDA no longer regulates what beef can be labeled as "grass-fed", so paying more may not always yield a better product. Your best bet is to patron a trusted butcher who knows where his product is raised.

Common Labels	Characteristics	Pros	Cons
Grain-Fed Beef	• Tends to be dark in color • Contains more fat • Has a milder flavor	• The streaks of intramuscular fat in grain-fed beef contributes to the mildly rich flavor of the meat.	• Lower in omega-3 fatty acids • Grain is used by farmers to supplement a cow's diet, but has an affect on the overall quality of its meat.

Common Labels	Characteristics	Pros	Cons
Grass-Fed Beef	• Contains less fat • Chewy texture • Has a gamey odor • Strong, complex flavor	• The meat has less intramuscular fat due to the nature of the animal's diet, thus, the meat is more on the chewy side and has a strong, pungent flavor and odor. • Has a broader range of beneficial fats and nutrients not found in grain-fed meat	• The pungent flavor may turn off some people. • Grass-fed beef tends to be more expensive than grain-fed beef.
Organic	• Raised without antibiotics or hormones • Animals live in conditions that accommodate their ability to graze on pasture • Fed 100% organic feed • Has a "USDA Organic" seal	• The "USDA Organic" seal ensures farmers have adhered to strict guidelines for raising these animals.	• Can be a little pricier than regular meats in the market.
Blade, mechanically or needle tenderized	• Meat has been passed through a machine that punctures it with small, sharp needles or blades to break the connective tissues and muscle fibers that results in a more chewy, tender cut.	• Blade-tenderized beef cuts when cooked tend are indeed more tender (when cooked at 160 degrees)	• The blades and needles used to tenderize the beef may transfer disease-causing bacteria such as E. coli. To counter this contamination, make sure to cook the beef to a safe temperature of 160 degrees.

BUYING BEEF BY CUT

Now that you are thoroughly familiar with the labels on those glorious packages of beautiful meat, it's time to get down to the nitty gritty. What cut do you use for smoking? Braising? Grilling?

PRIMAL CUTS OF BEEF AND OTHER CUTS

1. Beef Primal Cut: Chuck or Shoulder

Shoulder Steak

Characteristics: Relatively lean with a mild beef flavor

Flavor: ★★☆☆☆
Tenderness: ★★☆☆☆
Cost: $
Other name/s: Chuck steak
Recommended Cooking Method: Grilling
Notes & Tips: After cooking, meat should be thinly sliced on a bias.

Top Blade Roast

Characteristics: A boneless, flat cut with a mild flavor, which can sometimes be substituted for a chuck-eye roast.

Flavor: ★★★☆☆
Cost: $$
Other name/s: Chuck roast, first cut, blade roast, top chuck roast
Recommended Cooking Method: Braising, stewing
Notes & Tips: Top blade roasts reach their maximum flavor with long, slow, moist cooking. Try using this cut for your next pot roast for succulent meat and outstanding gravy.

Blade Steak

Characteristics: a small shoulder cut that has a rich flavor and is very tender

Flavor: ★★★☆☆
Tenderness: ★★★☆☆
Cost: $
Other name/s: Top blade steak, flat-iron steak
Recommended Cooking Method: Stir-frying, braising, stewing, broiling, grilling
Notes & Tips: Remove the gristle line at the middle of the meat and cut the steak into thin slices for stir-fries. Also makes great kebabs.

Chuck 7-Bone Roast

Characteristics: a cut based from a number seven-shaped bone that has a rich flavor

Flavor: ★★★☆☆
Cost: $$
Other name/s: Center-cut pot roast, center-cut chuck roast
Recommended Cooking Method: Braising, stewing
Notes & Tips: When braising, add less liquid than you would a top blade roast as this cut already has a deep flavor.

Chuck-Eye Roast

Characteristics: Boneless roast cut from the center (or "eye") of the first five ribs; extremely tender and juicy due to the abundance of fat in the meat

Flavor: ★★★☆☆
Cost: $$
Other name/s: Boneless chuck roll, boneless chuck fillet
Recommended Cooking Method: Braising, stewing, roasting
Notes & Tips: For pot roast, use kitchen twine to handle this cut effectively.

Chuck Shoulder Roast

Characteristics: Mild flavor, not a lot of fat or connective tissue.

Flavor: ★★☆☆☆
Cost: $$
Other name/s: Chuck shoulder pot roast, boneless chuck roast
Recommended Cooking Method: Braising, stewing.
Notes & Tips: Because of its low cost, chuck shoulder roast makes great stew meat. Cut in smaller chunks, brown the meat and cook slowly with root vegetables.

Under-Blade Roast

Characteristics: Its rich flavor is comparable to the seven bone roast but contains more connective tissue and ample amount of fat.

Flavor: ★★★☆☆
Cost: $$
Other name/s: Bottom chuck roast, California roast
Recommended Cooking Method: Braising, stewing, roasting
Notes & Tips: Meat tends to fall apart when carved because of its tenderness.

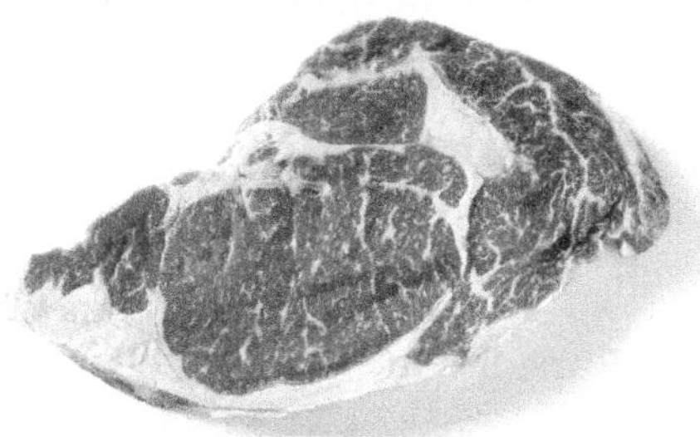

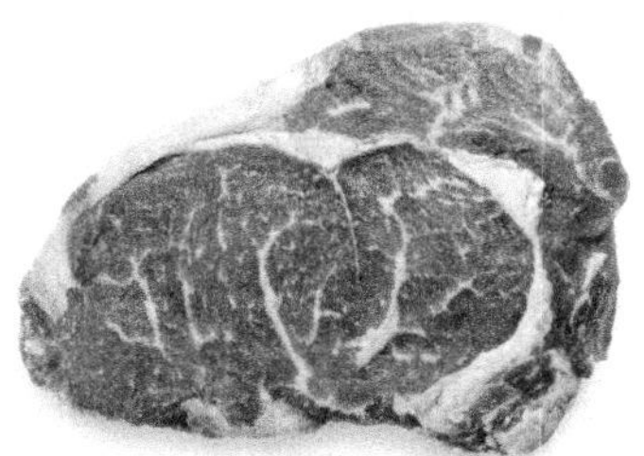

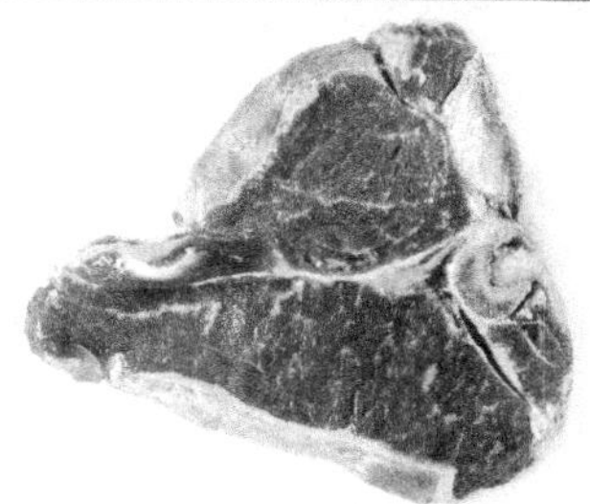

2. Beef Primal Cut: Rib

Rib Steak

Characteristics: A bone-in steak cut from a prime rib roast

Flavor: ★★★☆☆
Tenderness: ★★★☆☆
Cost: $$$
Other name/s: None
Recommended Cooking Method: Grilling, roasting, barbecuing

Rib-Eye Steak

Characteristics: A rib steak without the bone that has an oval shape and a narrow strip of meat that curves around one end; a beefy, tender and juicy cut of beef.

Flavor: ★★★★☆
Tenderness: ★★☆☆☆
Cost: $$$
Other name/s: Spencer steak, Delmonico steak
Recommended Cooking Method: Grilling, pan searing, barbecuing

Rib Roast, First Cut

Characteristics: Rib roast cut consisting of ribs 10 through 12 -- which have the big, single rib-eye section with less fat; closer to the loin end

Flavor: ★★★★☆
Cost: $$$$
Other name/s: Prime rib, loin end, small end
Recommended Cooking Method: Grill roasting, roasting, barbecuing

Rib Roast, Second Cut

Characteristics: A rib roast cut consisting of ribs 6 to 8 or 9, which contains more intramuscular fat that adds flavor into the roast

Flavor: ★★★★☆
Cost: $$$$
Other name/s: Large end
Recommended Cooking Method: Roasting, barbecuing

Beef Ribs

Characteristics: large rib cut from bones 6 to 12 of the prime rib, which are about 8 inches long and perfect for barbecuing

Flavor: ★★★☆☆
Cost: $$
Other name/s: Back ribs
Recommended Cooking Method: Barbecuing
Notes & Tips: Usually sold as a big slab of rib, but some retailers offer smaller cuts with just 3-4 bones per slab.

3. Beef Primal Cut:Short Loin

Strip Steak

Characteristics: A cut that runs along the shell muscle in the center of the steer's back; it is well marbled, has a tight grain with a strong beefy taste and a satisfying chewy texture

Flavor: ★★★★☆
Cost: $$$
Tenderness: ★★★☆☆
Other name/s: Shell steak, top loin steak, sirloin strip steak, New York Strip steak, Kansas City strip steak
Recommended Cooking Method: Grilling, pan searing

Tenderloin

Characteristics: The most tender cut of beef with a mild, almost non-beefy flavor

Flavor: ★☆☆☆☆
Cost: $$$$
Other name/s: Whole fillet, Chateaubriand
Recommended Cooking Method: Grilling, roasting
Notes & Tips: Unpeeled varieties of this cut come with a big layer of exterior fat that should be removed prior to cooking.

For peeled varieties, the fat is seen distributed throughout the cut and may be left as is.

T-Bone Steak

Characteristics: A cut named after the T-shaped bone that appears through the meat. The bone separates two different cuts of meat - the tenderloin on the right and the strip on the left.

Flavor: ★★★★☆
Cost: $$$
Tenderness: ★★★☆☆
Other name/s:
Recommended Cooking Method: Grilling, pan searing

Porterhouse Steak

Characteristics: A large T-bone steak with a bigger cut of tenderloin than a traditional T-Bone steak. It has a well-balanced texture and flavor like the T-bone steak.

Flavor: ★★★★☆
Cost: $$$
Tenderness: ★★★☆☆
Other name/s: None
Recommended Cooking Method: Grilling, pan searing

Filet Mignon

Characteristics: A cut from the narrow end of the tenderloin that is 1-2 inches thick. Filet Mignon has a very mild beef flavor and a pleasantly tender texture

Flavor: ★☆☆☆☆
Cost: $$$$
Tenderness: ★★★★☆
Other name/s: Chateaubriand, tenderloin steak, tournedo
Recommended Cooking Method: Grilling, pan searing
Notes & Tips: Because people tend to value texture over flavor, tenderloin is among the most expensive cuts of beef you can buy. It also goes by a few different names.

Chateaubriand is a center-cut steak cut from the largest part of the tenderloin, around 3 inches thick; it is big enough for two servings.

Tournedos are the smallest tenderloin cuts that come from the section toward the tip end of the tenderloin, around 1 inch thick only.

4. Beef Primal Cut: Sirloin

Sirloin Tri-Tip Roast

Characteristics: a small, triangular-shaped roast with a gentle flavor and moist, spongy texture.

Flavor: ★★☆☆☆
Cost: $$
Other name/s: Triangle roast
Recommended Cooking Method: Grilling, barbecuing
Notes & Tips: Tri-tip is a popular beef cut among West Coast butchers. East Coast butchers turn this cut into sirloin tips, or "steak tips".

5. Beef Primal Cut: Round

Cube Steak

Characteristics: A chewy cut of meat without a lot of fat or connective tissue.

Flavor: ★☆☆☆☆
Tenderness: ★☆☆☆☆
Cost: $
Other name/s: Minute steak
Recommended Cooking Method: Cube steaks are best when pounded with a meat tenderizer and pan seared. This cut is most popularly used for chicken fried steak.

Top Round Steak

Characteristics: A cut with a pleasant beefy taste and chewy texture.

Flavor: ★★★☆☆
Tenderness: ★★☆☆☆
Cost: $
Other name/s: Inside round cut, London broil
Recommended Cooking Method: Broiling, grilling
Notes & Tips: To reduce the chewiness of this steak, cook it to medium doneness and slice it super thin.

Bottom Round Rump Roast

Characteristics: A cut that is slightly less tender than the top round roast; juicy and has a mild flavor when cooked.

Flavor: ★★☆☆☆
Cost: $
Other name/s: Bottom round oven roast, bottom round pot roast, round roast
Recommended Cooking Method: Roasting

Top Round Roast

Characteristics: A cut similar to the top sirloin roast which has a good texture, flavor, and juiciness.

Flavor: ★★★☆☆
Cost: $
Other name/s: Top round steak roast, top round first cut
Recommended Cooking Method: Roasting
Notes & Tips: Upon serving, cut this roast into thinner slices as it tends to become chewy when sliced thick.

Eye-Round Roast

Characteristics: A boneless cut that slices nicely, the eye-round roast can be as flavorful as other top cuts with proper treatment.

Flavor: ★★☆☆☆
Cost: $
Other name/s: Round-eye roast
Recommended Cooking Method: Grilling, barbecuing
Notes & Tips: Because this roast reaches its maximum tenderness in a low-heat oven, barbecuing this roast to a medium doneness is ideal. Be sure to slice it thin when serving.

Bottom Round Roast

Characteristics: Because it doesn't have a distinct flavor of its own, bottom round roasts are ideal for stewing and braising.

Flavor: ★☆☆☆☆
Cost: $
Other name/s: None
Recommended Cooking Method: Braising, stewing
Notes & Tips: Braise or stew the bottom round roast in flavorful liquid. A combination of red wine and beef broth would be nice.

6. Beef Primal Cut: Brisket, Shank, Plate, Flank

Skirt Steak

Characteristics: A thin cut from the underside of the cow with more fat content than flank steak.

Flavor: ★★★☆☆
Tenderness: ★★★☆☆
Cost: $$$
Other name/s: Philadelphia steak, fajita steak
Recommended Cooking Method: Grilling, stir-frying, pan searing
Notes & Tips: Before cooking, remove the silverskin on the back of the steak for maximum tenderness. Grill quickly over a high heat and thinly slice across the grain for maximum tenderness.

Flank Steak

Characteristics: A wide, flat cut from the underside of the animal bearing a recognizable longitudinal grain.

Flavor: ★★★☆☆
Tenderness: ★★★☆☆
Cost: $$$
Other name/s: Jiffy steak
Recommended Cooking Method: Grilling, stir-frying, pan searing
Notes & Tips: This steak is quite thin for its size, so it cooks quickly. **Flank steak should never be cooked past medium doneness. Always thinly slice the steak across the grain, with a heavy bias.**

Hanger Steak

Characteristics: The hanger steak refers to the large muscle near the diaphragm on the underside of the cow that hangs down the center of the animal (thus the name hanger steak).

Flavor: ★★★☆☆
Tenderness: ★☆☆☆☆
Cost: $$
Other name/s: Butcher's steak, hanging tender, hanging tenderloin
Recommended Cooking Method: Grilling, pan searing
Notes & Tips: Hanger steak is around a third of the price of tenderloin with a lot more flavor. **Be sure to have your butcher remove all of the excess fat and silver skin that typically surrounds this cut of meat.**

Brisket

Characteristics: a large steak with a rectangular shake that weighs approximately 13 pounds and is further cut into 2 sub cuts: flat and point cuts.

Flavor: ★★★☆☆
Cost: $$
Other name/s: None
Recommended Cooking Method: Braising, barbecuing
Notes & Tips: The flat cut brisket is a thinner, leaner cut good for slow cooking.

If smoking is the name of the game, you will want a brisket with a nice fat cap on top to keep the meat moist.

Shank

Characteristics: A cut derived from the cross-section of the front leg with a rounded shape; a fatty, but tasty cut.

Flavor: ★★☆☆☆
Cost: $
Other name/s: Center beef shank
Recommended Cooking Method: Braising
Notes & Tips: This cut is available with or without the bone in.

The shank is equivalent to the osso buco of a calf's meat.

It is good to use in soups or simmered dinner recipes like pot-au-feu.

7. Beef Primal Cut: Brisket, Shank, Plate, Flank (cont.)

Short Ribs

Characteristics: A meaty cut that is usually taken from the underside of the cow (but can be cut in various parts, too) with each rib bone detached and cut crosswise.

Flavor: ★★★☆☆
Cost: $
Other name/s: English-style short ribs
Recommended Cooking Method: Stewing, braising, barbecuing

Flanken-Style Short Ribs

Characteristics: similar to the English-style short ribs, but are cut thinly into cross sections with 2-3 meaty bone pieces.

Flavor: ★★★☆☆
Cost: $$
Other name/s: Flanken
Recommended Cooking Method: Barbecuing, braising
Notes & Tips: These short ribs are more rare than the English style short ribs, but are generally sold in butcher shops.

Meat Facts:

- The leanest cuts of meat from four-legged animals almost always come from the loin. Look for words like sirloin or tenderloin

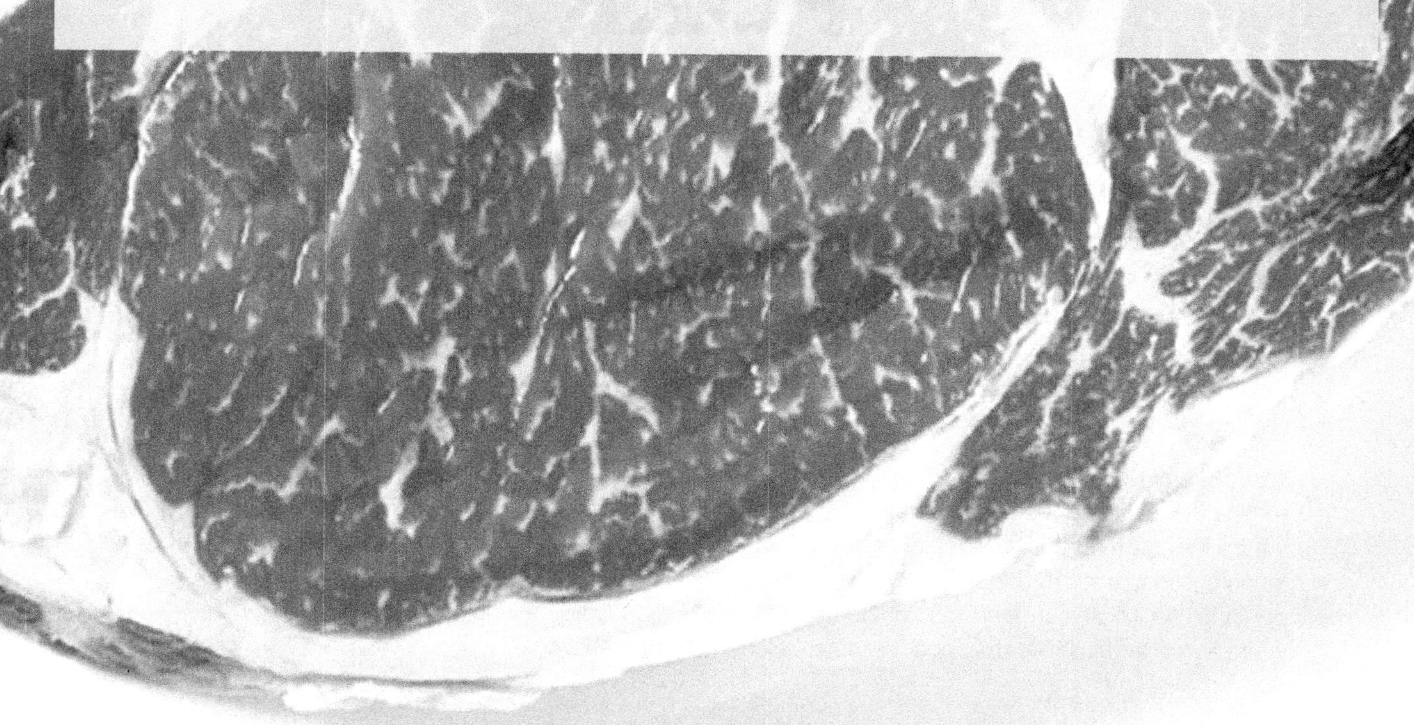

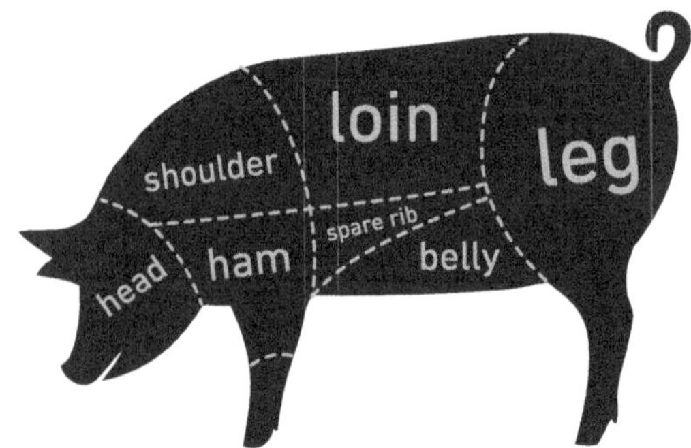

PORK

Once upon a time, American society really only ate pork for breakfast. Chicken was considered healthy, beef was thought to be luxurious, and pork was made into ham and bacon and the occasional pork chop. Thought to be too fatty to be eaten on a regular basis, ordinary citizens went about their days ignoring the thousands of ways pork could be transformed into delicious dishes.

Modern breeding systems and feeding techniques over the years created pigs with a third less fat than their porcine ancestors. Ingenious marketing in the early 1990s brought pork into American consciousness as "the other white meat" and just like that, pork became a relatively inexpensive, delicious, versatile protein addition to our daily diet.

Just like beef, there are a lot of different cuts and retailer labels for pork. Using our handy guide, you can become an expert pork purchaser.

LABELING

Heritage Breeds

Over the last decade, consumers have become more aware of how their pork is being raised and the effect the life of the animal has on the meat. The term "Heritage Breeds" has recently come into vogue when describing pork products, but what does it actually mean? According to The Livestock Conservancy, in order for pork to be labeled as a "Heritage Swine", it must be a true genetic breed of swine that has had a continuous breeding population in the US since 1925. However, the term "Heritage Breeds" when referring to meat is not USDA regulated and therefore open to interpretation.

For some farmers, heritage breed pork is a general term for meat from livestock that are raised as they would have been hundreds of years ago. Animals are allowed to feed on grass and grain and are raised without artificial hormones.

For other farmers, heritage breed pork comes from breeds common to the Americas hundreds of years ago, such as Berkshire and Duroc. The idea behind the propagation of heritage breeds is that they considerably more flavorful than their commercial counterparts and they protect the species as a whole. If all pigs were of one breed, a particularly nasty and widespread disease could wipe out the entire pork production industry.

While the USDA does not regulate the term "heritage breed pork", a high quality butcher who has a relationship with his farmers will be able to direct you to higher quality, more flavorful cuts of meat.

Quality and pH Level

According to Kenneth Prusa, Food Science professor at the Iowa State University, the color of pork is a strong indication of quality. Pork meat from both Berkshire and Duroc breeds have a vibrant pink to red tint to them (although Duroc isn't as red as the crimson-colored Berkshire breed of pork), which indicates that the meat has a higher pH than their supermarket pork counterparts. Prusa added that pH is the "overall driver of quality in pork." Hence, the higher the pH of the pork, the better the quality of the pork.

In fact, just a small difference in the pH level of pork greatly affects the texture and flavor of the meat. Berkshire breeds are strategically raised to have a little higher pH level than normal pigs; the normal pH for mammals is approximately 7. In effect, the slightly higher pH of Berkshire breeds makes the meat firmer, tastier a deeper red. Also, Prusa added that the pH level is more significant than the fat content of the pork in terms of assessing the flavor of the meat.

Factors Affecting pH Level

Husbandry. Berkshire pigs are grown in an environment with minimal stress. It is believed that when the animal experiences less stress and is more relaxed, its blood flows more evenly. This results in flavorful juices distributed well into its system.

Slaughtering methods. When Berkshire pigs are scheduled to be slaughtered, they are also subjected to little stress so that there wouldn't be a buildup of lactic acid in the muscles that results to a lower pH. The quality of the animal's last few days can greatly affect the final quality of the flavor and texture of its meat. Obviously, animals raised naturally are the least likely to be subject to high-stress environments like being locked in cages.

Blast chilling. Another way to avoid decreasing the pH level of the meat is by blast chilling it immediately after slaughter. It is important to note that once blood flow stops, the pH level of the meat rapidly decreases, so blast chilling it helps preserve the higher pH level of the pig.

ENHANCED PORK

Since regular pigs found in supermarkets are leaner and less flavorful than their heritage breed counterparts, many meat suppliers use flavor-enhancing meat injections to improve the overall flavor of modern pork.

Sodium Solution

Enhanced pork products are injected with sodium solution to improve the flavor of the meat. The solution is a mixture of water, salt, potassium lactate, sodium phosphates, sodium diacetate, sodium lactate, and other flavor-enhancing agents. Such an enhancers are often used in leaner cuts like loin and tenderloin to add flavor to an otherwise bland cut.

While sodium solution injections enhance the flavor of the pork, they do so at a price. Pork injected with a flavor-enhancing solution weighs 7-15 percent more than unenhanced pork products. As a result, the flavor tends to be salty and leave a spongy texture when it is cooked. Also, enhanced pork tends to lose almost six times its moisture content when frozen and thawed.

Nitrite and Nitrate Content

Nitrites and nitrates are food preservatives that fight bacteria in processed or cured meats. They are also the compounds that give meat its deep pink color. Both compounds are typically found in the brine of cured pork products such as ham, bacon, and lunch meat. Celery juice is often used as an alternative to chemical preservatives because of its naturally high nitrate content.

These compounds are generally considered safe to consume, although nitrites and nitrates have been linked to migraine headaches in some individuals. Even if pork products are labeled as "nitrite- or nitrate-free", these compounds are usually present in a natural form as a result of the curing process.

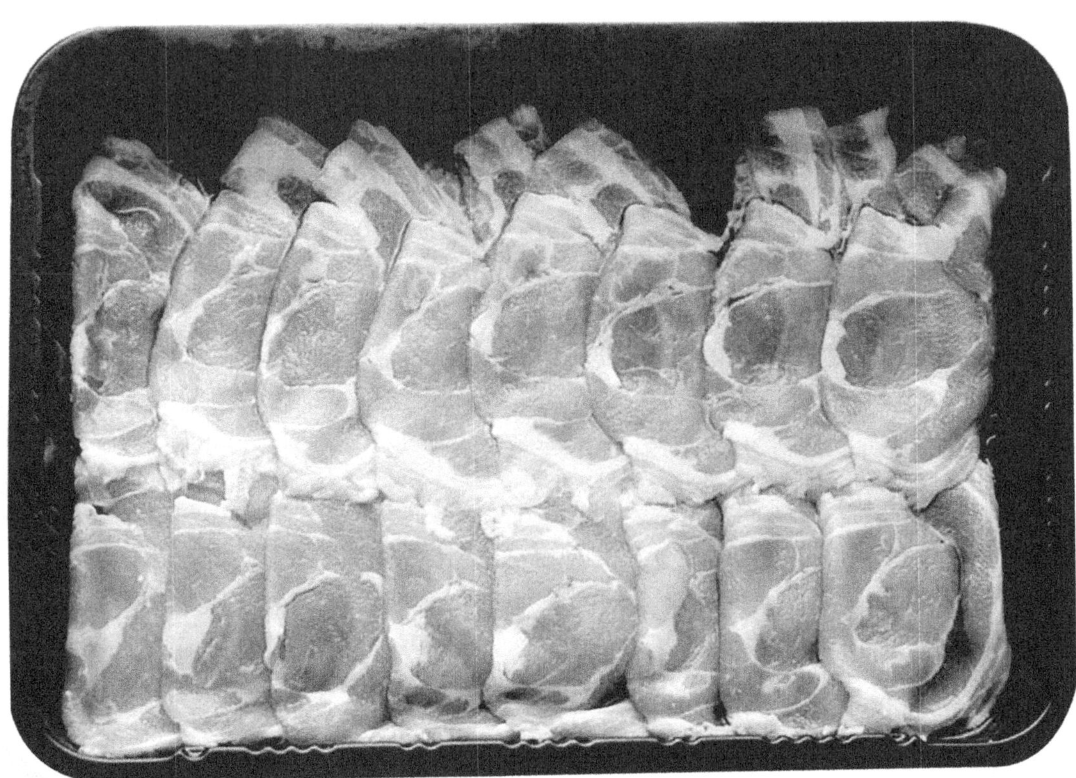

PRIMAL CUTS OF PORK

Pork is broken down into four initial series of cuts, more commonly known as "primal cuts" -- which include the shoulder, side or belly, loin, and leg. These primal cuts are wholesale items from the butcher level and are then sold in various cuts by supermarkets and local meat shops.

PRIMAL CUTS OF PORK

1. Shoulder

There are two basic portions from this cut of pork, -- the blade shoulder and picnic shoulder:

Blade shoulder - Cut from the upper section of the pork shoulder, a blade shoulder is evenly marbled with fat and holds a lot of connective tissue. Cuts from this portion of the pork shoulder are typically used for slow cooking methods like stewing, braising and barbecuing.

Picnic shoulder - Cut from the section near the front leg area of the pig. Cuts from this portion of the pork shoulder are quite similar to the cuts from the blade shoulder, but are considered to be more economical.

2. Side or Belly

As the name suggests, this portion contains the most fat of all of the cuts from the underside of the animal. This primal cut is where the spare ribs and bacon cuts are taken.

3. Loin

The cut from the section between the shoulder and the back legs is called the loin. It is the leanest and most tender part of the pig.

Popular cuts found in this area include loin chops, rib chops, loin roasts, and tenderloin roasts. Because of their lack of fat, it is important to cook them with a meat thermometer as they can become dry and lose flavor if overcooked.

4. Leg

The legs at the back of the animal are usually referred to as "ham". They are often sold as large roasts in fresh or cured varieties.

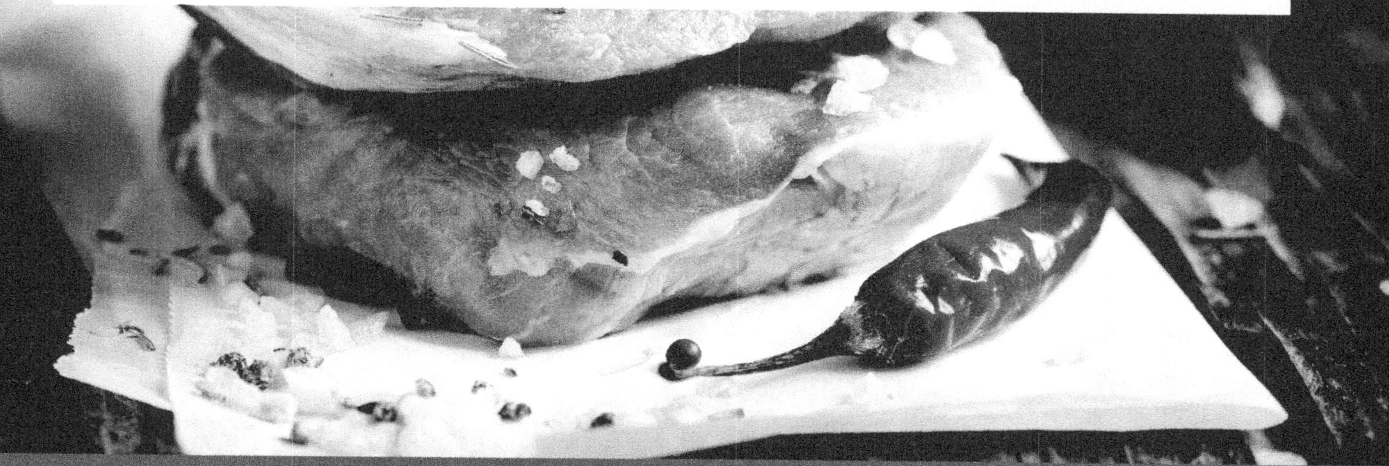

SHOPPING FOR PORK

At the supermarket or local meat shop level, each primal cut is sold in a variety of other cuts and under a litany of different labels. This handy guide will ensure you are familiar with the kind of cut you need before heading to the nearest supermarket or butcher.

1. Primal Cut: Shoulder

Pork Shoulder

Characteristics: Contains a lot of fat and connective tissue; sold either bone-in or boneless

Flavor: ★★★★☆
Cost: $
Other name/s: Fresh picnic roast, picnic roast, picnic shoulder, shoulder arm picnic roast
Recommended Cooking Method: Braising, roasting, grill roasting, barbecuing

Pork Butt Roast

Characteristics: Big cut weighing up to 8 pounds; can be sold with the bone in; has an excellent flavor

Flavor: ★★★★☆
Cost: $$
Other name/s: Boston butt, Boston shoulder, pork butt
Recommended Cooking Method: Stewing, braising, slow roasting, barbecuing
Notes & Tips: This roast can be sold in smaller cuts and is usually packaged in a mesh netting that holds the roast together.

2. Primal Cut: Side or Belly

St. Louis Style Spareribs

Characteristics: This style of cut uses whole ribs near the belly area of the animal; weighs about 5 pounds or more, as it consists of the brisket bone and meat.

Flavor: ★★★★☆
Cost: $$$
Other name/s: Spareribs
Recommended Cooking Method: Barbecuing, roasting
Notes & Tips: A popular cut for barbecuing because it can be easily managed on a grill or smoker. The connective tissue and fat on St. Louis style spareribs keep the meat moist during long, slow cooking.

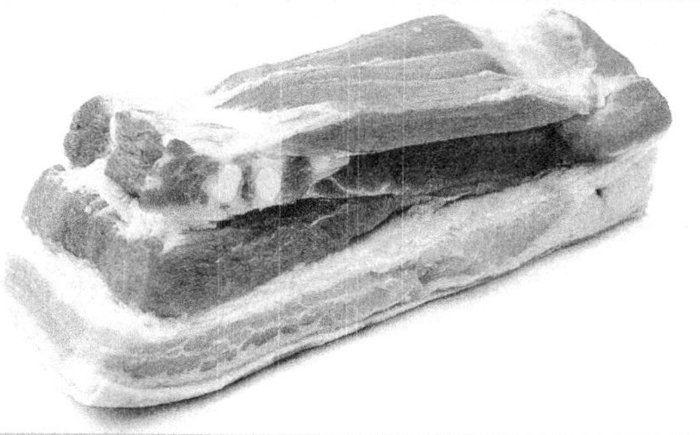

3. Primal Cut: Loin

Rib Chop

Characteristics: A cut taken from the rib area of the loin and has a recognizable bone running along one side and a big eye of loin muscle; these chops are fatty and juicy as long as they are not overcooked.

Flavor: ★★★☆☆
Cost: $$$
Other name/s: Pork chops end cut, rib cut chops
Recommended Cooking Method: Braising, roasting, pan searing, grilling
Notes & Tips: Rib chops can be sold boneless.

Blade Chop

Characteristics: A cut taken from the shoulder end of the loin, which contains a lot of fat and is quite tough; has a porky, pleasant flavor and is juicy

Flavor: ★★★☆☆
Cost: $$$
Other name/s: Pork chop end cut
Recommended Cooking Method: Braising, barbecuing

Center-Cut Chop

Characteristics: A chop with a distinct bone that divides the tenderloin muscle from the loin meat; contains less fat than rib chops, but have a mild pork flavor

Flavor: ★★☆☆☆
Cost: $$
Other name/s: Loin chops, top loin chops
Recommended Cooking Method: Grilling, searing
Notes & Tips: Cooking this chop can be challenging since the tenderloin portion tends to cook faster than the loin section.

Sirloin Chops

Characteristics: a chop cut from the sirloin or the hip end of the pig containing a piece of the hipbone, tenderloin, and loin meat.

Flavor: ★★☆☆☆
Cost: $
Other name/s: Sirloin steaks
Recommended Cooking Method: Pan searing, braising, barbecuing

Baby Back Ribs

Characteristics: Cut from the area of the rib cage nearest to the backbone, these ribs are smaller and leaner than spareribs.

Flavor: ★★★☆☆
Cost: $$$$
Other name/s: Riblets, loin back ribs
Recommended Cooking Method: Barbecuing, braising
Notes & Tips: Ribs benefit from low and slow cooking. Combine braising and smoking for optimum texture and flavor.

Country-Style Ribs

Characteristics: A boneless rib cut from the side just above the rib cage, from the blade end of the loin; the meat is tender with a rich flavor.

Flavor: ★★★☆☆
Cost: $$
Other name/s: Country ribs
Recommended Cooking Method: Grilling, braising, pan searing, barbecuing
Notes & Tips: Most butchers cut this type of ribs into several cuts and then place them in a single package.

3. Primal Cut: Loin (cont.)

Blade End Roast

Characteristics: The section of the loin nearest to the shoulder; it can be challenging to carve, as it has a lot of different fat pockets and muscles on the meat.

Flavor: ★★★☆☆
Cost: $$
Other name/s: Rib-end roast, pork five-rib roast, pork loin rib end, pork seven-rib roast
Recommended Cooking Method: Roasting, braising

Boneless Blade End Roast

Characteristics: A cut from the shoulder end of the loin; fatty, and more flavorful than the boneless center-cut loin roast.

Flavor: ★★☆☆☆
Cost: $$
Other name/s: Triangle roast
Recommended Cooking Method: Grilling, roasting
Notes & Tips: It may be quite difficult to find this type of cut in most meat shops.

Center-Cut Loin Roast

Characteristics: A cut similar to the boneless blade-end roast that can also be juicy and tender.

Flavor: ★★☆☆☆
Cost: $$$
Other name/s: Center-cut pork roast
Recommended Cooking Method: Grill roasting, roasting
Notes & Tips: Buy this roast with a nice fat cap on top and cook it with the fat cap on top. This allows the meat to self-baste and stay moist.

Center-Cut Rib Roast

Characteristics: A cut consisting of five to eight ribs with the bones and fat still encased within the meat; it has a good flavor and slightly tender texture similar to the prime rib or rack of lamb.

Flavor: ★★★☆☆
Cost: $$$$
Other name/s: Center-cut pork roast, pork loin rib half, rack of pork
Recommended Cooking Method: Grilling, roasting

Tenderloin Roast

Characteristics: A very small cut of meat that is boneless and lean with very little marbling; this cut is equivalent to beef tenderloin.

Flavor: ★☆☆☆☆
Cost: $$$
Other name/s: None
Recommended Cooking Method: Pan searing, sauteing, stir-frying, roasting

Sirloin Roast

Characteristics: A cut with lots of connective tissue, making it ideal for braising and barbecuing.

Flavor: ★☆☆☆☆
Cost: $$
Other name/s: None
Recommended Cooking Method: Braising, barbecuing
Notes & Tips: Sirloin roasts are ideal for slow cooking. For maximum flavor, be sure to marinate or rub prior to cooking.

Crown Roast

Characteristics: A cut from two bone-in center-cut rib or center-cut loin roasts attached together, usually containing 16 to 20 ribs.

Flavor: ★★★☆☆
Cost: $$$$
Other name/s: Crown rib roast
Recommended Cooking Method: Roasting
Notes & Tips: A crown rib roast is very impressive when served whole. Because of its shape and size, it is important to work with a meat thermometer to prevent overcooking.

4. Primal Cut: Leg

Fresh Ham (Shank End)

Characteristics: The first cut derived from the leg area is the shank end, which is covered with a thick layer of skin and fat.

Flavor: ★★★☆☆
Cost: $$
Other name/s: Shank end fresh ham
Recommended Cooking Method: Roasting, barbecuing
Notes & Tips: The fatty layer in this cut is just enough to keep the meat juicy and this cut will actually become more flavorful if you brine or marinate it first. Be sure to score the skin prior to brining or marinating to allow the liquid to penetrate the meat.

Spiral-Sliced Bone-in Half Ham

Characteristics: A wet-cured ham that is flavorful and easy to cut; a bone-in ham is tastier than a boneless ham since the bone also develops its flavor as it cooks.

Flavor: ★★★★☆
Cost: $
Other name/s: Spiral-cut ham
Recommended Cooking Method: Roasting
Notes & Tips: Buy the bone-in ham with the label "ham with natural juices".

Prepared hams also benefit from a slow reheating process making them ideal for parties or events.

Fresh Ham (Sirloin Half)

Characteristics: The second cut derived from the leg of the animal with a rounded shape because of the bone structure; a flavorful cut, but may be difficult to carve because of its shape.

Flavor: ★★★☆☆
Cost: $
Other name/s: None
Recommended Cooking Method: Roasting, barbecuing
Notes & Tips: Like its shank end cousin, this ham will take on the flavor of whatever marinade or brine you apply to it. Just be sure to purchase it with the skin on and score the skin prior to marinating.

Country Ham

Characteristics: A whole leg that is dry-cured with a salty, nutty flavor.

Flavor: ★★★☆☆
Cost: $$$
Other name/s: None
Recommended Cooking Method: Pan searing after slicing
Notes & Tips: It is important to think of country ham like prosciutto. It is delicious on its own, but very pungent. Ideally, country ham is served as a condiment rather than a main course. Top biscuits with very thin slices or use in place of prosciutto in pastas.

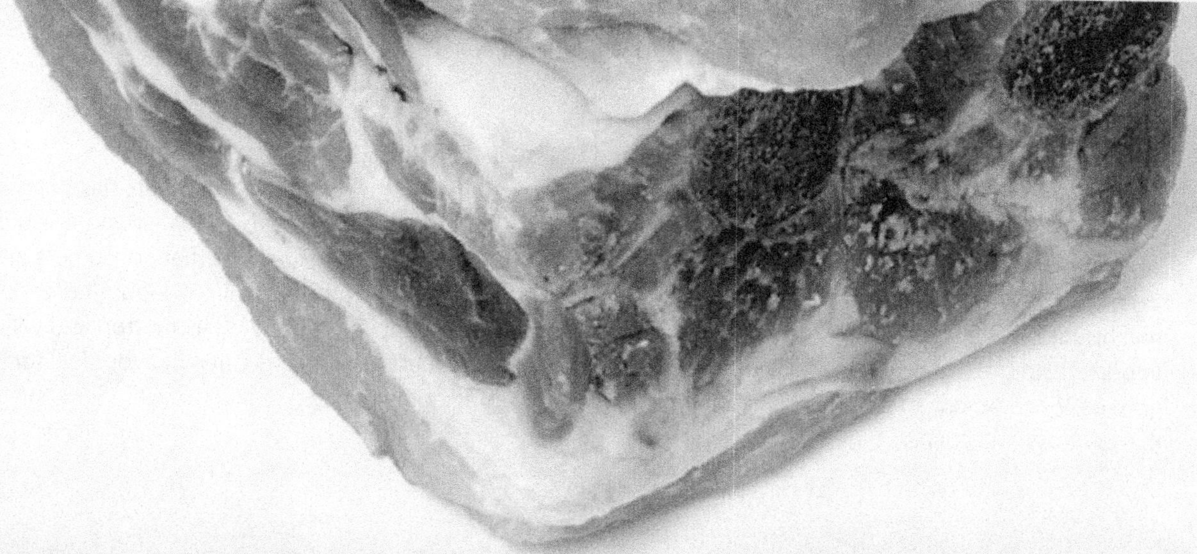

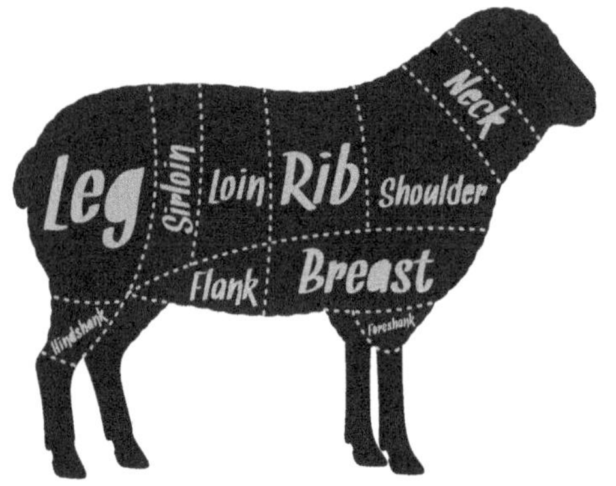

LAMB

Unlike beef and pork, lamb has typically been called the less popular option when buying meat. More recently, however, it has surged in popularity for three good reasons: price, taste, and versatility of cooking. Lamb is comparably more affordable than beef, and has a stronger flavor than pork. It can also be prepared using a variety of cooking methods, making it ideal for grilling, roasting, or even braising.

Consumers can buy domestic or imported lamb depending on the desired product. American lamb is larger and milder than lamb imported from New Zealand or Australia. The main reason for this difference is the diet the animals are fed. Imported lamb are grass-fed, usually on various grasses, while American lamb is raised on a mixed diet of grass and grain.

Often, lamb sold in supermarkets has been slaughtered at between six to twelve months old, to give the meat a mild flavor that consumers are accustomed to. If the animal is slaughtered as an adult, its meat will be labeled as mutton and will have a tough texture and gamey flavor ideal for braising and stewing.

PRIMAL CUTS OF LAMB

A lamb is divided into five major primal cuts that are then cut into smaller sections. Each cut has a recommended cooking method and varies in cost.

PRIMAL CUTS OF LAMB
Breast or Foreshank This cut consists of the underside portion of the animal: foreshank and breast. This includes the two front legs/shank, and the breast portion.
Shoulder This lamb section runs from the neck through the fourth rib of the animal. Because these muscles are worked a lot during the animal's life, this cut tends to be tough but flavorful making it ideal for braising and stewing.
Rib This area covers the section directly behind the shoulder from the fifth rib to the twelfth rib. All eight ribs from this portion are collectively called a rack. When the rack is cut into individual pieces, they are called rib chops, which have a fine, tender grain and pleasant flavor.
Loin This cut starts from the last rib and extends down to the hip area. The loin is considered to be the most popular cut, due to its tender texture and mild flavor, similar to the rib chops.
Leg This portion starts from the hip down to the hoof of the animal. Consumers can buy them whole or cut into smaller roasts and shanks (from the two back legs). They can also be bought bones in, boneless, or butterflied.

SHOPPING GUIDE FOR LAMB

If you haven't had lamb lately, now is the time to give it a try. Its unique flavor and varying texture naturally lends itself to a variety of cooking methods. It can be more expensive than other cuts of meat and purchasing the wrong cut can lead to a costly mistake on the barbecue. This handy guide will keep you on the right track when buying your next piece of lamb.

1. Primal Cut: Foreshank or Breast

Characteristics: Cut derived from the underside of the animal which includes the breast and the two front legs.

Flavor: ★★★☆☆
Cost: $$$$
Other name/s: None
Recommended Cooking Method: Roasting, grilling

2. Primal Cut: Shoulder

Blade Chops

Characteristics: A cut derived from the shoulder area, it has a thin part of the blade bone and a part of the chine or backbone; it contains more fat than round-bone chops but are pleasantly chewy and have a robust flavor.

Flavor: ★★★☆☆
Cost: $$
Other name/s: Shoulder chops
Recommended Cooking Method: Grilling, pan searing

Round-Bone Chops

Characteristics: Oval cuts taken from the shoulder portion; leaner than blade chops, these chops have a strong, lamby flavor.

Flavor: ★★★☆☆
Cost: $$
Other name/s: Arm chops
Recommended Cooking Method: Grilling, braising
Notes & Tips: Every round-bone chop consists of a cross section of the arm bone similar to a small ham steak and a small line of riblets of both sides of the chop.

3. Primal Cut: Loin

Loin Chops

Characteristics: A cut which contains meat from either side of the bone running down the center of the loin; it has a stronger lamb flavor than the rib chops and are firm, but not chewy.

Flavor: ★★★★☆
Cost: $$$$
Other name/s: None
Recommended Cooking Method: Grilling, pan searing
Notes & Tips: The small piece of meat at the right side of the loin chop bone is fine-grained and comparably tender to the tenderloin of a pig or cow. The larger piece of meat on the other side of the loin chop bone is more chewy.

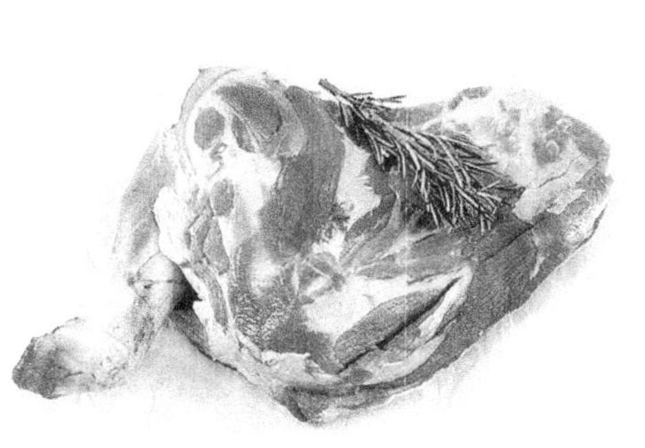
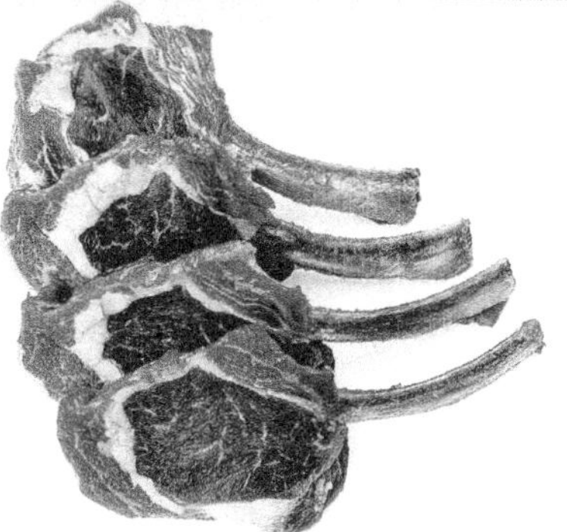

4. Primal Cut: Rib

Rib Chops

Characteristics: A cut that has a recognizable bone on one side of the chop. Rib chops usually have a lot of fat, especially near the bone; ribs chops have a refined, slightly sweet taste and a tender texture.

Flavor: ★★★★☆
Cost: $$$$
Other name/s: Frenched chops, rack chops
Recommended Cooking Method: Pan searing, grilling, roasting
Notes & Tips: If you want leaner rib chops, you can ask the butcher to "french" or scrape the fat away from the tip of the bone, and thus the alternate name "Frenched chops".

To get the best results, do not cook these chops past medium-rare for a mildly sweet flavor.

Rack of Lamb

Characteristics: A cut that consists of eight to nine bones; this cut is very tender and flavorful comparable to the prime rib of a cow.

Flavor: ★★★★☆
Cost: $$$$
Other name/s: Rib roast, rack roast
Recommended Cooking Method: Roasting

5. Primal Cut: Leg

Leg of Lamb

Characteristics: A cut derived from the wider sirloin end and the narrower shank end consisting of the butt end (sirloin or hip meat) and the shank end or ankle at the bottom part of the animal; it usually weighs six to ten pounds and is ideal for a variety of preparations.

Flavor: ★★★☆☆
Cost: $$$
Other name/s: Sirloin-on leg, whole leg
Recommended Cooking Method: Grilling, barbecuing, roasting, braising

Notes & Tips: A leg of lamb is ideal for marinades and rubs. Ask your butcher to bone and butterfly the leg if you are looking to grill this cut to a medium rare. For braises, the lamb leg can be stuffed, rolled, and tied. Or barbecue the whole leg, bone and all, for a tasty treat.

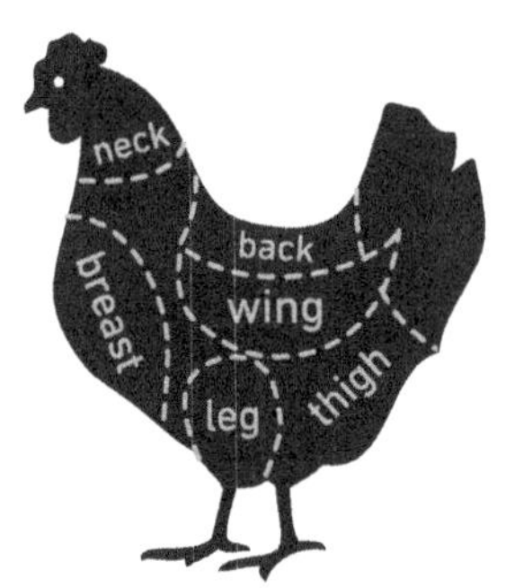

POULTRY

Poultry is the most popular meat in the U.S. because of its low cost and pleasant flavor. As consumers have become more aware of where their poultry comes from and how it is raised, new cooks may be confused by the variety of labels on their chicken or turkey.

LABELING

POULTRY PACKAGING TERMS THAT YOU SHOULD KNOW

USDA Organic

In order to be labeled as "USDA Organic", farmers have to adhere to guidelines set forth by the USDA for the care, feeding, and slaughtering of poultry animals. Animals must be raised on an organic feed diet without animal byproducts, antibiotics, or growth hormones. They must be given year-round access to the outdoors, shade, shelter, and clean water. Any bedding must be made from organic materials and shelters must allow for adequate exercise and normal behaviors.

Raised Without Antibiotics

The term "Raised Without Antibiotics" is a marketing term and is not regulated by the USDA. It generally means that animals were not given any medications classified as antibiotics for disease prevention or treatment. Since the USDA requires that an animal treated with antibiotics cannot be slaughtered until the substance has left the animal's system, all poultry is technically antibiotic free when it reaches the market.

Hormone-Free

"Hormone-Free" is also a marketing term used on poultry packaging. Contrary to popular belief, the USDA prohibits the use of steroids or hormones in all poultry or pork production. Companies that use "hormone-free" labeling are free to do so, but it is not indicative of a better quality product than poultry without the designation.

Natural and All Natural

The USDA requires that poultry products carrying these labels have no artificial ingredients, artificial colors or chemical preservatives. However, "natural" and "all natural" labels still allow for the injection of sodium solutions to enhance the flavor of the product.

Vegetarian-Fed and the Vegetarian Diet

The USDA has no specific regulation regarding this claim. Traditional poultry feed is made from corn and soybean meal but may be enhanced with protein, fats, and oils from animal byproducts. Farmers may choose to use a feed that does not contain animal products, but chickens are not naturally vegetarians. Wild birds consume a diet rich in insects and other small creatures in addition to seeds and plant matter.

Air-Chilled

"Air-chilled" poultry products refer to the way the meat was treated after slaughter. In the US, most poultry is chilled in large, chlorinated ice water baths before packaging. While this process is fast, it also uses a tremendous amount of water, dilutes the poultry's flavor, and causes the finished product to weigh more due to water retention. Air-chilling poultry is a much slower process, where the product is hung individually on a conveyor belt and circulated around a chilling room. Not only is it more environmentally friendly, it results in a more flavorful final product.

Free Range

The only USDA requirement for a poultry producer to label its product as "free range" or "free roaming" is that the animal has access to the outside. Unfortunately, this does not guarantee that the flavor or quality of the meat be grossly affected in any way.

SHOPPING GUIDE FOR POULTRY

Chicken and turkey is generally easier to shop for than beef, pork, or lamb. However, there are still some factors to consider when buying poultry products.

CHICKEN

Types of Chicken Packaging

Whole: Roasters, Broilers, and Fryers

Whole chickens come in three varieties: roasters, broilers and fryers.

Roasters - Older chickens that typically weigh between five to seven pounds.

Broilers and fryers - Younger chickens that weigh between 2 ½ to 4 ½ pounds.

Avoid labels that say the chicken is "enhanced". This means it may contain unnecessary "flavor enhancers" that may affect the flavor and texture of the chicken. Not to mention, you are actually paying for the water solution they inject the chicken with. Buy birds labeled "air chilled" or "USDA Organic" for the most flavorful chicken.

Ground

Ground chicken in supermarkets is prepared in one of two ways: prepackaged or ground to order.

Prepackaged - ground chicken meat from either dark or white meats

Ground to order - ground meat from buyer's choice of chicken

Because chicken must be cooked thoroughly, choosing ground chicken with a large amount of dark meat will yield a juicier, more flavorful end product.

Boneless, Skinless Breasts and Cutlets

Boneless, skinless breasts and cutlets are the most popular cuts in the US. Lean, versatile, and neutral in flavor, they are a staple in households throughout the country. Just be sure to use a meat thermometer when cooking them as they become dry and rubbery when they are overcooked.

Next time, give boneless, skinless chicken thighs a try in place of the breasts. They are packed with chicken flavor and won't dry out as quickly.

Bone-In Parts

Chefs generally agree that roasting chicken with the bone in and skin on will yield the juiciest, most flavorful outcome.

Bone-in, skin-on parts are ideal for the barbecue or grill.

TURKEY

Types of Turkey Packaging

Whole

Most whole turkeys available in the market today do not contain as much fat as they did fifty years ago, leaving the birds dry and flavorless.

Heritage birds are purebred or cross bred descendants of wild turkeys that roamed freely decades ago. These turkeys have a rich flavor and texture but may be difficult to find in a supermarket.

To combat the lack of flavor in traditional birds, some processors "prebaste" the turkey with a sodium solution to improve the flavor. It is always better to buy a bird that has not been injected with water and brine it yourself. Not only can you control the ingredients in the brine, you do not pay for the additional weight of the sodium solution.

Bone-In Breasts

Bone-in breasts found in supermarkets are available in two varieties:

(1) Regular or True Cut
(2) Hotel or Country-Style

Regular or True Cut
The cut which includes the whole bone-in breast section with ribs and parts of the wing meat, back, and neck skin.

Hotel or Country-Style
This cut is basically the same as regular turkey breast, except that it comes with the neck, wings, and giblets.

Ground

When buying ground turkey, be sure to buy a variety that contains a mixture of white meat and dark meat for extra flavor and added juiciness.

The Sad Truth

- Most of the meat in the United States is produced industrially. Cramped living conditions, artificial diets, and growth hormones are utilized in many facilities to produce more livestock or poultry for consumption. Unfortunately, this affects the quality of the meat you find in the supermarket. Your best bet is to befriend a trusted butcher who sources his products from local farmers. Not only are you supporting your local agricultural industry, you will have access to high quality meat and poultry raised in more humane conditions.

Tool Guide

In addition to your Big Green Egg® accessories, there are a few tools of the trade that will make your grilling experience even more enjoyable.

Tool	What It Is Used For	Approximate Cost
Meat Thermometer	A meat thermometer is necessary to check the doneness of meat. In order to cook to temperature rather than time, you must know what the internal temperature of your meat is.	Varies according to features. $5-$150
Heat Proof Gloves	Heat-proof gloves are perfect for handling briskets, pulling pork, or moving meat into or out of the EGG®. They are also ideal for adjusting the airflow at the Dual Function Metal Top or Precision Flow Draft Door	$5-$20
Chef's Knife	Just because you never EVER check the doneness of your meat by cutting into it, doesn't mean you won't need a knife for carving it after it is finished. Look for a knife that is comfortable in your hand.	A good quality knife can be found in the $30-$50 range.
Filet Knife	Ideal for butterflying meat you intend to stuff and tie.	A good quality knife can be found in the $30-$50 range.
Small saucepot	Simmering mop sauce or glazing sauces for application. Look for a pot that can be used over a gas fire.	$20-30
Dutch Oven	Cast iron Dutch ovens, when properly cared for, can become family heirlooms. Look for one that is at least 10 quarts in capacity for maximum versatility.	$50
Heat proof tongs	Just like you never cut into a piece of meat to check if it is done, you also never poke it to turn it over.	$10-$20
Heat proof spatula	Perfect for flipping burgers of all types and removing fish from the grill.	$10-$20
Flavor Injector	This tool looks like an ancient torture device but is actually ideal for injecting large cuts of meat with flavorful marinades.	$10-$20

Is It Done Yet?

Every chef will tell you that, when it comes to cooking meat, temperature matters more than time. Investing in a high quality meat thermometer will ensure thousands of successful roasts, steaks, briskets, and chickens for decades to come. But how do you know when your meat is ready?
First, it is important to understand a little about what happens to meat at different temperatures.

Temperature	What Happens to Meat
0°F (-18°C)	Ideal freezer temperature.
25°F (-4°C)	Meat freezes. Since the water in meat contains proteins, meat freezes at a lower temperature than plain water.
32°F (0°C)	Water freezes.
34-39°F (1-4°C)	Water is not frozen and microbial growth is minimized making this the ideal refrigerator temperature.
41-135°F (5-57°C)	The USDA refers to this as the "danger zone" for bacterial growth. At these temperatures, bacteria can double in as little as 20 minutes increasing the likelihood of food-borne illness.
95-130°F (35-54°C)	Animal fat starts to melt.
120°F (49°C)	Myosin, the protein involved in muscle contraction, begins to lose its structure in a process called "denaturing".
130°F (54°C)	Many pathogens begin to die, slowly. At this temperature it takes over two hours to pasteurize meat, meaning all of the pathogenic bacteria is dead.
130-135°F (54-57°C)	Medium rare doneness. Fats begin to render, or liquefy, albeit slowly.
140°F (60°C)	Collagen begins to contract pushing pink juice from the muscle fibers onto the surface of the meat. Red or pink juices begin to turn clear and bead up on the surface of the meat.
150°F (66°C)	The muscle protein actin begins to denature making the meat tough and dry.
150-165° (66-74°C)	When you are cooking large cuts of meat, such as pork butt or beef brisket, this is what is known as "the stall zone". Meat seems to get stuck in this temperature range for hours because moisture evaporates on the surface of the meat and cools it like sweat. Once evaporation slows, the meat's temperature will start to rise again.
160-165°F (71-74°C)	The "instant kill zone". Most meat is safe to eat long before this temperature because the majority of the bacteria is on the surface. However, in the case of ground meats, it is necessary to cook them beyond well done in order to ensure their safety.
160-205°F (71-96°C)	Tough collagens melt and form tender gelatin. Dehydrated fibers begin to fall apart and pull away from any bones and the meat is easy to shred.

Temperature Guide By Cut

To accurately test the temperature of your meat, insert an instant-read meat thermometer into the thickest portion. For poultry, this will be the meatiest part of the thigh, being careful not to touch the bone. If your smoker is equipped with a temperature probe, by all means, use it. This will not only prevent heat from escaping the smoker, it will give you a digital reading throughout the cooking process.

Cut of meat	Desired Internal Temperature
BEEF	
Brisket	190-200°F (190°F for sliced, 200°F for pulled)
Chuck Roast	190-200°F
Ribs	185-190°F
Short Ribs	190-200°F
Beef Country Style Ribs	175-180°F
Meatloaf	160°F
Burgers	160°F
Steaks	135°F (Medium Rare), 145°F (Medium)
Prime Rib	130-135°F (Medium Rare)
Tri Tip	130-135°F (Medium Rare)
PORK	
Pork Butt	205°F
Baby Back Ribs	180°F
Spare Ribs	180-185°F
Loin	145°F
Tenderloin	145°F
POULTRY	
Whole Chicken	165°F
Chicken Legs/Thighs	165°F
Chicken Wings	165°F
Chicken Quarters	165°F

Cut of meat	Desired Internal Temperature
Whole Turkey	165°F
Turkey Breast	165°F
Turkey Legs	175-180°F
Quail/Pheasant	165°F
Cornish Hens	165°F
FISH & SEAFOOD	
Salmon	145°F
Tilapia	145°F
Whole Trout	145°F
Lobster Tails	140°F
Oysters	Oysters that have been shucked, rinsed, and smoked in a shell half are done when the edges start to curl.
Scallops	145°F
Shrimp	Shrimp are done when they turn bright pink and opaque.
MISCELLANEOUS	
Sausages	175°F
Corn on the cob	Cook until kernels change color
Whole potatoes	Cook until soft
Tomatoes	Cook until skin splits

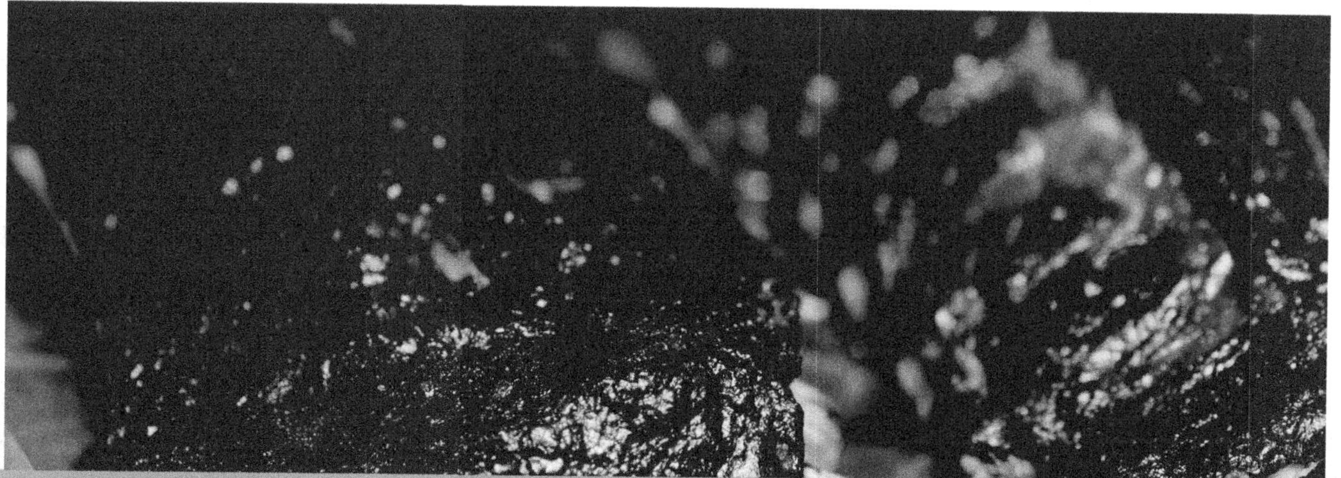

A WORD ABOUT COOKING OUTDOORS

Before we get into actual recipes, it's important that we all pause for a moment to appreciate why we cook outside. In the summer. In the heat. It's hot outside, it takes effort, and for the novice, seems pretty overwhelming.

But there's something magical about the experience.

Cooking outside is quiet. Rather than deal with the cacophony of pots and pans, timers, and buzzers, there is something serene about standing over an open flame, turning ingredients into something delicious and special. Not to mention the zen nature of drinking a cold beverage on a hot summer day while the smell of melting pork fat and real charcoal wafts through the air.

Cooking outside is also great for the environment. Imagine all of the water you use to wash pots and pans that you don't have to worry about with a grill. You can enjoy the smell of dripping fat hitting charcoal, the sound of a steak hitting the grids, and charred veggies without dirtying a single pot or heating up your kitchen unnecessarily.

But unintended benefits aside, we get to connect to our primal ancestors when we cook over fire. In that singular moment we get are feeding our family and friends the same way the cavemen did. We get to connect with bygone generations of pioneers who cooked over open flames on the prairies of the wild west. With the convenience of modern technology we are able to do something that has been done for generations - cook over an open flame.

These recipe sections are divided into major food groups, with recipes categorized by cut. If you want to cook a whole chicken, there is a recipe for the method that you can customize with our Rubs, Marinades, and Sauces section. If you want to cook pork ribs, there is a recipe that, once you are familiar with the method, can be customized to your taste.

Most exciting of all is the Dutch oven section that will introduce you to a different way of thinking about your Big Green Egg®. Imagine not having to turn on the oven again. With a cast iron Dutch oven and the EGG®, it's possible. We'll show you how.

So, grab a cold one, kick up your feet, and imagine the delicious meals you are about to enjoy.

Rubs, Marinades, and Sauces

A choose your own guide to flavor

There is one thing that sets home cooks apart from restaurants - seasoning. Whether it is in the form of a rub, marinade, or sauce, restaurants understand that properly seasoning food will make the difference between a good dish and a great dish. We have made it easy for you with this handy "choose your own" chart. Simply pick a rub, marinade, or brine and pair it with a sauce for an easy, delicious grilled dish. But how do you know if it will turn out?

1. Choose a sauce that shares some of the ingredients in your rub. The flavor notes in the rub will carry through the sauce creating a harmonious combination.
2. If you choose a spicy rub, pair it with a sweeter sauce. Even if you enjoy spicy food, there is a difference between waking up your tastebuds and blowing your head off. By pairing spicy with sweet, you will be assured of having the right "kick" without blowing your mind.
3. Don't mix regions of the world. If you use an Asian rub, stick with an Asian sauce for the maximum deliciousness.

CHOOSE ONE OF THESE		FINISH WITH ONE OF THESE (OPTIONAL)
RUBS	**MARINADES & BRINES**	**SAUCES**
Adobo Rub	Apple Cider Vinegar Pork Brine	Besto Pesto
Asian Rub	Basic Steak Marinade	Catalan Vinaigrette
Basic BBQ Rub	Beef Kebab Marinade	Chimichurri
Berbere Spice Mix	Carne Asada Marinade	Chinese Barbecue Sauce (Char Sui)
Cajun Dry Rub	Cuban Mojo	Chipotle Mango Lime Sauce
Carne Asada Rub	Greek Marinade	Classic Texas Barbecue Sauce
Chile Rub	Italian Chicken Marinade	Coffee Spice Barbecue Sauce
Classic American Brown	Lemon Rosemary Marinade	Compound Herb Butter
Sugar Rub	Korean Barbecue (Bulgogi) Marinade	East Carolina Barbecue Sauce
Coffee Rub	Maple Brine	Frank's Buffalo Sauce
Country Style Rub	Maple Mustard Marinade	Garlic Grill Sauce
English Pub Rub	Memphis Marinade	Kansas City Barbecue Sauce
Indian Spice Rub	Not-so-basic Chicken Marinade	Peach Mustard Sauce
Garlic Lover's Rub	Overnight Beef Marinade	Peanut Sauce
Habanero Rub	Salmon Brine	Romesco Sauce
Malaysian Rub	Spicy Thai Marinade	Sweet and Sour Hoisin Sauce
Mediterranean Rub	Teriyaki Marinade	White Barbecue Sauce
North African Rub	Texas Hillbilly Marinade	Z-10 Steak Sauce
Spicy Tunisian Rub	Turkey Brine	
Tuscan Spice Rub	Veggie Marinade	

RUBS

Adobo Rub

Ingredients:

- 1 Tablespoon (Tbsp) ancho chili powder
- 1 teaspoon (tsp). ground cumin
- 1 tsp onion powder
- 1 tsp garlic powder
- 1 tsp salt
- ½ tsp pepper
- The juice of 1 lime
- 2 Tbsp extra-virgin olive oil

1. Thoroughly combine ingredients in a small bowl and rub on chicken or pork.
2. Allow to sit for 4-6 hours or overnight before smoking.

Asian Rub

Ingredients:

- ¼ c paprika (Spanish or sweet paprika works best)
- 2 Tbsp dry mustard
- 2 Tbsp Chinese Five Spice Powder
- 2 Tbsp ground ginger
- 1 Tbsp salt
- 1 Tbsp pepper
- 1 Tbsp crushed red pepper flakes

1. Combine all ingredients in a small bowl.
2. May be stored in an airtight container for up to 6 months.

TIP: Once you have mastered a few rubs, try adding new ingredients to see what new combinations you can come up with. Tomato powder, green chile powder, or even smoked orange zest are all available through online retailers and make delicious additions to a basic barbecue rub.

Basic Barbecue Rub (Also known as 4-3-2-1 rub)

The idea behind this versatile rub is really just the proportions. 4 parts salt, 3 parts sugar, 2 parts paprika, and 1 part of one or several spices.

Basic Ingredients:

- 4 Tbsp salt
- 3 Tbsp brown sugar
- 2 Tbsp paprika
- 1 Tbsp cayenne powder

1. Combine ingredients in a small bowl.
2. Rub onto meat and skin and allow to sit at least one hour before smoking.
3. Unused portions can be kept in an airtight container for up to 6 months.

NOTE: For ribs, try brown sugar, smoked paprika, and 1 Tbsp each garlic powder, onion powder, chili powder, black pepper, and cayenne pepper.

Basic Beef Rub

This rub contains no salt, but rather relies on a hefty kick from black and cayenne peppers for a powerful flavor.

Ingredients:

- 3 Tbsp coarsely ground black pepper
- 1 Tbsp white sugar
- 1 Tbsp onion powder
- 2 tsp dried mustard
- 2 tsp garlic powder
- 2 tsp chili powder
- 1 tsp cayenne pepper

1. Combine ingredients in a small bowl.
2. Rub onto meat and skin and allow to sit at least one hour before smoking.
3. Unused portions can be kept in an airtight container for up to 6 months.

Berbere Spice Mix

This sweet and spicy rub is perfect for chicken or pork to give it a Middle Eastern flair.

Ingredients:

- 1 Tbsp paprika
- 1 ½ tsp cayenne pepper
- 1 ½ tsp ground ginger
- 1 tsp ground allspice
- 1 tsp ground cumin
- ½ tsp nutmeg
- ½ tsp ground cinnamon
- ½ tsp dried oregano
- ¼ tsp ground cloves

1. Combine ingredients in a small bowl.
2. Rub onto meat and skin and allow to sit at least one hour before smoking.
3. Unused portions can be kept in an airtight container for up to 6 months.

Big Bold Barbecue Rub

Sweeter than most, the heat in this rub is offset somewhat by the sugar.

Ingredients:

- ½ cup brown sugar
- 1/4 c sweet paprika
- 1 Tbsp ground black pepper
- 1 Tbsp lemon pepper
- 1 Tbsp kosher salt
- 1 Tbsp chili powder
- 1 Tbsp garlic powder
- 1 Tbsp onion powder
- 1 Tbsp cayenne pepper

1. Combine ingredients in a small bowl.
2. Rub onto meat and skin and allow to sit at least one hour before smoking.
3. Unused portions can be kept in an airtight container for up to 6 months.

Cajun Dry Rub

Cajun doesn't always mean super spicy. Although this rub has a fair amount of heat, the herbs serve to bring a little something extra to the party.

Ingredients:

- 2 Tbsp Kosher salt
- 2 Tbsp sweet paprika
- 2 tsp dried thyme
- 2 tsp dried oregano
- 2 tsp black pepper
- 2 tsp granulated garlic
- 2 tsp dried onion
- 1 tsp cayenne pepper
- 1 bay leaves, ground

1. Combine ingredients in a small bowl.
2. Unused portions can be kept in an airtight container for up to 6 months.

Carne Asada Rub

In Latin America, "carne asada" literally means "grilled meat". While the flavors in the rubs and marinades for carne asada vary, this zippy rub adds a Latin flare with very few ingredients. This is a wet rub and should be made no more than a day in advance.

Ingredients:

- 2 cloves garlic, crushed
- 2 Tbsp lime juice
- 2 Tbsp orange juice
- 2 Tbsp extra-virgin olive oil
- 1 Tbsp lime zest
- 1 Tbsp orange zest
- 1 tsp ancho chili powder
- 1 tsp cumin
- 1 tsp salt
- ½ tsp pepper
- ½ tsp Mexican oregano

1. Combine in a small bowl.
2. Slather on the meat and allow it to sit at least 30 minutes before smoking or grilling.

TIP: If you cannot find ancho chili powder, pick up whole ancho chilis and buzz them in your coffee grinder until they are a powder consistency. Just be sure to thoroughly clean your coffee grinder with warm water and soap before using it again for coffee. To make sure it is extra clean, grind a piece of bread before washing.

Chile Rub

Ingredients:

- 4 dried New Mexico chiles
- 4 dried guajillo chiles
- 4 dried ancho chiles
- ½ c cumin seeds
- ¼ c dried oregano
- ¼ c paprika
- 3 Tbsp kosher salt
- 1 Tbsp onion powder
- 2 tsp garlic powder

1. Combine all ingredients into a spice grinder and pulse until thoroughly ground.
2. Then add onion powder and garlic powder.
3. Combine ingredients in a small bowl.
4. Rub onto meat and skin and allow to sit at least one hour before smoking.
5. Unused portions can be kept in an airtight container for up to 6 months.

TIP: What we know as "chili powder" is actually a combination of ground chiles and other spices. If you cannot find a particular chile in the Latin foods aisle of your supermarket, feel free to substitute any chiles that are available.

Classic American Brown Sugar Rub

This sweet and smoky rub is exactly what you imagine a Kansas City style rub to be.

Ingredients

- ½ cup light brown sugar
- ¼ c smoked paprika
- 4 Tbsp kosher salt
- 3 Tbsp black pepper
- 2 tsp onion powder
- 2 tsp garlic powder
- 2 tsp celery seed
- 1 tsp red pepper flakes

1. Combine ingredients in a small bowl.
2. Rub onto meat and skin and allow to sit at least 30 minutes before smoking or grilling.
3. Unused portions can be kept in an airtight container for up to 6 months.

Coffee Rub

This rub is a strong, slightly bitter addition to any piece of beef or pork.

Ingredients:

- 3 Tbsp ground coffee
- 2 Tbsp dark brown sugar
- 1 Tbsp kosher salt
- 1 Tbsp paprika
- 1 Tbsp black pepper
- ½ tsp ground coriander

1. Combine ingredients in a small bowl.
2. Rub onto meat and skin and allow to sit at least one hour before smoking.
3. Unused portions can be kept in an airtight container for up to 6 months.

Country Style Rub

The addition of celery seed gives this rub a floral background perfect for chicken and fish

Ingredients:

- 1 c white sugar
- ½ c kosher salt
- ¼ c sweet paprika

- 2 Tbsp garlic powder
- 1 Tbsp ground cumin
- 1 Tbsp cayenne pepper
- 1 Tbsp black pepper
- 1 tsp ground celery seed

1. **Combine ingredients in a small bowl.**
2. **Rub onto meat and skin and allow to sit at least one hour before smoking.**
3. **Unused portions can be kept in an airtight container for up to 6 months.**

English Pub Rub

This rub is ideal for steak of any kind. The beef bouillon enhances the steak flavor while the aromatics send the flavor to a whole new level.

Ingredients:
- 1 beef bouillon cube, pulverized
- 2 cloves garlic, crushed
- 1 small shallot, finely diced
- 1 tsp kosher salt
- ¼ c extra-virgin olive oil

1. **Combine ingredients in a small bowl and slather on the steaks.**
2. **Allow to sit at least 30 minutes before smoking.**

Garlic Lover's Rub

This rub is for the garlic lover in all of us. It's so versatile you can use it on any piece of meat, seafood, poultry, or vegetable.

Ingredients:
- 8 cloves garlic, minced
- 1 Tbsp extra-virgin olive oil
- 2 tsp dijon or stone-ground mustard
- 1 tsp kosher salt
- ½ tsp black pepper
- The zest of one lemon

1. **Combine ingredients in a small bowl and slather on your protein of choice at least 30 minutes before smoking.**

Habanero Rub

This jerk-inspired rub is sweet, spicy, and super flavorful. It can be made as a dry rub as written, or as a wet rub by blending the first nine ingredients with a chopped habanero chile, the juice of one lime, and ¼ cup of extra-virgin olive oil. Either way, break out the flip flops and sunglasses because you're headed to the Caribbean.

Ingredients:
- 3 Tbsp onion powder
- 2 Tbsp garlic powder
- 2 Tbsp paprika
- 2 Tbsp light brown sugar
- 1 Tbsp ground allspice
- 1 Tbsp ground chipotle chile powder
- 2 tsp ground cinnamon
- 2 tsp ground thyme
- 1 tsp ground habanero chile powder
- 1 tsp ground dried lemon peel
- ½ tsp ground nutmeg

1. **Combine ingredients in a small bowl.**
2. **Rub onto meat and skin and allow to sit at least one hour before smoking.**
3. **Unused portions can be kept in an airtight container for up to 6 months.**

TIP: You can find habanero chile powder online, but if you are in a pinch, substitute cayenne pepper and increase the dried lemon peel to 1 ½ tsp.

Indian Spice Rub

Ingredients:
- 6 Tbsp curry powder
- 3 Tbsp kosher salt
- 1 Tbsp crushed red pepper flakes
- 1 Tbsp ground cumin
- 1 Tbsp ground coriander
- 2 tsp turmeric

- 2 tsp ground ginger
- 1 tsp garam masala

1. Combine ingredients in a small bowl.
2. Rub onto meat and skin and allow to sit at least one hour before smoking.
3. Unused portions can be kept in an airtight container for up to 6 months.

TIP: Garam masala is the northern India equivalent of "chili powder" in the US. It is a combination of spices that varies from one brand to another and is readily available in supermarkets. It is also commonly used in the Indian dishes khorma and tikka masala.

Malaysian Rub

Malaysian cooking is known for balancing four things - salt, sour, bitter, and sweet. This rub reflects that sensibility. If you cannot find lemongrass at your Asian market, substitute zest and juice of one lemon and 3 Tbsp of chopped flat leaf parsley.

Ingredients:

- 1 Tbsp fish sauce
- 2 Tbsp fresh grated ginger
- 2 Tbsp lemongrass, minced
- 1 Tbsp turmeric
- 1 Tbsp sugar
- 2 cloves garlic, crushed
- 2 limes, zested and juiced

1. Combine ingredients in a small bowl.
2. Slather on meat, chicken or fish and allow to sit for at least 30 minutes before smoking.

Mediterranean Spice Rub

This rub will remind you of oceanside afternoons in Greece. This is perfect as a dry rub on chicken, fish, or lamb, or can be made as a wet rub with fresh herbs, fresh garlic, and ¼ cup extra-virgin olive oil.

Ingredients:

- 3 Tbsp dried rosemary
- 2 Tbsp ground cumin
- 2 Tbsp ground coriander
- 1 Tbsp dried oregano
- 2 tsp ground cinnamon
- 2 tsp garlic powder
- 1 tsp kosher salt

1. Combine ingredients in a small bowl.
2. Rub onto meat and skin and allow to sit at least one hour before smoking.
3. Unused portions can be kept in an airtight container for up to 6 months.

North African Rub

Harissa paste is a spicy chile paste. If you cannot find it, you can substitute sriracha or sambal.

Ingredients:

- 2 Tbsp chili powder
- 1 Tbsp harissa paste or other chile paste
- The juice and zest of one orange
- 2 Tbsp salt
- 1 clove garlic, finely minced
- 1 tsp extra-virgin olive oil

1. Combine ingredients in a small bowl.
2. Slather onto meat at least 30 minutes prior to smoking.

Spicy Tunisian Rub

Ingredients:

- 2 tsp coriander seeds
- 2 tsp caraway seeds
- ¾ tsp crushed red pepper flake
- ¾ tsp garlic powder
- ½ tsp kosher salt

1. Combine ingredients in a spice grinder and grind until it forms a consistent powder.

2. Rub onto meat and skin and allow to sit at least one hour before smoking.
3. Unused portions can be kept in an airtight container for up to 6 months.

Tuscan Spice Rub

Ingredients:

- 1 Tbsp fennel seeds
- 3 Tbsp dried basil
- 3 Tbsp garlic powder
- 2 Tbsp kosher salt
- 2 Tbsp dried rosemary
- 2 Tbsp dried oregano

1. Rub onto meat and skin and allow to sit at least one hour before smoking.
2. Unused portions can be kept in an airtight container for up to 6 months.

MARINADES

The difference between a brine and a marinade is simple - salt. A brine is a salt-based solution consisting of water, salt, and other flavorings. A marinade is a combination of acid, fat, and any seasonings you would like. While marinades are great for any meat or veggies, it is only recommended that you brine pork, poultry, and fatty fish.

Apple Cider Vinegar Pork Brine

Most apple cider vinegar you buy in the store is actually distilled vinegar with sugar and color added. Real apple cider vinegar is made from apple juice and gives this brine a sweet, apple flavor.

Ingredients:

- 1 cup real apple cider vinegar
- 1 cup apple cider
- 1 cup salt
- 1 cup brown sugar
- 1 Tbsp whole peppercorns
- 4 cloves garlic, smashed

1. In a medium saucepan, heat ingredients until the salt and sugar are dissolved.
2. Cool to room temperature or add 4 cups ice cubes to chill the brine.
3. Soak pork in the brine for a minimum of 30 minutes before cooking.

Basic Steak Marinade

While many steaks do not need anything more than salt and pepper, some cuts lend themselves to a little more seasoning. Use this marinade on your next flank steak for an extra level of flavor

Ingredients:

- ½ cup olive oil
- 2 Tbsp Dijon mustard
- 2 Tbsp Worcestershire sauce
- 1 Tbsp fresh rosemary, chopped
- 4 cloves garlic, smashed
- The juice and zest of 1 lemon

1. Whisk all ingredients together and pour over steak.
2. Let marinate for 30 minutes before grilling.

Beef Kebab Marinade

Marinate chunks of tenderloin, strip steak, or ribeye in this flavorful marinade for 30 minutes before threading on skewers with chunks of onion, bell pepper, and mushrooms. Better yet, marinate the meat and veggies.

Ingredients:

- ¼ cup olive oil
- 2 Tbsp soy sauce
- 1 tsp kosher salt
- 1 tsp paprika
- 1 tsp black pepper
- 1 tsp granulated garlic
- 1 tsp granulated onion
- 1 tsp dried dill

1. **Combine ingredients in a zip top bag and marinate chunks of beef for 30 minutes before grilling.**

Carne Asada Marinade

This citrusy, spicy marinade is perfect for every cut of meat and seafood.

Ingredients:

- ¾ cup orange juice
- ½ cup lime juice
- ½ cup olive oil
- ⅓ cup lemon juice
- ¼ cup soy sauce
- 1 Tbsp chili powder
- 1 Tbsp cumin
- 1 Tbsp paprika
- 1 tsp oregano
- 4 cloves garlic, minced
- 1 chipotle in adobo sauce, finely chopped

1. **Whisk all ingredients together in a bowl and marinade the meat for a minimum of 30 minutes, up to overnight.**

Cuban Mojo

Anyone who has spent time in Miami is familiar with this tangy marinade and its resultant pork dishes. Mojo (pronounced: mo-ho) and its variants are found all over the Caribbean, but this simple version gets its flavor from citrus juices and a hefty dose of garlic.

Ingredients:

- 1 cup freshly squeezed orange juice
- ½ cup freshly squeezed lime juice
- 2 t cumin
- 2 t salt
- 1 t pepper
- 10 cloves of garlic, smashed

1. **Combine all ingredients and pour over pork or chicken.**
2. **Refrigerate 1 hour or as long as overnight before cooking.**

Greek Marinade

This super flavorful marinade is ideal for souvlaki.

Ingredients:

- ¼ cup extra virgin olive oil
- 2 Tbsp minced fresh oregano
- 2 Tbsp minced fresh parsley
- 5 cloves of garlic, minced
- 3 lemons, zested and juiced

1. **Combine ingredients in a small bowl and marinate chicken, fish or vegetables for 30 minutes to 2 hours before grilling.**

Italian Chicken Marinade

This marinade actually doubles as a lovely salad dressing. Make extra to serve on a bed of leafy greens.

Ingredients:

- ½ cup olive oil
- 2 Tbsp finely grated parmesan cheese
- 2 Tbsp Dijon mustard
- 1 tsp Kosher salt
- ½ tsp black pepper
- 1 small shallot, finely chopped
- The zest and juice of 1 lemon

1. Whisk all ingredients in a small bowl.
2. Pour over chicken in a shallow, glass pan and allow to sit for 30 minutes before grilling.

Lemon Herb Marinade

Ingredients:

- ¼ cup olive oil
- 2 Tbsp fresh rosemary, chopped
- 2 Tbsp fresh thyme, chopped
- 1 tsp salt
- ½ tsp black pepper
- 2 lemons, juiced and zested
- 2 cloves garlic, minced

1. Combine ingredients in a small bowl and pour over poultry, fish, pork, or vegetables for 30 minutes or more.

Korean Barbecue Marinade (Bulgogi)

Fans of Korean barbecue will recognize this sweet and spicy beef. But this marinade also makes fantastic chicken wings, pork chops, and veggies!

Ingredients:

- ¼ cup soy sauce
- ¼ cup chopped green onion
- 2 ½ Tbsp white sugar
- 2 Tbsp minced garlic
- 2 Tbsp sesame seeds
- 2 Tbsp sesame oil
- 1 Tbsp sriracha (more if you would like it hotter)

1. Combine ingredients and marinade meat or veggies overnight for maximum flavor.

Maple Brine

This brine is perfect for pork or poultry.

Ingredients:

- 1 quart water
- ½ cup salt
- ⅓ cup real maple syrup
- 4 cloves garlic, smashed
- 2 Tbsp peppercorns
- 2 tsp dried rosemary
- 1 inch fresh ginger, grated

1. In a small saucepan, combine ingredients over medium heat until salt is dissolved.
2. Cool with ice cubes or bring the brine to room temperature before submerging the pork or poultry for a minimum of 1 hour. Overnight is even better.

Did you know that what most people think of as maple syrup is actually corn syrup with maple flavoring? Real maple syrup is thinner than pancake syrup and is a delicious go-to natural sweetener.

Maple Mustard Marinade

This four ingredient marinade may sound like a strange combination, but covering chicken, pork, veggies, or fish, it is the best damn thing you have put in your mouth.

Ingredients:

- ¼ cup Dijon mustard
- ¼ cup real maple syrup
- 4 clove garlic, minced
- ½ tsp black pepper

1. In a small bowl, combine ingredients and pour over vehicle of your choice.
2. Let sit a minimum of 30 minutes, but overnight is even better.

NOTE: Be sure to set the temperature lower than you would think. This marinade will burn easily because of the sugar content in the maple syrup.

Memphis Marinade

Try marinating ribs in this delightful concoction then mopping them during cooking to keep them moist and tender.

Ingredients:

- 1 cup water
- ½ cup apple cider vinegar
- 3 Tbsp paprika
- 2 Tbsp dry mustard
- 1 Tbsp onion powder
- 1 Tbsp garlic powder
- 1 Tbsp crushed red pepper flake
- 2 tsp black pepper
- 1 tsp dried thyme

1. Combine ingredients in a small saucepan over medium heat for 10 minutes to allow flavors to combine.
2. Cool before applying to meat halfway through smoking.

Not-so-basic Chicken Marinade

The yogurt in this marinade actually keeps the chicken from drying out on the grill.

Ingredients:

- 1 cup plain yogurt
- ¼ cup fresh squeezed lemon juice
- 3 Tbsp olive oil
- 2 cloves garlic, minced
- 1 inch fresh ginger, grated
- 1 tsp salt
- 1 tsp smoked paprika
- ½ tsp pepper
- ½ tsp cumin
- ¼ tsp ground coriander

1. Combine all ingredients and pour over chicken.
2. Marinade for 4-8 hours or overnight.

Overnight Marinade

For leaner, tougher cuts, this marinade is ideal to impart a little more flavor before grilling. It is also ideal for veggies!

Ingredients:

- ½ cup olive oil
- ¼ cup balsamic vinegar
- 2 Tbsp Worcestershire sauce
- 2 Tbsp soy sauce
- 1 tsp Dijon mustard
- 1 clove garlic, minced

1. Whisk together ingredients and pour over meat or veggies in a zip top bag.
2. Refrigerate overnight before grilling.

Salmon Brine

This brine is ideal for a pre-smoke treatment for salmon or other hearty fish.

Ingredients:

- 1 quart water
- ½ cup brown sugar
- ¼ cup kosher salt
- 2 Tbsp Old Bay seasoning
- 2 cloves garlic, minced
- 1 lemon, sliced
- 1 lime, sliced
- 1 onion, sliced

1. In medium saucepan over medium heat, combine water, brown sugar, salt, and seasoning, stirring frequently until salt and sugar are dissolved.
2. Remove from the heat and add onion, garlic, and lemon and lime slices.
3. Allow the brine to cool completely before submerging the fish for 12-24 hours before smoking.

Spicy Thai Marinade

Thai food is known for being sweet, spicy, sour, and salty. All four flavors can be found in this simple marinade. If you can't find fish sauce, you can substitute soy, but it is definitely worth the trip to the Asian market to find it.

Ingredients:

- ½ cup vegetable oil
- ¼ cup cilantro leaves
- 2 Tbsp Asian fish sauce
- 1 Tbsp sriracha or sambal oelek (an Asian chile sauce)

- 1 Tbsp brown sugar
- 8 cloves garlic, peeled
- 2 green onions
- 1 inch ginger, peeled
- The zest and juice of 1 lime

1. In a food processor, pulse all ingredients until a paste forms.
2. Rub on chicken, fish, or shrimp and allow to sit for up to overnight.

Teriyaki Marinade

This marinade can be made thin, without the cornstarch, or thick, with it.

Ingredients:

- ½ cup soy sauce
- ½ cup mirin (Japanese rice wine)
- ¼ cup water
- 2 tsp brown sugar
- ½ inch ginger, finely grated
- 2 cloves garlic, minced
- 2 tsp cornstarch (optional)
- 2 tsp cold water (optional)

1. In a small sauce pan, combine soy sauce, mirin, water, brown sugar, ginger, and garlic and cook over medium heat until the brown sugar has dissolved.
2. Allow to cool and pour over desired meat or veggies.
3. If you would like a thicker marinade, combine cornstarch and remaining water in a separate cup and pour into the marinade.
4. Bring to a boil until the sauce thickens slightly.

Texas Hillbilly Marinade

Because this marinade doesn't have any sugar, it won't burn in low and slow applications.

Ingredients:

- 2 cups apple cider vinegar
- 1 cup (2 sticks) melted butter
- ⅔ cup Worcestershire sauce
- ½ cup water
- ½ cup lemon juice
- 2 Tbsp hot sauce
- 1 Tbsp paprika
- 1 Tbsp chili powder
- 6 bay leaves, crushed
- 2 cloves garlic, minced

1. Heat all ingredients together in a medium saucepan for 10 minutes to combine flavors.
2. Allow to cool before marinating or mopping meat.

Turkey Brine

The best part of the Big Green Egg® is the ability to cook an entire turkey to perfection. This brine ensures your bird stays juicy and flavorful throughout the cooking process

Ingredients:

- 1 gallon cold water
- 1 cup Kosher salt
- 1 cup brown sugar
- ¼ cup Worcestershire sauce
- 1 Tbsp peppercorns
- 4 cloves garlic, smashed
- 2 lemons, cut in pieces

1. Combine water, salt and sugar and stir until both the salt and sugar are dissolved.
2. Add remaining ingredients and submerged turkey.
3. Brine your bird for a minimum of 2 hours or up to overnight.

Veggie Marinade

While any of the marinades in this book are ideal for vegetables, this one is particularly perfect. Sure, you can use it on chicken or pork, but why?

Ingredients:

- ¼ cup olive oil
- ¼ cup white wine vinegar
- ¼ cup red onion, chopped
- 2 Tbsp chopped parsley
- 2 Tbsp minced garlic

- 2 tsp brown sugar
- ½ tsp dried oregano
- ½ tsp dried basil
- ½ tsp Kosher salt
- ¼ tsp black pepper

1. Combine ingredients and pour over vegetables.
2. Allow to sit 1-2 hours before grilling.

SAUCES

Besto Pesto

Pesto can be made with any combination of soft herbs. Try using this same method with a combination of mint and basil or a combination of basil and tarragon.

Ingredients:

- 2 cups packed basil leaves
- 2 cloves garlic
- ⅔ cup olive oil
- ½ cup parmesan cheese
- ¼ cup pine nuts
- ½ tsp salt
- ¼ tsp black pepper

1. In a food processor, pulse pine nuts, garlic, and basil together until just chopped.
2. With the blade running, stream in olive oil until a paste forms.
3. Add parmesan, salt, and pepper and pulse to combine.

TIP: Pesto can be stored in the fridge for up to a week or in the freezer for up to 3 months. Simply add a layer of olive oil to the top of the pesto to prevent it from turning brown and store in an air-tight container.

Catalan Vinaigrette

This sauce is found all over Spain, liberally splashed on a variety of grilled meats and seafoods for an extra zip. Best part, you can customize it to your liking. Don't like Spanish olives? Substitute cornichon. Don't know what a cornichon is? Add green onion.

Ingredients:

- 1 cup olive oil
- ¼ cup onion, finely chopped (Vidalia or red onions work particularly well)
- ¼ cup Spanish olives, finely chopped
- ¼ cup red wine vinegar
- 3 Tbsp water
- 3 Tbsp flat leaf parsley, finely chopped
- 1 Tbsp capers, with juices
- 2 tsp Dijon mustard
- 1 tsp kosher salt
- 1 small tomato, finely chopped
- 1 clove garlic, mashed into a paste

1. Combine red wine vinegar, water, mustard and garlic in a bowl.
2. While whisking, stream in olive oil until the vinaigrette thickens.
3. Add remaining ingredients and stir to combine.
4. Check for seasonings.
5. Liberally brush over meat, seafood, poultry, pork, or veggies once they come off the grill.

Chimichurri

This ubiquitous sauce is found on grilled meats throughout South America and can be customized the same way you would its Italian cousin, pesto. The trick is to not overthink it.

Ingredients:

- ¾ cup olive oil
- ¼ cup red wine vinegar
- 1 Tbsp diced red onion

- 1 tsp dried oregano
- ½ tsp salt
- ¼ tsp black pepper
- ⅛ tsp crushed red pepper flake
- 8 cloves garlic
- 1 bunch curly parsley (Yes, curly. Trust us on this.)

1. In a food processor, pulse parsley, garlic, and red onion until finely chopped.
2. Add vinegar, oregano, salt, pepper, and red pepper flake.
3. With the blade running, stream in olive oil until combined.

For a twist on Chimichurri, add fresh oregano and substitute balsamic vinegar for a new taste experience!

Chinese Barbecue Sauce (Char Sui)

Ingredients:

- ⅔ cup hoisin sauce
- ⅔ cup soy sauce
- ½ cup sugar
- 2 tsp black bean paste
- 1 ½ tsp Chinese five spice powder
- 1 tsp salt
- 4 cloves garlic, minced

1. Combine all ingredients in a small sauce pan and heat over low, stirring constantly.
2. Once mixture thickens, allow it to cool a few minutes before using.

Chipotle Mango Lime Sauce

Ingredients:

- ½ cup ketchup
- 1 Tbsp melted butter
- 1 Tbsp brown sugar
- ½ tsp Kosher salt
- 2 cloves garlic
- 1 mango, peeled, cored and cubed
- 1 chipotle pepper in adobo sauce
- The juice and zest of 1 lime

1. Place all ingredients into a food processor and puree until smooth.
2. Brush on chicken, pork or fish in the last 10-15 minutes of cooking.

Classic Texas Barbecue Sauce

Texas barbecue sauce is sweet, tangy, and just a little spicy. Since beef is the name of the game in Texas barbecue, this sauce can stand up to any brisket or burger but won't overpower pork or chicken.

Ingredients:

- 1 cup water
- 1 cup ketchup
- ½ cup apple cider vinegar
- ½ cup chopped celery
- ¼ cup (half a stick) butter
- ¼ cup minced onion
- 2 Tbsp Worcestershire sauce
- 2 Tbsp spicy mustard
- 2 Tbsp honey
- 2 Tbsp chili powder
- 1 Tbsp beef base or 1 beef bouillon cube
- ½ tsp salt
- ½ tsp pepper
- ¼ tsp cayenne pepper
- 2 cloves garlic, minced

1. Melt the butter in a medium-sized saucepan.
2. Add onion and celery and cook until translucent.
3. Add water and bouillon and stir until bouillon is dissolved.
4. Add remaining ingredients and cook until the mixture has reduced by ⅓ and is thickened, around 15 minutes.
5. Blend in a blender or food processor until smooth.
6. Brush onto meat the last 15-30 minutes of cooking.

Coffee Spice Sauce

Red eye gravy is found all over the south as an accompaniment to breakfast food. It is made from the drippings of ham, sausage, or bacon, spiked with coffee, and thickened with flour.

This sauce is a wink and a nod to that southern tradition only spicier and with a tomato backbone.

Ingredients:

- ¾ cup brown sugar, packed
- ½ cup ketchup
- ½ cup strong coffee
- ½ cup apple cider vinegar
- ½ cup finely chopped red onion
- ½ cup Thai sweet chile sauce
- 2 Tbsp Worcestershire sauce
- 2 Tbsp smoked paprika
- 1 Tbsp bacon fat (you can substitute olive oil, but why?)
- 2 tsp sriracha
- 1 tsp cumin
- 2 cloves garlic, smashed
- 1 8-ounce can tomato sauce

1. **In a medium saucepan, heat bacon fat or olive oil over medium heat.**
2. **Add onion and garlic and cook until translucent.**
3. **Add remaining ingredients and simmer over low for 15-20 minutes.**

Compound Herb Butter

This trick can be customized to any taste preference and is perfect for adding a finishing touch to meat, fish, or veggies.

Ingredients:

- ½ cup (1 stick) butter, softened
- 2 Tbsp fresh chopped parsley
- 1 Tbsp fresh chopped tarragon
- 1 clove garlic, smashed into a paste

1. **Combine all ingredients, wrap in plastic and refrigerate until ready to use.**

East Carolina Barbecue Sauce

Barbecue sauce in the eastern part of the Carolinas is made up of three basic items - apple cider vinegar, sugar, and crushed red pepper flake. Ours takes advantage of the garlicky flavor of Sriracha or sambal to kick the heat up a notch without sacrificing flavor. Unlike traditional thick barbecue sauces, this sauce is meant to be served on the table as the perfect complement to fatty pork dishes.

Ingredients:

- 2 cups apple cider vinegar
- 1 cup sugar
- ½ cup (1 stick) butter
- 1 Tbsp Worcestershire
- 1 Tbsp ground dry mustard
- 1 Tbsp Sriracha or sambal
- 1 tsp crushed red pepper flake

1. **In a medium saucepan, heat ingredients until sugar has dissolved.**
2. **Cool and serve in a squeeze bottle alongside pulled pork.**

Frank's Buffalo Sauce

Taking a cue from buffalo wings, this sauce has a bit more complexity than the traditional buffalo sauce.

Ingredients:

- 1 cup Frank's red hot sauce
- ½ cup ketchup
- ¼ cup apple cider vinegar
- 2 Tbsp butter
- 2 tsp Worcestershire
- ¼ tsp celery seed

1. **Combine ingredients in a small sauce pan over medium heat until thoroughly combined and heated through, around 5 minutes.**
2. **Allow to cool before applying to meat.**

Garlic Sauce

Garlic lovers unite!

Ingredients:

- ½ cup (1 stick) butter
- ¼ cup minced garlic
- ¼ cup lemon juice
- 2 Tbsp soy sauce

- 1 Tbsp honey
- Black pepper, to taste
- Cayenne pepper, to taste

1. In a small saucepan, melt butter and add garlic.
2. Cook until the garlic is softened.
3. Add remaining ingredients and season with black pepper and cayenne for a kick.
4. Serve brushed over chicken, fish, or veggies.

Kansas City Barbecue Sauce

Traditional Kansas City barbecue sauce is sweet and thick with a touch of heat. This sauce does not disappoint and is perfect for ribs.

Ingredients:

- 1 ½ cup ketchup
- 1 cup water
- ⅓ cup apple cider vinegar
- ¼ cup dark brown sugar
- 2 Tbsp molasses
- 1 Tbsp onion powder
- 1 Tbsp garlic powder
- 1 Tbsp black pepper
- 1 tsp celery salt
- 1 tsp allspice
- 1 tsp cayenne

1. Combine all ingredients in a small saucepan over medium heat until thoroughly combined.
2. Reduce heat to a simmer until thickened, around 10 minutes.
3. Allow to cool before applying to meat.
4. Brush meat with the sauce the last 15-30 minutes of cooking to prevent it from burning.

TIP: Allspice is actually not a combination of spices as the name suggests. Even though it tastes like a combination of cinnamon, nutmeg, and clove, it is the berry from the allspice bush.

Peach Mustard Sauce

If you're tired of tomato based barbecue sauces, this sweet and tangy sauce is the perfect out-of-the-ordinary barbecue sauce for chicken, fish, or pork.

Ingredients:

- 1 cup peach jam or preserves
- ¼ cup butter (½ stick)
- ¼ cup minced onion
- ¼ cup apple cider vinegar
- ½ cup whole grain mustard
- ¼ cup Dijon mustard
- ½ tsp salt
- 3 cloves garlic, minced

1. In a medium saucepan over medium heat, melt butter until foamy.
2. Add onion and garlic and cook until translucent.
3. Add remaining ingredients and simmer for 10 minutes until thick.
4. For a smoother sauce, puree in a food processor or blender.
5. Brush sauce on chicken, pork, or fish during the last 15-30 minutes of cooking.

Peanut Sauce

Not only does this sauce make a fantastic barbecue sauce on chicken, it is also a phenomenal dipping sauce for egg rolls or chicken wings.

Ingredients:

- 1 cup Thai sweet chile sauce
- ½ cup cocktail peanuts, finely chopped
- 3 Tbsp fresh lime juice
- 2 Tbsp soy sauce
- 2 Tbsp toasted sesame oil
- 1 Tbsp ginger, freshly grated
- 2 tsp Asian hot chili sauce or Sriracha
- 2 garlic cloves, minced
- 2 green onions, finely chopped

1. Combine all ingredients in a bowl and allow to sit at least 30 minutes before using.

Romesco Sauce

This Spanish sauce is popular on grilled meats and gets its consistency from almonds and day-old bread.

Ingredients:

- 1 cup day old bread cubes
- ½ cup olive oil
- 2 Tbsp water
- 2 Tbsp red wine vinegar
- 2 Tbsp blanched almonds
- ½ tsp salt
- 2 cloves garlic
- 1 large red bell pepper, roasted and peeled
- 1 large tomato, cored
- 1 chipotle in adobo sauce, finely chopped

1. In a blender, combine all ingredients and blend until smooth.
2. Use on poultry, seafood, or veggies.

Sweet and Sour Hoisin Sauce

This Asian-inspired sauce is a great addition to spare ribs that have been rubbed with our Asian rub.

Ingredients:

- ½ cup dry sherry
- ½ cup hoisin sauce
- ½ cup ketchup
- ¼ cup rice wine vinegar
- 2 Tbsp finely grated peeled fresh ginger
- 2 Tbsp sugar
- 1 Tbsp extra-virgin olive oil
- 2 tsp sambal or Sriracha
- 2 tsp soy sauce
- 2 tsp sesame oil
- 2 cloves garlic, chopped

1. In a saucepan, heat olive oil.
2. Add garlic and ginger and cook until fragrant.
3. Add remaining ingredients and simmer over low heat for 10 minutes.
4. Allow to cool before applying to meat.

White Barbecue Sauce

White barbecue sauce is ideal for poultry. Marinate your birds in it for tender, flavorful meat or brush it on during the last 30 minutes of cooking.

Ingredients:

- 1 cup mayonnaise
- ½ cup apple cider vinegar
- ¼ cup lemon juice
- ¼ cup apple juice
- 2 Tbsp horseradish
- 1 Tbsp garlic powder
- 1 Tbsp onion powder
- 1 Tbsp ground black pepper
- 1 tsp dry mustard powder
- ½ tsp salt
- ½ tsp cayenne pepper

1. Combine all ingredients in a medium bowl.
2. Cover and chill at least one hour before using.

Z10 Steak Sauce

You know that popular steak sauce brand, right? This sauce is an homage to that one, but with a devilish twist.

Ingredients:

- ¾ cup balsamic vinegar
- ½ cup ketchup
- ¼ cup honey
- ¼ cup finely diced red onion
- 2 Tbsp Worcestershire sauce
- 1 Tbsp olive oil
- 1 Tbsp dijon mustard
- 1 tsp sriracha
- ¼ tsp cracked black pepper
- ¼ tsp allspice

1. In a small saucepan, heat olive oil.
2. Add onion and cook until translucent.
3. Add remaining ingredients and simmer on low 10 minutes.
4. For a smoother sauce, blend in a blender until smooth.

Beef

Beef rules the barbecue and grilling landscape in areas like Texas where Brisket reigns supreme and brontosaurus-sized beef ribs are rule the day. If you haven't tried the larger cuts on the grill, now is the time and The Big Green Egg® is the perfect vehicle.

ROASTS	BURGERS	STEAKS
Holiday Sirloin Roast	Breakfast Burger	Asian Flank Steak
New York Style Pastrami	Classic American Burger	Korean Short Ribs
Perfectly Smoked Texas Style Brisket	Oahu Burger	London Bridge London Broil
Prime Rib Roast	Quesadilla Burger	New York Strip Steaks
Rouladen	The Crowned Jewels Burger	Pitmaster Ribeyes
Round Roast Cheesesteaks	"The Masterpiece"	Serious Tenderloin Kebab
Shredded Chuck Roast Tacos		Skirt Steak Fajitas

ROASTS

Roasts are the unsung heroes of the grill. Most of the time we think of grilling as the method for steaks, chicken, and sausages. But the best part of the Big Green Egg® is its ability to mimic an oven in its temperature consistency and efficiency.

HOLIDAY SIRLOIN ROAST

Sirloin roasts are a delicious, less expensive alternative to standing rib roasts.

Preparation Time: 20 minutes
Cooking Temperature: 325°F
Cooking Time: 2-3 hours
Serves: 6-8

Meat	Seasoning
▸ 1 5-8 lb sirloin roast	▸ ¼ cup Dijon mustard ▸ 2 Tbsp fresh rosemary, chopped ▸ ½ tsp salt ▸ ¼ tsp pepper ▸ 3 cloves garlic, minced

Preparation:

1. Bring the roast to room temperature for 30 minutes before cooking.
2. Sprinkle the roast with salt and pepper.
3. Spread liberally with Dijon and press rosemary and garlic into the mustard. .Grilling:
1. Heat the EGG® to 325°F.
2. Place the roast directly on the grid and close the dome for 2 ½ to 3 hours or until the internal temperature reaches 130°F.
3. Remove from the EGG® onto a board and allow it to rest for 20 minutes before carving.

Beef | Roasts

NEW YORK STYLE PASTRAMI

When you can't make it to Katz's deli, bring that deli flavor to you. Homemade pastrami takes some time, but it is definitely worth it.

Preparation Time: 4 days
Cooking Temperature: 250°F
Cooking Time: 8-10 hours
Serves: 8-10

Meat	Cure	Rub
▸ 1 (12-lb.) whole beef brisket	▸ ¼ cup curing salt ▸ 3 Tbsp garlic, granulated ▸ 2 Tbsp pickling spice ▸ 2 Tbsp ground coriander	▸ 1 cup water ▸ 3 Tbsp black pepper, coarsely ground ▸ 1 Tbsp coriander seeds, toasted and ground ▸ 1 tsp garlic, granulated

Preparation:

1. Wash the brisket and pat-dry.
2. Trim the fat evenly across the surface of the brisket, leaving ½ inch of fat on the meat.
3. In a bowl, combine all cure ingredients. Coat the brisket entirely with the cure.
4. Place the cured brisket in a 2-gallon resealable bag . Refrigerate it for 4 days, turning the brisket 1-2 times per day.
5. After 4 days, remove the brisket from the bag. Wash it well and pat-dry.
6. In a mixing bowl, mix together all of the rub ingredients.
7. Coat the brisket evenly with the rub.
8. Let it sit for at room temperature for 30 minutes before smoking.

Smoking:

1. Preheat the EGG® to 250°F. Add 2 cups of soaked wood chips to the lit natural lump charcoal. (We like cherry or hickory.)
2. Set the brisket directly on the grid, fat side up.
3. Smoke the meat for 4-5 hours, or until the internal temperature registers 165°F.
4. Remove the brisket from the smoker.
5. Wrap the brisket tightly in aluminum foil, adding ¼ cup of water to the pouch before sealing the foil.
6. Place the pastrami back on the grid and cook until the internal temperature registers 190°F.
7. For best results, let the pastrami rest for 20-30 minutes before slicing.

Beef | Roasts

PERFECTLY SMOKED TEXAS STYLE BRISKET

Brisket is a versatile slab of beef, perfect for beginner smokers. Be sure to purchase a brisket with a layer of fat and smoke it fat-side up.

Preparation Time: 6 hours
Cooking Temperature: 250°F
Cooking Time: 8-10 Hours (1 hour per lb.)
Serves: 8-10

Meat	From This Book
▸ 1 (8-10 lb) brisket	▸ 1 cup Basic Barbecue Rub

Preparation:

1. Set the brisket in an aluminum pan, fat side-up.
2. Sprinkle liberally with Basic Barbecue Rub.
3. Cover the aluminum pan and refrigerate for at least 6 hours or overnight.
4. Let the brisket come to room temperature in the aluminum pan for 30 minutes.
5. Preheat the EGG® to 250°F adding 2 cups of soaked wood chips to the heated coals.

Smoking:

1. Set the brisket directly on the grid. Close the dome.
2. Begin checking the internal temperature of the brisket after 8 hours. Remove the brisket from the smoker when the internal temperature reaches 190°F.
3. Let the meat rest for 15-20 minutes before carving.

PRIME RIB ROAST

Prime Rib Roasts, also known as a standing rib roast, are widely available around the holidays. These roasts are basically several ribeye steaks before they are cut. While expensive, there is nothing more impressive for a special occasion than beautiful slices of prime rib.

Preparation Time: 25 min
Cooking Temperature: 425°F
Cooking Time: 4 ½ - 5 hours
Serves: 8-10

Meat	From This Book
▸ 1 14-pound rib roast	▸ ¼ cup English Pub Rub

Preparation:

1. Remove from fridge and allow the roast to come to room temperature, about 30 minutes.
2. Dry the roast with paper towels and season liberally with English Pub Rub.

Smoking:

1. Preheat the EGG® to 425°F.
2. Place the roast directly on the grid and close the dome.
3. Cook for 20 minutes per pound, or until the internal temperature reaches 130°F (for medium).
4. Remove from the EGG® and allow the roast to rest for 30 minutes before carving.

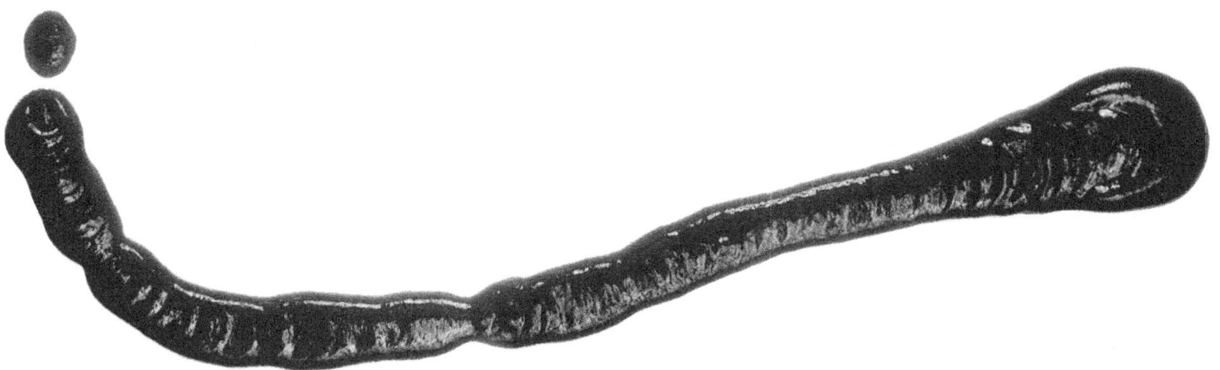

ROULADEN

Rouladen is a traditional German dish that is almost always stuffed with onion, bacon, and dill pickle. While it is usually browned, braised, and served with gravy, this version on the grill comes together quickly and is sure to please.

Preparation Time: 20 minutes
Cooking Time: 30-45 minutes
Serves: 6

Meat	Filling
▸ 1 1½-2lb flank steak	▸ ½ cup chopped onion ▸ ⅓ cup chopped dill pickle ▸ ¼ cup German mustard ▸ ½ tsp salt ▸ ¼ tsp pepper ▸ 6 strips of bacon, separated

Preparation:

1. In a medium skillet, brown 3 strips of bacon until crisp. Remove from the pan.
2. Remove all by 2 Tbsp of the bacon fat and cook the onion over medium heat or until the onion is translucent. Set aside to cool.
3. Pound flank steak into an 8 inch by 10 inch rectangle.
4. Spread the meat with the mustard.
5. Top the meat with the onion, dill pickle, and crumbled cooked bacon.
6. Roll the meat around the filling lengthwise.
7. Wrap the roast with the remaining raw bacon and secure with metal skewers.

Grilling:

1. Heat the EGG® to 425°F. Place the roast on the grid and cook for 30-45 minutes or until the internal temperature reaches 130°F.
2. Allow the rouladen to rest for 20 minutes before carving.

ROUND ROAST CHEESESTEAKS WITH PEPPER JACK CHEESE SAUCE

Philadelphians take their cheesesteaks seriously. So much so a rivalry has brewed for generations between those who like their cheesesteaks "with" or "without". This take on a classic has a spicy twist on the traditional melted cheese product so popular throughout Philly.

Meat & Fixings	From This Book	Pepper Jack Cheese Sauce
▸ 1 2-3 lb Round Roast ▸ 2 Tbsp olive oil ▸ 6 crusty hoagie rolls ▸ 1 large onion, sliced	▸ ¼ cup Garlic Lovers' Rub	▸ 2 cups whole milk ▸ 1 cup Pepper Jack cheese ▸ 2 Tbsp butter ▸ 2 Tbsp flour ▸ ½ tsp salt ▸ ¼ tsp sriracha

Preparation:

1. Bring round roast to room temperature.
2. Spread liberally with Garlic Lover's' Rub.
3. In a medium skillet, heat olive oil and cook onion slowly until caramelized, about 20 minutes.
4. Meanwhile, in a small sauce pan, melt butter and stir in flour. Cook an additional 1 minute.
5. Slowly add milk, whisking continually until thickened.
6. Remove the sauce from the heat, add salt, sriracha, and cheese, and stir to combine.

Grilling:

1. Preheat the EGG® to 475°F.
2. Place the roast on the grid and close the dome for 10 minutes.
3. Reduce the heat inside the EGG® to 325°F and continue to cook for 25-30 minutes or until the internal temperature reaches 130°F.
4. Remove from the EGG® and set aside to rest while cooking the onions and making the cheese sauce.
5. Thinly slice the beef, adding several slices to a hoagie roll. Top with onion and cheese sauce and serve.

SHREDDED CHUCK ROAST TACOS

Chuck roast is the ideal roast for pot roast, but this particularly fatty cut also makes great shredded beef tacos.

Preparation Time: 20 minutes
Cooking Temperature: 225°F
Cooking Time: 4-5 hours
Serves: 6-8

Meat	From This Book	Taco Fixings
▸ 1 3-4 lb chuck roast	▸ ¼ cup Adobo Rub	▸ 12 taco-size flour or corn tortillas ▸ Shredded lettuce ▸ Shredded cheese ▸ Salsa ▸ Sour cream ▸ Guacamole

Preparation:

1. Bring chuck roast to room temperature for 30 minutes.
2. Sprinkle liberally with Adobo Rub.

Grilling:

1. Preheat the EGG® to 225°F.
2. Place the roast on the grid and close the dome.
3. Cook for 4-5 hours or until the roast is tender.
4. Use two forks to shred the meat. Serve on tortillas with toppings.

BURGERS

There is nothing like a burger cooked over an open flame but the same old burger gets tiresome. Try these new takes on a classic to mix things up a bit. We like to use 80/20 ground beef, which is 80 percent meat and 20 percent fat. This keeps the burger moist and juicy when cooked.

BREAKFAST BURGER

What could possibly be better than a burger? A burger for breakfast. Think of this as breakfast on an eggy, buttery bun.

Preparation Time: 20 minutes
Cooking Temperature: 400°F
Cooking Time: 11-13 minutes
Serves: 4

Burgers	Fixings
▸ 1 ½ lb ground beef	▸ 2 Tbsp butter
▸ ½ lb ground pork breakfast sausage	▸ 8 strips bacon
	▸ 4 slices sharp cheddar cheese
	▸ 4 Brioche buns
	▸ 4 eggs
	▸ 4 thick slices tomato

Preparation:
1. In a medium bowl, mix ground beef and sausage until just combined.
2. Form into 4 patties and refrigerate while the EGG® heats.
3. Melt butter in a large skillet and fry the eggs for 2 minutes on each side.

Grilling:
1. Preheat the EGG® to 400°F.
2. Place bacon on a small cookie sheet and place on the grid in the EGG®. Cook until crispy.
3. Place the patties on the grid and close the dome for 3 minutes.
4. Flip the burgers and replace the dome for an additional 3 minutes.
5. Close all of the vents and allow the burgers to sit for an additional 5 minutes. The internal temperature of the burger should be 150°F.
6. Place cheese on top of the burgers and cover for 1 more minute.
7. Assemble the burgers by placing a burger on the bottom bun, topping with bacon, tomato, and a fried egg.

CLASSIC AMERICAN BURGER

This classic burger will be the perfect centerpiece of every barbecue.

Preparation Time: 20 minutes
Cooking Temperature: 500°F
Cooking Time: 10-12 minutes
Serves: 4

Burgers	Fixings
▸ 2 lbs ground beef ▸ ½ tsp salt ▸ ¼ tsp pepper	▸ 4 slices American cheese ▸ 4 hamburger buns ▸ Green Leaf Lettuce ▸ Sliced Tomato ▸ Ketchup ▸ Mustard ▸ Sliced Pickle

Preparation:

1. Form ground beef into four patties and season both sides with salt and pepper.

Grilling:

1. Preheat the EGG® to 500°F.
2. Place burgers on the grid and close the dome for 3 minutes.
3. Flip burgers and close the dome for 2 more minutes.
4. Close all of the vents and allow the burgers to sit for 5 minutes.
5. Top each burger with a slice of cheese and close the dome for 1 more minute.
6. Build burgers with lettuce, tomato, pickle, mustard, and ketchup.

OAHU BURGER

When we think of Oahu, we think of pineapple and teriyaki. This burger delivers on both.

Preparation Time: 10 minutes
Cooking Temperature: 500°F
Cooking Time: 10-12 minutes
Serves: 4

Burger	Fixings
▸ 2 lbs ground beef ▸ ¼ cup thickened Teriyaki Marinade	▸ ¼ cup mayonnaise ▸ ½ tsp sambal or sriracha ▸ 4 slices fresh pineapple, cored ▸ 4 slices tomato ▸ 4 slices butter lettuce ▸ 4 Hawaiian hamburger buns

Preparation:

1. Form ground beef into four patties and season both sides with salt and pepper.
2. In a small bowl, mix mayonnaise with hot chile sauce and spread on buns.
3. Top each bun with a burger, slice of pineapple, lettuce and tomato.

Grilling:

1. Preheat the EGG® to 500°F.
2. Place burgers on the grid and close the dome for 3 minutes.
3. Flip burgers, baste with Teriyaki Marinade, and place the pineapple slices on the grid. Close the dome for 2 more minutes.
4. Flip the burgers again and baste with remaining Teriyaki Marinade. Close the dome.
5. Close all of the vents and allow the burgers to sit for 5 minutes.

QUESADILLA BURGER

When you can't decide between a burger or tacos, why not have both?

Preparation Time: 20 minutes
Cooking Temperature: 500°F
Cooking Time: 10-12 minutes
Serves: 4

Burger	**Fixings**
▸ 2 lbs ground beef ▸ 2 Tbsp Adobo Rub	▸ 1 cup shredded cheddar cheese ▸ 4 large flour tortillas ▸ Sour Cream ▸ Guacamole ▸ Salsa

Preparation:

1. Form ground beef into four patties and season both sides with Adobo Rub.
2. Serve each burger with sour cream, guacamole, and salsa.

Grilling:

1. Preheat the EGG® to 500°F.
2. Place burgers on the grid and close the dome for 3 minutes.
3. Flip burgers and close the dome for 2 more minutes.
4. Close all of the vents and allow the burgers to sit for 5 minutes.
5. Remove burgers and place flour tortillas on the grid.
6. Top each tortilla with shredded cheese and close the dome for 1 minute until the cheese melts.
7. Place a hamburger in the center of each tortilla and begin folding the tortilla around the burger like an envelope.

Beef | Burgers

THE CROWNED JEWELS BURGER

High in the mountains of Utah sits a local chain of restaurants called "Crown Burger". Their signature burger that bears the same name is a beacon of meat in the desert. This version is an homage, piled high with pastrami and a mysterious sauce known in the intermountain west as "fry sauce". Go ahead and make more for your fries.

Preparation Time: 20 minutes
Cooking Temperature: 500°F
Cooking Time: 10-12 minutes
Serves: 4

Burger

- 2 lbs ground beef
- ½ tsp salt
- ¼ tsp pepper

Fixings

- 1 lb thinly sliced pastrami
- 1 cup shredded Romaine lettuce
- ¼ cup mayonnaise
- 2 Tbsp ketchup
- ⅛ tsp onion powder
- 4 slices Sharp Cheddar cheese
- 4 hamburger buns
- 1 tomato, sliced

Preparation:

1. Form ground beef into four patties and season both sides with salt and pepper.
2. Meanwhile, mix together mayonnaise, ketchup, and onion powder. Smear on each bun.
3. Place each pastrami and cheese covered burger on the prepared buns and top with shredded lettuce and tomato.Grilling:
1. Preheat the EGG® to 500°F.
2. Place burgers on the grid and close the dome for 3 minutes.
3. Flip burgers and close the dome for 2 more minutes.
4. Close all of the vents and allow the burgers to sit for 5 minutes.
5. Top each burger with ¼ of the pastrami and a slice of cheese and close the dome for 1 more minute.

"THE MASTERPIECE"

When you start looking at burgers as a vehicle for any flavor, you start to realize the possibilities are endless. This masterpiece takes all of the favorite toppings for a burger and stuffs them inside.

Preparation Time: 30 minutes
Cooking Time: 10-12 minutes
Serves: 4

Burgers	Fixings
▸ 2 lbs ground beef ▸ 6 ounces sliced mushrooms ▸ 4 Tbsp shredded smoked Gouda ▸ 2 Tbsp butter ▸ 2 Tbsp olive oil ▸ 2 Tbsp Dijon mustard ▸ ½ tsp salt ▸ ¼ tsp pepper ▸ 8 slices bacon, cooked and crumbled	▸ 4 slices Swiss cheese ▸ 4 brioche buns ▸ 1 small onion, sliced

Preparation:

1. Heat a skillet over medium heat and add 1 Tbsp butter and 1 Tbsp olive oil.
2. Place mushrooms in the pan and DO NOT MOVE THEM. Saute for 5-7 minutes or until the mushrooms are browned. Remove from the pan and set aside.
3. In the same skillet, heat remaining butter and olive oil and add onions. Saute over medium heat until they become translucent and begin to brown, about 10 minutes. Remove from the heat and set aside to cool.
4. Mix onion, mushrooms, and crumbled bacon.

Grilling:

1. Preheat the EGG® to 425°F.
2. Form ground beef into eight patties and season both sides with salt and pepper.
3. Place a generous spoonful of the mushroom and onion mixture in the center of four patties and top with smoked Gouda.
4. Top with additional patty and press sides to seal the mixture inside.
5. Place burgers on the grid and close the dome for 5 minutes.
6. Flip burgers and close the dome for 3 more minutes.
7. Close all of the vents and allow the burgers to sit for 5 minutes.
8. Top each burger with a slice of Swiss cheese and close the dome for 1 more minute.
9. Spread buns with mustard, top with burgers and bun tops.

STEAKS

Going to a high quality steakhouse is an experience, a bank-busting experience. Next time you crave a steak, give these tasty recipes a try and keep more money in your pocket.

ASIAN FLANK STEAK

The trick to flank steak is to cook it medium rare to medium, let it rest, and slice it thinly on a bias.

Preparation Time: 30 minutes - overnight
Cooking Temperature: 500°F
Cooking Time: 12-14 minutes
Serves: 4-6

Meat	From This Book
▸ 1-1 ½ -pound flank steak	▸ 1 recipe Spicy Thai Marinade

Preparation:
1. Pour marinade into a large zip top bag and place steak inside. Refrigerate at least 30 minutes or up to overnight.
2. Remove the meat from the fridge while you preheat the EGG® to 500°F..

Grilling:
1. Place flank steak on the grid and close the dome for 3 minutes.
2. Flip the steak over and cook an additional 2 minutes.
3. Close all of the vents and let the steak sit for 5 minutes or until the internal temperature reaches 130°F.
4. Remove the steak and allow it to rest for 10 minutes before slicing thinly on the bias.

KOREAN SHORT RIBS

Okay, so these aren't technically steaks, but they are best cooked quickly over a high heat. Your butcher can cut your short ribs "flanken style" meaning cross-sections of bone are held together by rib meat. This ensures the meat stays tender and tasty.

Preparation Time: 4 hours - overnight
Cooking Temperature: 500°F
Cooking Time: 6 minutes
Serves: 4-6

Meat	From This Book
▸ 12 flanken style beef short ribs (about 4 lbs)	▸ 1 recipe Korean Barbecue Marinade

Preparation:
1. Pour the marinade in a large zip top bag. Add short ribs. Seal and let sit in the fridge at least 4 hours, preferably overnight.
2. Remove short ribs from the oven before preheating the EGG®.

Grilling:
1. Preheat the EGG® to 500°F.
2. Place the ribs directly on the grid and close the dome for 3 minutes.
3. Turn the ribs and cook an additional 2 minutes.
4. Remove the ribs, close all vents to extinguish the fire, and serve.

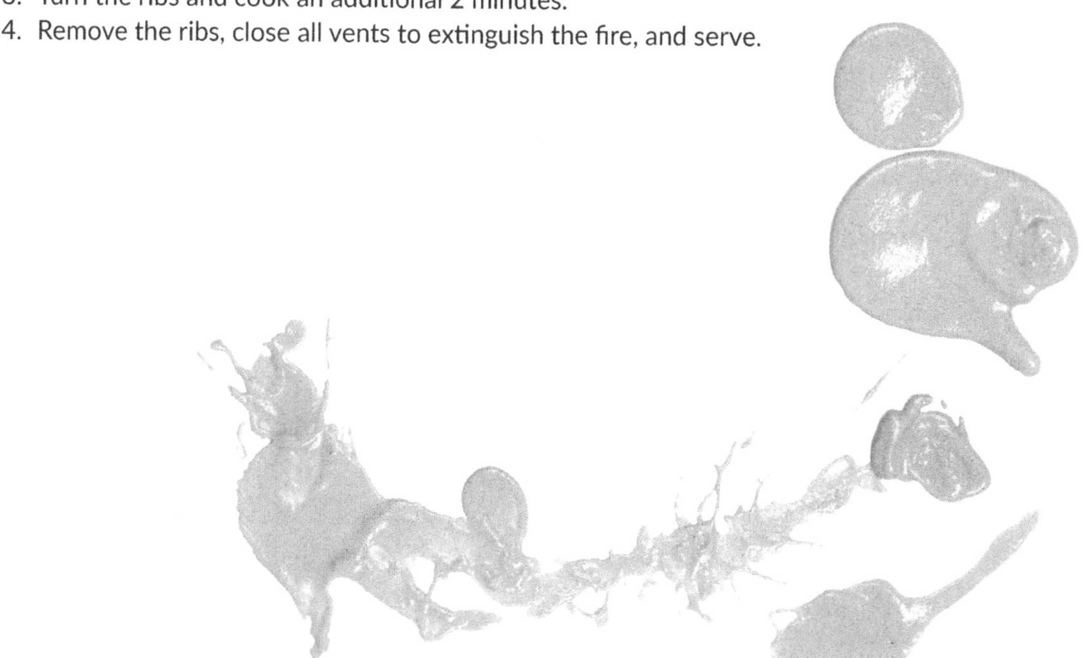

Beef | Steaks

LONDON BRIDGE LONDON BROIL

London Broil was the "en vogue" cut of meat in the 50's and 60's with highly acidic marinades to cover the gamey flavor of this particular cut. That led to rubbery meat that was often overcooked. However, when it is treated like a normal steak and cut thinly across the grain, this inexpensive cut provides delicious beefy flavor.

Preparation Time: 5 minutes
Cooking Temperature: 500°F
Cooking Time: 10 minutes
Serves: 4-6

Fajitas	From This Book
▸ 1 1 ½ -2 pound London Broil ▸ ½ tsp salt ▸ ¼ tsp pepper	▸ 4 Tbsp Herb Compound Butter

Preparation:

1. Season both sides with salt and pepper.

Grilling:

1. Preheat the EGG® to 500°F.
2. Place London Broil on the grid and close the dome for 3 minutes.
3. Flip the steak over and cook an additional 2 minutes.
4. Close all of the vents and let the steak sit for 5 minutes or until the internal temperature reaches 130°F.
5. Remove the steak and immediately top with dots of Herb Compound Butter.
6. Allow it to rest for 10 minutes before slicing thinly across the grain.

NEW YORK STRIP STEAKS

Look at this as the "method" looking for a little madness. Check out our spice rub guide for new flavor combinations for this meaty favorite. Looking to stretch your steak further? Plan on two people per steak and slice them before serving.

Preparation Time: 5 minutes
Cooking Temperature: 500°F
Cooking Time: 10 minutes
Serves: 8

Meat	From This Book
▸ 4 New York Strip Steaks	▸ ¼ cup spice rub of your choice

Preparation:

1. Season both sides of all steaks with spice rub and allow to sit for 15 minutes.

Grilling:

1. Preheat the EGG® to 500°F.
2. Place steaks on the grid and close the dome for 3 minutes.
3. Flip the steaks over and cook an additional 2 minutes.
4. Close all of the vents and let the steaks sit for 5 minutes or until the internal temperature reaches 130°F.
5. Allow the steaks to rest for 10 minutes before slicing.

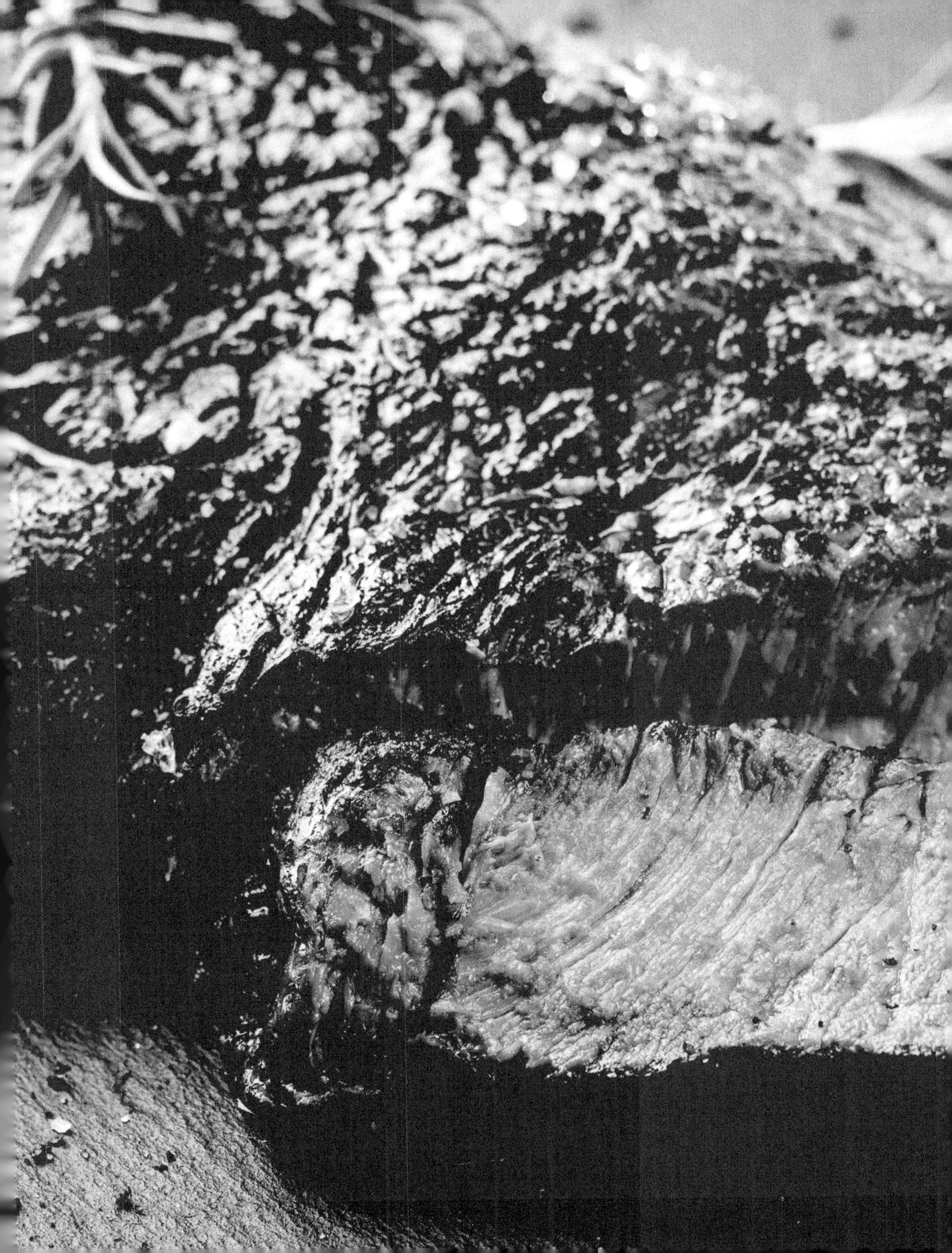

PITMASTER RIBEYES

In barbecue competitions around the country, ribeye steaks are the steak of choice. These are smoked then seared giving the intramuscular fat a chance to melt making the meat succulent.

Preparation Time: 30 minutes
Cooking Temperature: 225°F
Cooking Time: 1 hour 15 minutes
Serves: 4-8

Meat	From This Book
▸ 4 ribeye steaks	▸ ¼ cup spice rub

Preparation:

1. Season both sides of all steaks with spice rub and allow to sit for 15 minutes.

Grilling:

1. Preheat the EGG® to 225°F. Add soaked wood chips to the charcoal. (We like pecan or apple.)
2. Place the steaks on the grid and allow to smoke for 1 hour.
3. Remove the steaks from the grill.
4. Heat the EGG® to 500°F.
5. Place steaks on the grid and close the dome for 3 minutes.
6. Flip the steaks over and cook an additional 2 minutes.
7. Close all of the vents and let the steaks sit for 5 minutes or until the internal temperature reaches 130°F.
8. Allow the steaks to rest for 5-10 minutes before slicing.

Beef | Steaks

SERIOUS TENDERLOIN KEBABS

The secret to great kebab is to soak the skewers, don't overcrowd the meat, and cook meat on one skewer and veggies on another. This will prevent the veggies from overcooking while the meat stays undercooked, or vice versa.

Preparation Time: 30 minutes
Cooking Temperature: 500°F
Cooking Time: 10 minutes
Serves: 6-8

Meat	From This Book
▸ 2-3 lbs beef tenderloin	▸ 1 recipe Beef Kebab Marinade

Preparation:

1. Cut tenderloin into 2 inch cubes and marinate in the Beef Kebab Marinade for a minimum of 30 minutes.
2. Thread cubes onto soaked wooden or metal skewers and set aside.

Grilling:

1. Preheat the EGG® to 500°F.
2. Place skewers on the grid and close the dome for 3 minutes.
3. Flip the skewers over and cook an additional 2 minutes.
4. Close all of the vents and let the skewers sit for 5 minutes or until the internal temperature reaches 130°F.

SKIRT STEAK FAJITAS

Skirt Steak is a super popular cut for fajitas because it is relatively inexpensive and serves a lot of people. Be sure to remove all of the stringy tendon on the back of the skirt steak for maximum tenderness.

Preparation Time: 30 minutes
Cooking Temperature: 500°F
Cooking Time: 10 minutes
Serves: 4-6

Meat	From This Book	Fixings
▸ 2 skirt steaks (about 1 ½ pounds)	▸ 1 recipe Carne Asada Marinade	▸ 2 green bell peppers, sliced ▸ 1 onion, sliced ▸ 1 Tbsp olive oil ▸ Flour Tortillas ▸ Guacamole ▸ Sour Cream ▸ Pico de Gallo

Preparation:

1. In a large zip top bag, combine skirt steaks and Carne Asada Marinade. Refrigerate for a minimum of 30 minutes.
2. In a medium skillet, preheat olive oil and saute onions and peppers over medium heat for 10-15 minutes or until they soften and begin to brown.
3. Remove steak from the fridge and preheat the EGG® to 500°F.

Grilling:

1. Place the steaks directly on the grid and close the dome for 3 minutes.
2. Turn the steaks and cook an additional 2 minutes.
3. Remove the steaks, close all vents to extinguish the fire, and slice across the grain.
4. Serve with tortillas, guacamole, sour cream, and pico de gallo.

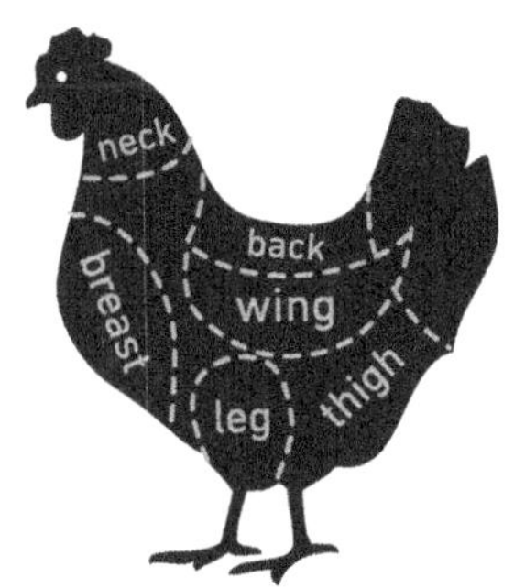

Poultry

While I don't object to cooking a boneless, skinless chicken breast on the grill, it takes a lot more work to make sure it stays moist, juicy, and tasty. If you are tired of dried out, flavorless poultry, give these methods a try and fall in love with white meat all over again.

WHOLE BIRDS	WINGS & THINGS	OTHER POULTRY
Beer Can Chicken Chicken Under a Brick Rotisserie Style Chicken Whole Smoked Barbecue Chicken	Bacon Wrapped Chicken Bites Chicken Keema Burgers Classic Hot Wings Greek Chicken Kebabs Hoisin Glazed Wings Jerk Chicken Drums Lemon Scented Chicken Thighs Stuffed Chicken Breasts with Sundried Tomatoes and Artichokes Thai Stuffed Chicken Drums "Walk the Plank" Chicken Quarters Wicked Wings	Amusement Park Turkey Legs Company Cornish Game Hens Grilled Pheasant with Chimichurri Peking Duck The Best Turkey Burger Ever Whole Smoked Turkey

BEER CAN CHICKEN

Cooking a chicken over a can of beer creates a delicious steam that helps the chicken cook inside as well as outside.

Preparation Time: 10 minutes
Cooking Temperature: 375°F
Cooking Time: 45 minutes - 1 hour
Serves: 6-8

Meat	From This Book	Other Seasonings
▸ 1 (4-5 lb) chicken	▸ ¼ cup Country Style Rub	▸ 1 12-ounce beer in a can ▸ 1 sprig rosemary ▸ 2 cloves garlic, smashed

Preparation:

1. Open the beer, drink half.
2. Add rosemary and garlic cloves to the remaining beer.
3. Sprinkle Country Style Rub on every surface, inside and out, of the chicken.
4. Situate the chicken on top of the beer can until the can is firmly inside of the cavity.

Grilling:

1. Preheat the EGG® to 375°F and add the convEGGtor® for indirect heat.
2. Place the chicken with the beer can standing up on the grid.
3. Close the dome and allow the chicken to cook for 45 minutes to 1 hour or until the internal temperature of the thigh reaches 170°F.
4. Allow the chicken to rest off the heat for 10 minutes before removing the beer can and carving.

To cut the spine out of a chicken is called to "spatchcock". This not only allows you to place a brick on top of the bird, but also speeds up the cooking process. Using kitchen sheers, cut up one side of the spine and down the other removing it completely. Then, flip the chicken breast side up and press firmly to flatten.

CHICKEN UNDER A BRICK

For this recipe, you will need to triple wrap a garden brick in heavy duty aluminum foil. This allows for maximum contact between the chicken and the grill, speeding the cooking process. This same method can be done in a cast iron skillet with the convEGGtor® in the EGG®.

Preparation: 30 minutes
Cooking Temperature: 350°F
Cooking Time: 40-55 minutes
Serves: 6-8

Meat	From This Book	Other Ingredients
▸ 1 4-5 pound whole chicken	▸ ¼ cup Berbere Spice Mix	▸ 2 Tbsp olive oil ▸ 1 garden brick, triple wrapped in aluminum foil

Preparation:

1. Spatchcock the chicken by removing the backbone with poultry shears or a sharp knife. Turn the chicken over and press to break the cartilage in the breast.
2. Rub both sides of the chicken with olive oil and sprinkle the spice mix generously over the entire bird. Set aside.

Grilling:

1. Preheat the EGG® for direct cooking at 350°F.
2. Place the chicken, skin side down, on the grid and place the foil covered brick on top. Close the dome for 20 minutes.
3. Remove the brick and flip the chicken bone side down. Replace the brick and close the dome for 25 to 30 minutes or until the internal temperature of the breast and thigh reach 160°F.
4. Remove the brick and set aside to cool. Remove the chicken and allow it to rest for 10 minutes before carving.

ROTISSERIE STYLE CHICKEN

There is a popular bulk foods chain that has not changed the price of their rotisserie chicken in nearly 20 years. There is something alluring about walking past the meat counter and seeing hundreds of chickens lined up on spits, rotating to golden brown perfection. This recipe recreates that beauty but without an expensive rotisserie.

Preparation Time: 2-8 hours
Cooking Temperature: 375°F
Cooking Time: 45 minutes - 1 hour
Serves: 4-6

Meat	From This Book
▸ 1 (4-5 lb) whole chicken	▸ ½ recipe Turkey Brine ▸ 1 cup White Barbecue Sauce

Preparation:
1. Place chicken in Turkey Brine for 2 hours or overnight.
2. Rinse the chicken and pat dry.

Grilling:
1. Preheat the EGG® to 375°F and add the convEGGtor® for indirect heat.
2. Place the chicken on the grids, breast side up, and close the dome for 20 minutes.
3. Flip the chicken over and cook for an additional 20 minutes.
4. Baste the chicken with White Barbecue Sauce, flip the chicken, and replace the dome for 5 minutes.
5. Repeat until the internal temperature of the thigh reaches 170°F.
6. Allow the chicken to rest off the heat for 10 minutes before carving.

WHOLE SMOKED BARBECUE CHICKEN

Novice smokers always panic when their chicken is still pink after reaching the correct internal temperature. This is largely due to a chemical reaction where nitrogen dioxide penetrates the meat creating a pink "smoke ring". It is safe, and delicious, to eat.

Preparation Time: 20 minutes
Cooking Temperature: 225°F
Cooking Time: 3 hours
Serves: 4-6

Meat	From This Book	Wood Chips
▸ 2 (2-3 lb) whole chickens	▸ 1 recipe Basic Barbecue Rub	▸ 2 cups apple wood chips, soaked for 30 minutes in water

Preparation:

1. Generously sprinkle chickens with Basic Barbecue Rub inside and out and set aside.

Grilling:

1. Preheat the EGG® to 225°F.
2. Add wood chips to the charcoal and replace the grid.
3. Place the chickens directly on the grid and close the dome.
4. Cook at 225°F for 3 - 3 ½ hours or until the internal temperature of the thigh reaches 170°F.
5. Remove the chickens from the EGG® and allow them to rest for 10 minutes before carving.
6. Serve with your favorite barbecue sauce (we like our Kansas City Barbecue Sauce).

BACON WRAPPED CHICKEN BITES

This recipe is the perfect appetizer for a party and comes together in minutes.

Preparation: 15 minutes
Cooking Temperature: 400°F
Cooking Time: 10 minutes
Serves: 8-10

Meat	From This Book
▸ 2 lbs boneless, skinless chicken breasts ▸ ½ lb bacon	▸ ¼ cup Classic American Brown Sugar Rub

Preparation:

1. Cut chicken into bite sized pieces, about 1 ½ to 2 inches large.
2. Cut bacon slices into quarters.
3. Wrap bacon slices around chicken pieces and secure with a toothpick.
4. Sprinkle all chicken pieces liberally with Classic American Brown Sugar Rub.

Grilling:

1. Preheat the EGG® to 400°F.
2. Place the chicken bites onto the grid and close the dome for 5 minutes.
3. Turn the chicken bites and replace the dome for an additional 5 minutes or until the chicken is cooked through and the bacon is crispy.
4. Serve with the barbecue sauce of your choice. (We like the Peach Mustard Sauce.)

CHICKEN KEEMA BURGERS

Keema is an Indian dish made from ground mutton and a variety of spices and served with Naan. This take on this delicious dish is served in burger form on Naan but is also tasty on a traditional hamburger bun.

Preparation: 20 minutes
Cooking Temperature: 500°F
Cooking Time: 11-12 minutes
Serves: 4

Burgers	From This Book	Raita
▸ 2 lbs ground chicken ▸ ½ cup fresh breadcrumbs ▸ 1 Tbsp olive oil ▸ 2 cloves garlic, finely chopped ▸ 1 small onion, finely chopped ▸ 1 egg ▸ 4 pieces Naan	▸ 2 Tbsp Indian Spice Rub	▸ ½ cup Greek style yogurt ▸ ½ cup finely chopped, seeded, cucumber ▸ 2 Tbsp chopped fresh cilantro ▸ 1 tsp finely chopped green onion ▸ ¼ tsp ground cumin

Preparation:

1. In a small bowl, combine ingredients for the raita and set aside. The raita can be made a day in advance, covered, and refrigerated.
2. In a small skillet, heat olive oil over medium and add onion and garlic. Cook until soft and translucent. Set aside to cool.
3. In a medium bowl, combine ground chicken, bread crumbs, onion mixture, egg, and Indian Spice Rub until combined. Form 4 patties and return to the fridge to chill for 10 minutes.

Grilling:

1. Preheat the EGG® to 500°F.
2. Place burgers on the grid and close the dome for 3 minutes.
3. Flip burgers and close the dome for 3 more minutes.
4. Close all of the vents and allow the burgers to sit for 5-6 minutes or until the internal temperature reaches 170°F.
5. Serve burgers on naan, topped with raita.

CLASSIC HOT WINGS

There is nothing like hot wings and beer while you're watching the big game. These alternatives to fried wings are easier on the waistline, leaving you more room for beer!

Preparation Time: 10 minutes
Cooking Temperature: 400°F
Cooking Time: 30 minutes
Serves: 3-4

Meat	From This Book
▸ 3-4 pounds chicken wings	▸ ¼ cup Cajun Dry Rub ▸ 2 cups Frank's Buffalo Sauce

Preparation:
1. Liberally sprinkle the wings with the Cajun Dry Rub

Grilling:
1. Preheat the EGG® to 400°F.
2. Place the wings on the grid with the dome closed for 20-30 minutes, turning once halfway through cooking.
3. When the juices run clear, place the wings in a large bowl and pour the Franks Buffalo Sauce over them. Toss to coat.
4. Replace the wings on the grid and close all of the vents. Allow the wings to finish for 5 minutes.
5. Toss in the sauce once more and serve.

GREEK CHICKEN KEBABS

Also known as Souvlaki, this dish is delicious served with pita and tzatziki sauce.

Preparation Time: 30 minutes - 4 hours
Cooking Temperature: 400°F
Cooking Time: 15 minutes
Serves: 4-6

Meat	From This Book	Tzatziki Sauce
▸ 2 lbs boneless, skinless chicken breasts, cut into large chunks (about 2 inches large) ▸ Wooden Skewers, soaked for 30 minutes (or Metal skewers)	▸ 1 recipe Greek Marinade	▸ 6-ounces Greek style yogurt ▸ ½ cup shredded cucumber ▸ ¼ tsp fresh oregano ▸ ¼ tsp salt ▸ ⅛ tsp pepper ▸ 2 cloves garlic, finely chopped

Preparation:

1. Place the chicken breast pieces in a large zip top bag. Pour in Green Marinade.
2. Refrigerate the chicken for as little as 30 minutes or up to 4 hours before cooking.
3. Remove the chicken from the fridge. Thread the chicken onto the skewers without overcrowding them, and set aside.

Grilling:

1. Preheat the EGG® to 400°F.
2. Place chicken skewers on the grids and close the dome for 5 minutes.
3. Turn the skewers and replace the dome for an additional 5-7 minutes or until the chicken is cooked through.
4. Meanwhile, combine ingredients for tzatziki sauce in a small bowl. Serve chicken with warmed pita bread and tzatziki sauce.

HOISIN GLAZED WINGS

Hoisin, also known colloquially as Chinese Barbecue Sauce, is a sweet and savory blend of soy, ginger, honey, and other traditionally Asian flavors. Widely available at supermarkets everywhere, the sugar content gives the wings a sticky texture sure to please.

Preparation Time: 10 minutes
Cooking Temperature: 400°F
Cooking Time: 25-30 minutes
Serves: 3-4

Meat	From This Book
▸ 3-4 lbs chicken wings	▸ 1 cup Chinese Barbecue Sauce ▸ ¼ cup Asian Rub

Preparation:

1. Liberally dust the wings with the Asian Rub. Set aside.

Grilling:

1. Preheat the EGG® to 400°F.
2. Place the wings on the grid with the dome closed for 20-30 minutes, turning once halfway through cooking.
3. When the juices run clear, place the wings in a large bowl and pour the Chinese Barbecue Sauce Sauce over them. Toss to coat.
4. Replace the wings on the grid and close all of the vents. Allow the wings to finish for 5 minutes.
5. Toss in the sauce once more and serve.

Poultry | Wings & Things

JERK CHICKEN DRUMS

Jerk Chicken is everywhere in Jamaica. This spicy, citrusy grilled dish will light a fire in your mouth and leave you coming back for more.

Preparation Time: 4 hours - Overnight
Cooking Temperature: 400°F
Cooking Time: 30-40 minutes
Serves: 8-10

Meat	From This Book	Other Seasonings
▸ 3 lbs chicken drumsticks	▸ 1 recipe Habanero Rub	▸ ¼ cup olive oil ▸ The juice of two limes

Preparation:

1. In a large zip top bag, combine Habanero Rub with olive oil and lime juice. Add chicken and refrigerate 4 hours or overnight.
2. Remove from fridge and allow to come to room temperature for 15 minutes.

Grilling:

1. Preheat the EGG® to 400°F.
2. Shake off any excess marinade and place on the grid of the EGG®.
3. Close the dome and cook for 20 minutes.
4. Turn drumsticks and close the dome for an additional 15 minutes or until the juices run clear.

LEMON SCENTED CHICKEN THIGHS

Chicken thighs are quickly becoming more popular than their leaner cousin, chicken breasts, for their rich flavor and tendency to stay moist through any cooking process.

Preparation Time: 30 minutes
Cooking Temperature: 375°F
Cooking Time: 30-40 minutes
Serves: 8-10

Meat	From This Book	Other Ingredients
▸ 2-3 lbs bone in, skin on chicken thighs	▸ 1 recipe Lemon Rosemary Marinade	▸ 1 lemon, thinly sliced

Preparation:

1. In a large zip top bag, pour marinade over chicken thighs and refrigerate for 30 minutes.

Grilling:

1. Preheat the EGG® to 375°F.
2. Remove the thighs from the marinade and gently slide thinly sliced lemon between the skin and the meat.
3. Place thighs directly on the grid, skin side down, and close the dome for 20 minutes.
4. Turn the thighs and close the dome for an additional 15-20 minutes or until the internal temperature reaches 170°F.

STUFFED CHICKEN BREASTS WITH SUNDRIED TOMATOES AND ARTICHOKES

Consider this recipe a throwback to the early 2000s when everything was stuffed with sundried tomatoes and artichokes. Come on. It was delicious then and it is delicious now.

Preparation Time: 40 minutes
Cooking Temperature: 375°F
Cooking Time: 30-40 minutes
Serves: 4

Meat	Stuffing
▸ 4 boneless, skin on chicken breasts	▸ ½ cup feta cheese ▸ ¼ cup frozen spinach, thawed and squeezed dry ▸ ¼ cup sundried tomatoes, roughly chopped ▸ 1 (6 oz) jar marinated artichoke hearts, roughly chopped

Preparation:

1. Combine cheese, spinach, tomatoes, and artichokes. Set aside.
2. Using a sharp knife, cut a pocket into the middle of each chicken breast and stuff with the cheese mixture.
3. Season the skin with salt and pepper.

Grilling:

1. Preheat the EGG® to 375°F with the convEGGtor® and grid in place.
2. Place the chicken breasts on the grid and close the dome for 30-40 minutes or until the chicken is cooked through and the skin is crispy.

THAI STUFFED CHICKEN DRUMSTICKS

Stuffed chicken wings are a favorite appetizer at many Thai restaurants, but by using drumsticks these delights become a meal.

Preparation Time: 1 hour
Cooking Temperature: 375°F
Cooking Time: 30-40 minutes
Serves: 8-10

Meat	Stuffing	Dipping Sauce
▸ 3 lbs chicken drumsticks	▸ ½ lb ground pork ▸ 6 oz mushrooms, finely chopped ▸ 4 oz rice vermicelli noodles ▸ 2 Tbsp fish sauce ▸ 1 Tbsp freshly grated ginger ▸ 1 Tbsp minced garlic (about 3 cloves) ▸ 2 tsp cornstarch ▸ 1 bunch green onions, finely chopped ▸ 1 egg	▸ 1 cup Thai sweet chili sauce ▸ 2 Tbsp soy sauce ▸ 1 tsp fish sauce ▸ The juice of 1 lime

Preparation:

1. Rinse and dry the drumsticks. Using your fingers, gently separate the skin from the meat beginning at the thickest part of the drumstick and leaving the skin attached at the bone.
2. In a large bowl, soak the vermicelli according to the package directions. When they are soft, cut into small pieces.
3. Mix noodles, ground pork, mushrooms, green onion, ginger, garlic, fish sauce, cornstarch, and egg. Divide into equal portions according to the number of drumsticks you intend to cook.
4. Gently work the stuffing under the skin of each drumstick.

Grilling:

1. Preheat the EGG® to 375°F with the convEGGtor® in place under the grid.
2. Place the drumsticks onto the grid and close the dome for 20 minutes.
3. Flip the drumsticks over and continue to cook an additional 20-25 minutes or until the skin is crispy and the juices of the chicken run clear.
4. Remove from the grid and mix ingredients for the dipping sauce. Serve.

WALK THE PLANK CHICKEN QUARTERS

Cooking on a cedar plank is a centuries old technique that imparts a beautiful smoked flavor to food without actual smoke. Be sure to use an untreated cedar plank, available at grocery and hardware stores, and soak it in water for 10-20 minutes before cooking.

Preparation: 2 hours
Cooking Temperature: 350°F
Cooking Time: 1 hour
Serves: 4

Meat	From This Book	Wood
▸ 4 chicken leg quarters (drumstick and thigh)	▸ 4 cups Maple Brine ▸ ¼ cup Coffee Spice Barbecue Sauce	▸ 2 untreated cedar planks

Preparation:

1. In a large zip top bag, pour cool Maple Brine over chicken leg quarters and allow them to sit, refrigerated, for 2 hours.
2. Remove the chicken from the brine, pat dry, and allow to come to room temperature while the EGG® is heating.

Grilling:

1. Preheat the EGG® to 350°F. Place the cedar planks on the grid for 3 minutes, with the dome closed.
2. Flip the plank and place the chicken on the heated side. Close the dome for 45 minutes to 1 hour or until the thigh registers 170°F.
3. Generously brush the thighs with Coffee Spice Barbecue Sauce and close the dome for an additional 5 minutes. Serve with additional sauce.

WICKED WINGS

This recipe is perfect for the chile heads in your life.

Preparation Time: 10 minutes
Cooking Temperature: 375°F
Cooking Time: 30-40 minutes
Serves: 4

Meat	From This Book	Other Seasonings
▸ 3-4 lbs chicken wings	▸ 1 cup Chipotle Mango Lime Sauce ▸ ½ cup Habanero Rub	▸ 2 Tbsp sambal or sriracha ▸ 1 jalapeño pepper, finely chopped

Preparation:

1. Liberally season the wings with the Habanero Rub.
2. Combine Chipotle Mango Lime Sauce with sambal (or sriracha) and jalapeño.

Grilling:

1. Preheat the EGG® to 375°F.
2. Place the wings on the grid and close the dome for 15 minutes.
3. Flip the wings and close the dome for another 15 minutes or until the juices in the chicken run clear and the internal temperature reads 165°F.
4. Toss cooked wings in the sauce and return to the grill for an additional 5 minutes with the dome closed.
5. Toss the wings in the sauce again and serve with pickled jalapeños.

WILD BIRDS

Chicken isn't the only poultry perfect for your EGG®. Give these birds a shot next time you're in the mood for something a little different.

AMUSEMENT PARK TURKEY LEGS

There's nothing quite like walking around an amusement park with a giant hunk of meat on a stick. These turkey legs are so large, they can be shared with a friend.

Preparation Time: 2 hours - overnight
Cooking Temperature: 250°F
Cooking Time: 3-4 hours
Serves: 4

Meat	From This Book	Wood Chips
‣ 2 fresh turkey drumsticks	‣ 4 cups Turkey Brine	‣ 2 cups apple or cherry wood chips, soaked in water for 30 minutes

Preparation:
1. Submerge drumsticks into the turkey brine for as few as 2 hours and as long as overnight.
2. Remove the drumsticks and discard the brine. Pat the turkey dry.

Grilling:
1. Preheat the EGG® To 250°F. Add soaked, drained wood chips to the burning coals.
2. Put the convEGGtor® in place and place the grid on top.
3. Place the turkey legs on the grid and close the dome for 3-4 hours or until the turkey registers 170°F.
4. Remove the drumsticks and pretend to walk around an amusement park or renaissance fair.

COMPANY CORNISH GAME HENS

Cornish Game Hens, although fancy in name, are actually small chickens. However, there is nothing quite so impressive as serving your guests their own bird on a platter.

Preparation Time: 30 minutes
Cooking Temperature: 450°F
Cooking Time: 40 minutes
Serves: 4

Meat	From This Book
▸ 4 Cornish Game Hens (about 1 ¼ to 1 ½ pounds each)	▸ 1 recipe Lemon Rosemary Marinade

Preparation:
1. Pour Lemon Rosemary Marinade over the hens and allow them to marinade for 30 minutes in the refrigerator.
2. Remove from the fridge and allow to come to room temperature while the EGG® heats.

Grilling:
1. Preheat the EGG® to 450°F.
2. Place the hens on the grid and cover with the dome for 20 minutes.
3. Reduce the heat inside the EGG® to 350°F and cook for 20 more minutes, or until the internal temperature reaches 165°F.
4. Remove and let rest before serving.

GRILLED PHEASANT WITH CHIMICHURRI

Whole pheasants are smaller than chickens and are more gamey than turkeys. But if you have an opportunity to cook one (or 2 in this case) take it!

Preparation Time: 2 hours
Cooking Temperature: 400°F
Cooking Time: 30 minutes
Serves: 4

Meat	From This Book
▸ 2 pheasants (about 1 ¼ to 1 ½ pounds each)	▸ 4 cups Turkey Brine ▸ 1 cup Chimichurri

Preparation:

1. Cover pheasants with Turkey Brine and allow to sit a minimum of 2 hours or up to overnight.

Grilling:

1. Preheat the EGG® to 400°F. Put the convEGGtor® in place along with the grid.
2. Place the dried pheasants on the grid and cover for 30 minutes or until the internal temperature of the thigh reaches 160°F.
3. Remove the pheasants from the grill and cover with chimichurri. Serve.

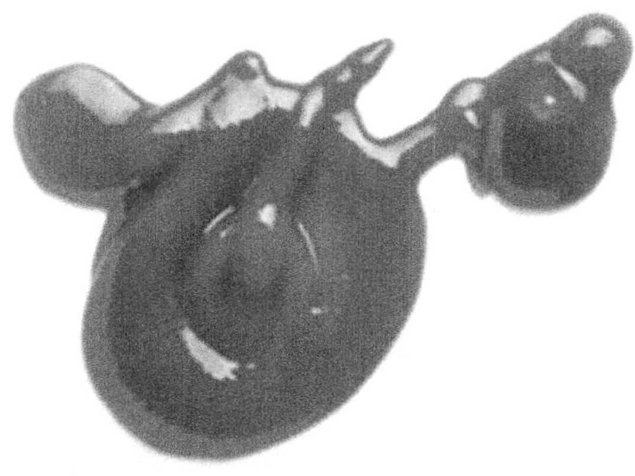

PEKING DUCK

Peking Duck is known for its crispy skin, a process that usually takes days of drying. In our case, we use indirect heat and low temperature to encourage the fat to render out of the duck, leaving the meat moist and the skin crispy.

Preparation: 1 hour
Cooking Temperature: 300°F
Cooking Time: 4 hours 10 minutes
Serves: 6-8

Meat	From This Book
▸ 1 (5 lb) duck	▸ ¼ cup Asian Rub ▸ 1 cup Chinese Barbecue Sauce (optional)

Preparation:

1. Pat the duck dry.
2. Score the duck skin in one direction, then the other so you end up with a diamond pattern on the skin. (Scoring means you only cut through the skin, not the fat or meat.)
3. Liberally season all sides and the cavity with Asian Rub.
4. Allow the duck to rest in the fridge for 1 hour, bringing it back to room temperature while the EGG® preheats.

Grilling:

1. Preheat the EGG® to 300°F, placing the convEGGtor® and grids inside.
2. Place the duck, breast side up, on a rack, in a roasting pan that will fit inside the EGG®. The duck will render about 1 ½ cups of fat.
3. Place the roasting rack inside the EGG® and close the dome for 1 hour.
4. Flip the duck back side up and close the dome for 1 hour.
5. Flip the duck breast side up and close the dome for 1 hour.
6. Finally, flip the duck back side up and close the dome for 1 hour.
7. Baste the duck with Chinese Barbecue Sauce (if desired). Adjust the temperature to 400°F. Close the dome for a final 5-7 minutes to crisp the skin, and remove.
8. Allow to sit uncovered for 10 minutes before carving.

Substitute duck fat for olive oil when cooking potatoes, root vegetables, or even eggs. Once rendered, strain the fat of any solids and save it in an airtight container in the fridge for up to 1 week.

THE BEST TURKEY BURGER EVER

If you have ever had a turkey burger, chances are it was dry and flavorless. This recipe remedies that by using shredded apple and onion in the patty to keep it moist and a aioli to keep it flavorful.

Preparation: 20 minutes
Cooking Temperature:450°F
Cooking Time: 10-12 minutes
Serves: 4

Burger	Aioli	Fixings
▸ 1 ½ pounds ground turkey (a mixture of white and dark meat is best) ▸ ½ cup fresh breadcrumbs ▸ ¼ cup shredded onion ▸ ¼ cup shredded Granny Smith apple ▸ ½ tsp salt ▸ ¼ tsp pepper ▸ 1 egg, beaten ▸ 1 clove garlic, grated	▸ ¼ cup mayonnaise ▸ 2 Tbsp Besto Pesto ▸ ½ tsp sriracha	▸ 1 cup arugula ▸ 4 brioche buns ▸ 1 Granny Smith apple, thinly sliced

Preparation:
1. In a large bowl, combine burger ingredients well. Form into 4 patties and refrigerate while the EGG® comes to temperature.

Grilling:
1. Preheat the EGG® to 450°F.
2. Place turkey burgers onto the grid and close the dome for 3 minutes.
3. Flip the burgers and close the dome for another 3 minutes.
4. Close all of the vents and allow the burgers to sit for 5 minutes more or until the internal temperature reaches 170°F.
5. Stir together aioli mixture.
6. Remove the burgers and serve on a toasted brioche bun with arugula, thinly sliced apple, and a healthy smear of the aioli.

WHOLE SMOKED TURKEY

There are a few tricks to a juicy smoked turkey. Use a small bird, brining is best, and spatchcock the bird by cutting out the backbone and pressing the breast down until the cartilage breaks. This is the only way to ensure the meat reaches the appropriate temperature before it dries out.

Preparation Time: 4 hours - overnight
Cooking Temperature: 275°F
Cooking Time: 3 ½ - 4 ½ hours
Serves: 12-14

Meat	From This Book	Wood Chips
▸ 1 (10-12 lb) turkey, spatchcocked	▸ 1 recipe Turkey Brine	▸ 2 cups wood chips, soaked in water (we like fruit wood chips)

Preparation:
1. Submerge the spatchcocked turkey into the Turkey Brine and refrigerate for a minimum of four hours, or up to overnight.
2. Remove the turkey from the brine and pat try 30 minutes before smoking.

Grilling:
1. Preheat the EGG® to 275°F, adding smoked wood chips, and place the convEGGtor® and grid in place.
2. Place the turkey, breast side up, on the grids and close the dome for 3 ½ hours.
3. Begin checking the temperature of the meat in the thigh. Continue cooking until the temperature in the meatiest part of the thigh reaches 165°F.
4. Allow the turkey to rest for 20 minutes before carving.

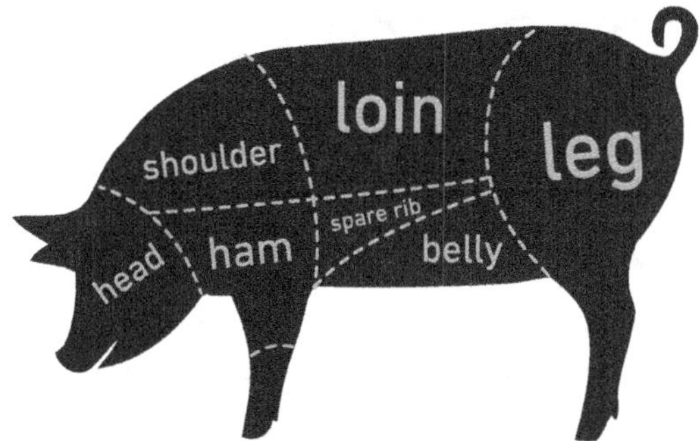

Pork

Barbecue and pork are synonymous in the south. Certain regions are loyal to the whole hog while others focus on shoulders and ribs. While we feature some fantastic barbecue recipes, pork has truly become "the other white meat" in the US and a favorite for quick preparations on the grill.

ROASTS	CHOPS	RIBS
Barbecue Pork Shoulder	Beer Brined Loin Chops	Caribbean St. Louis Style Ribs
Cedar Plank Pork Tenderloin	Center Cut Pork Loin Chops	Chinese St. Louis Style Ribs
Christmas Gingersnap Ham	Chops with Pineapple Salsa	Classic Barbecue Ribs
Crown Roast of Pork	Maple Mustard Loin Chops	Korean Pork Riblets
Cuban Pork (Lechon Asado)	PLTs - Pork, Lettuce and Tomato Sandwiches	
Garlic Studded Sirloin Roast	Spanakopita Stuffed Loin Chops	
Homemade Bacon	Teriyaki Bone-in Loin Chops	
Pomegranate Pork Roast		
Spanish Pork Tenderloins		
Sunday Dinner Loin Roast		

ROASTS

BARBECUE PORK SHOULDER

Pork shoulder, also known as "picnic roast" or "Boston Butt" is one of four cuts of its kind on the hog. Known for its fat and connective tissue, it is a fool proof beginner's cut for low and slow smoking.

Preparation: 4 hours - overnight
Cooking Temperature: 225°F
Cooking Time: 12-14 hours
Serves: A small army

Meat	From This Book	Wood Chips
▸ 1 (6-8 lb) pork shoulder	▸ 2 cups East Carolina Barbecue Sauce ▸ 1 cup Basic BBQ Rub	▸ 2 cups wood chips, soaked in water for a minimum of 1 hour (any wood is great for this recipe)

Preparation:

1. Score the skin of pork shoulder with a knife, cutting only through the skin, not the meat.
2. Liberally sprinkle the pork with BBQ Rub, cover tightly in an aluminum pan and refrigerate 4 hours or up to overnight.
3. Remove the pork shoulder from the refrigerator 1 hour before cooking.

Grilling:

1. Preheat the EGG® to 225°F. Add the drained wood chips to the coals and place the convEGGtor® and grid inside the EGG®.
2. Place the pork shoulder on the grid and close the dome.
3. The EGG® will hold its heat at this temperature for up to 18 hours, so you can literally set it and forget it.
4. After 12 hours, check the internal temperature of the roast. It will be a deep mahogany color, but if the temperature has been maintained, it will not be burned or dried out. When the internal temperature reaches 200°F, carefully remove the roast with two forks.
5. Gently pull the meat apart and sprinkle with East Carolina Barbecue Sauce. Serve with additional sauce.

CEDAR PLANK PORK TENDERLOIN

Pork tenderloin, while lean, does not have much of a flavor of its own. The cedar plank and Basic Steak Marinade imparts flavor at every level.

Preparation Time: 30 minutes
Cooking Temperature: 425°F
Cooking Time: 15-20 minutes
Serves: 6-8

Meat	From This Book	Wood
▸ 2 pork tenderloins	▸ 1 cup Basic Steak Marinade (not just for steaks!)	▸ 2 cedar planks (Be sure they are untreated cedar)

Preparation:

1. Place the pork tenderloins and Basic Steak Marinade in a zip top bag for 30 minutes.

Grilling:

1. Preheat the EGG® To 425°F.
2. Place the cedar planks directly on the grid and close the dome for 3 minutes.
3. Turn the planks and place the tenderloins directly on the heated planks.
4. Close the dome for 10 minutes.
5. Turn the tenderloins once and close the dome for another 5-10 minutes or until the internal temperature reaches 155°F.
6. Remove the tenderloins and allow them to rest for 5 minutes before slicing.

CHRISTMAS GINGERSNAP HAM

Spiral sliced ham is made extra special with a Dijon mustard schmear and gingersnap crust.

Preparation Time: 10 minutes
Cooking Temperature: 350°F
Cooking Time: 1 - 1 ½ hours
Serves: 15-18

Meat	Topping
▸ 1 8-10 pound spiral sliced ham	▸ 2 cups gingersnap cookies, crushed ▸ ¼ cup brown mustard

Preparation:

1. Remove the ham from its wrapper, thoroughly rinse it and pat it dry.
2. Place the ham in a heat-proof roasting pan.
3. Brush the outside liberally with mustard.
4. Press the gingersnap cookies into the mustard coating.

Grilling:

1. Preheat the EGG® to 350°F with the convEGGtor® and grid in place.
2. Place the ham inside the EGG® and close the dome for 1 to 1 ½ hours.
3. Allow the ham to rest for 20 minutes before carving and serving.

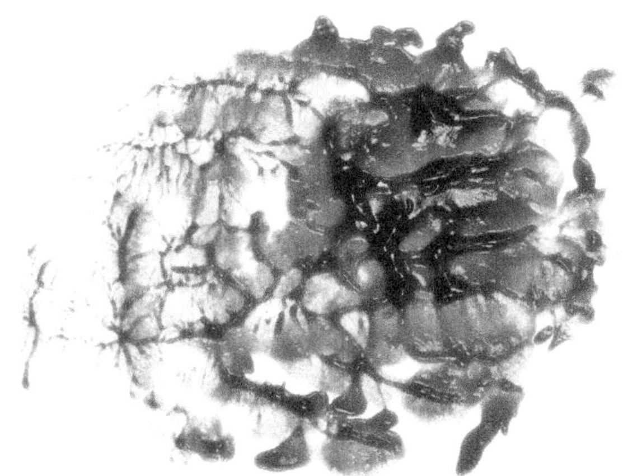

BONE-IN LOIN ROAST

In the same way several steaks make up a roast in beef, several uncut chops make up a roast in pork. A crown roast of pork is actually several bone-in pork loin chops that have been Frenched (the bones are exposed) and tied into the shape of a crown. Ask your butcher to "French" the roast, but there is no need to tie it.

Preparation: 40 minutes
Cooking Temperature: 400°F
Cooking Time: 1 ½ - 2 hours
Serves: 8

Meat	Seasoning
▸ 1 5-pound bone-in pork loin roast	▸ ½ cup olive oil ▸ ⅓ cup fresh rosemary ▸ ⅓ cup fresh thyme ▸ 2 tsp salt ▸ 1 tsp black pepper ▸ 6 cloves garlic, minced ▸ 4 lemons, juiced and zested

Preparation:

1. Remove the pork loin from the fridge, rinse, and pat dry.
2. In a food processor, combine olive oil, herbs, lemon juice and zest, and garlic and pulse to combine into a paste.
3. Slather the pork loin on all sides with the oil and herb mixture and set aside for 30 minutes.

Grilling:

1. Preheat the EGG® to 400°F.
2. Place the roast on the grid and close the dome for 1 ½ hour. The roast is done when a thermometer inserted into the center of the meat reaches 150°F.
3. Remove the roast and allow it to rest for 20 minutes before carving.

CUBAN PORK (LECHON ASADO)

Deep in the heart of Miami sits a neighborhood known as "Little Havana". On any given holiday, thousands of families marinate pork shoulders (or whole pigs!) in sour orange juice and garlic then slow roast them until they are tender and succulent. Since sour orange juice is not a common ingredient, lime juice and freshly squeezed orange juice work as substitutes.

Preparation Time: 4 hours to overnight
Cooking Temperature: 225°F
Cooking Time:10-12 hours
Serves: A Small Army

Meat	From This Book
▸ 1 (7-9 lb) pork shoulder	▸ 1 recipe Cuban Mojo

Preparation:
1. Score the skin and fat on the pork shoulder by cutting in one direction, then the other to form cross hatches.
2. Pour Cuban Mojo over the pork shoulder, cover, and refrigerate at least four hours, preferably overnight, turning once.
3. Remove the pork from the marinade 30 minutes before cooking.

Grilling:
1. Preheat the EGG® to 225°F, placing the convEGGtor® and grid inside.
2. Place the pork shoulder on the grid and close the dome. The EGG® is designed to maintain this temperature for up to 18 hours.
3. After 10 hours, check the internal temperature of the pork. Remove the roast when it reads 200°F.
4. Carefully remove the pork shoulder from the EGG® and allow it to rest 30 minutes before slicing/pulling it apart.

GARLIC STUDDED SIRLOIN ROAST

Slicing into this roast is like playing hide and seek for garlic lovers. Whole cloves of garlic become sweet and flavorful in this delightfully simple roast.

Preparation Time: 30 minutes
Cooking Temperature: 350°F
Cooking Time: 1 hour
Serves: 6-8

Meat	From This Book
▸ 1 (3 lb) pork sirloin roast	▸ ¼ cup olive oil ▸ 2 Tbsp fresh thyme, chopped ▸ 2 Tbsp Worcestershire sauce ▸ ½ tsp salt ▸ ¼ tsp black pepper ▸ 12 whole cloves garlic, peeled ▸ The zest and juice of 1 lemon

Preparation:

1. Rinse and pat the sirloin roast dry.
2. Using a paring knife, make 12 slits into the roast, filling each with a single clove of garlic.
3. Combine remaining ingredients and brush all sides of the roast. Set aside.

Grilling:

1. Preheat the EGG® to 350°F with the convEGGtor® and grid in place.
2. Place the prepared roast on the grid and close the lid for 45 minutes to 1 hour or until an internal thermometer reads 150°F.
3. Remove the roast from the EGG® and allow it to rest for 15 minutes before thinly slicing.

HOMEMADE BACON

Making homemade bacon is a long process, but not a difficult one. The recipe does call for something called, "pink curing salt" which is a combination of salt and sodium nitrate, a preservative. This is easily found at kitchen supply stores and online retailers.

Preparation Time: 2 weeks (mostly curing and drying)
Cooking Temperature: 200°F
Cooking Time: 3 - 3 ½ hours
Yields: 3 ½ pounds of bacon

Meat	Cure	Wood
▸ 5 pounds pork belly, skin on	▸ ¼ cup Kosher salt ▸ ¼ cup dark brown sugar, packed ▸ ¼ cup honey ▸ 2 Tbsp sweet paprika ▸ 2 Tbsp chili powder ▸ 1 Tbsp cracked black pepper ▸ 2 tsp pink curing salt	▸ 2 cups wood chips, soaked in water for 30 minutes

Preparation:
1. Rinse the pork and pat it dry.
2. Mix the cure together and liberally spread it on the pork belly.
3. Place the pork in a large zip top bag, close it and refrigerate it for 7-10 days, flipping every day until the pork feels firm. (7 days for a 1 ½ inch thick pork belly)
4. Remove the pork from the bag and rinse and dry it thoroughly.
5. Place the pork on a rack over a pan back in the fridge, uncovered, for 48 hours to allow the skin to dry out.

Grilling:
1. Preheat the EGG® to 200°F putting the drained wood chips on top of the charcoal and putting the convEGGtor® and grid in place.
2. Place the pork belly on the grid and close the dome. Cook for 3 - 3 ½ hours or until the internal temperature of the pork reaches 150°F.
3. Allow the bacon to cool then remove the rind.
4. Store the bacon wrapped in plastic in the fridge for up to 1 week or in the freezer for up to 2 months.

POMEGRANATE PORK ROAST

Pomegranate molasses is found in many high-quality grocery stores. But in a pinch, reduce 2 cups of pomegranate juice in a sauce pan until it reaches ½ cup. This sweet and spicy roast not only makes a great fall supper, it makes amazing sandwiches too!

Preparation Time: 30 minutes
Cooking Temperature: 500°F
Cooking Time: 1 hour
Serves: 6-8

Meat	Seasoning
▸ 1 (5 lb) pork loin roast	▸ ½ cup pomegranate molasses ▸ 2 Tbsp fresh rosemary, minced ▸ 1 Tbsp hot Chinese mustard ▸ 1 tsp salt ▸ ½ tsp pepper ▸ 4 cloves garlic, minced

Preparation:

1. In a small bowl, combine molasses, mustard, garlic, and rosemary..
2. Pat the pork loin roast dry and season with salt and pepper.

Grilling:

1. Preheat the EGG® to 500°F and place the convEGGtor® and grid inside.
2. Set the pork roast on the grid and close for 25 minutes.
3. Reduce the temperature to 375°F and roast for 20 minutes.
4. Generously brush the glaze on the roast and continue cooking for 10 minutes.
5. Brush the roast again and cook 10 minutes more. Continue the process until the internal temperature reaches 155°F.
6. Remove the roast from the EGG® and allow it to rest for 15 minutes before carving.

SPANISH PORK TENDERLOINS

Pimenton (smoked sweet paprika) gives this dish a Spanish flair.

Preparation: 20 minutes
Cooking Temperature: 450°F
Cooking Time: 15 minutes
Serves: 6-8

Meat	Rub	From This Book
▸ 1 pound pork tenderloin	▸ 2 tsp olive oil ▸ ¾ tsp smoked sweet paprika (pimenton) ▸ ½ tsp garlic powder ▸ ¼ tsp salt ▸ ¼ tsp ground cumin	▸ 1 cup Romesco Sauce

Preparation:

1. In a blender, combine all ingredients and blend until smooth. Set aside. The sauce can be made up to 3 days in advance.
2. Combine rub ingredients.
3. Brush tenderloins with olive oil and sprinkle liberally with the rub. Set aside.

Grilling:

1. Preheat the EGG® to 450°F.
2. Place the tenderloins on the grid and close the dome for 10 minutes.
3. Flip the tenderloins and cook another 10 minutes or until the internal temperature reaches 150°F.
4. Remove from the EGG® and allow to rest for 10 minutes before slicing and serving with the Romesco sauce.

SUNDAY DINNER PORK ROAST

This dish requires the convEGGtor® and a roasting pan that will fit inside the EGG®. Both items will enable you to cook thousands of dishes without turning on your oven.

Preparation Time: 20 minutes
Cooking Temperature: 425°F
Cooking Time: 45 minutes - 1 hour
Serves: 6-8

Meat	Seasonings	Vegetables
▸ 1 (3-4 lb) boneless pork loin roast	▸ ¼ cup olive oil, separated ▸ 2 Tbsp fresh thyme, chopped ▸ 2 Tbsp Worcestershire sauce ▸ 1 Tbsp soy sauce ▸ 4 cloves garlic, minced	▸ 2 lb small potatoes, halved (we like Yukon golds) ▸ 1 lb carrots, cut into 2 inch chunks ▸ 1 onion, cut into 2 inch chunks

Preparation:
1. In a small bowl, combine Worcestershire sauce, soy sauce, thyme, garlic, and 2 Tbsp olive oil.
2. Rinse and pat the pork loin dry.
3. In the bottom of a roasting pan, toss onion, potatoes and carrots with 2 Tbsp olive oil, salt, and pepper.
4. Place the pork loin on top of the vegetables, fat side up and brush with the Worcestershire sauce mixture.

Grilling:
1. Preheat the EGG® to 425°F with the convEGGtor® in place.
2. Place the roasting pan on the grid and close the dome for 45 minutes to 1 hour or until the roast reaches an internal temperature of 150°F.
3. Allow the roast to rest for 10 minutes before slicing and serve with roasted vegetables on the side.

BEER BRINED LOIN CHOPS

Always use a beer you like to drink for any of your cooking preparations.

Preparation Time: 2 hours - overnight
Cooking Temperature: 425°F
Cooking Time: 12-15 minutes
Serves: 6

Meat	From This Book
▸ 6 boneless pork loin chops, cut 1 to 1 ¼ inch thick	▸ 2 cups water ▸ 2 cups ice ▸ ¼ cup coarse salt ▸ 2 Tbsp brown sugar ▸ 6 cloves garlic, minced ▸ 1 (12 oz) beer (we like Samuel Adams Cherry Wheat for its sweet and tart fruity flavor)

Preparation:
1. In a small sauce pan, heat water, salt, and sugar together until salt and sugar are dissolved. Add cold beer, garlic, and ice.
2. Submerge pork chops into brine and allow to sit in the refrigerator for at least 2 hours and as long as overnight.
3. Remove the chops from the fridge and brine and pat dry.

Grilling:
1. Preheat the EGG® to 425°F.
2. Place the pork chops on the grid and close the dome for 5 minutes.
3. Flip the pork chops and close the dome for another 5 minutes.
4. Close all vents and allow the pork to sit for another 3-5 minutes or until the internal temperature reaches 150°F.

CENTER CUT PORK LOIN CHOPS WITH PINEAPPLE SALSA

This salsa is good enough to eat on its own with a bag of tortilla chips. You might want to double the recipe

Preparation Time: 1 hour - Overnight
Cooking Temperature: 425°F
Cooking Time: 20-22 minutes
Serves: 6

Meat	Brine	Salsa
▸ 6 center cut, bone in pork loin chops cut 1 to 1 ¼ inch thick	▸ 3 cups water ▸ 2 cups ice ▸ 1 cup apple juice ▸ ¼ cup Kosher salt ▸ 1 Tbsp whole peppercorns ▸ 4 cloves garlic, smashed	▸ 2 cups pineapple, diced into ¼ inch cubes ▸ ½ cup red onion, finely diced ▸ 2 Tbsp lime juice ▸ 1 jalapeño, finely diced ▸ ¼ tsp salt

Preparation:

1. In a small saucepan, heat water and salt until the salt dissolves. Add apple juice, ice, garlic, and peppercorns.
2. Submerge the pork chops for a minimum of 1 hour or up to overnight in the fridge.
3. Remove the pork chops from the brine and pat dry.

Grilling:

1. Preheat the EGG® to 425°F.
2. Place the pork chops on the grid and close the dome for 10 minutes.
3. Meanwhile, combine salsa ingredients and set aside.
4. Turn pork chops and close the dome for an additional 10-12 minutes or until the internal temperature near the bone reaches 150°F.
5. Remove the chops and top with the salsa.

MAPLE MUSTARD LOIN CHOPS

This four ingredient marinade is so simple and delicious it will be your go-to marinade for everything.

Preparation Time: 30 minutes
Cooking Temperature: 400°F
Cooking Time: 12-15 minutes
Serves: 6

Meat	From This Book
▸ 6 boneless loin chops, cut 1 to 1 ¼ inch thick	▸ ¼ cup Dijon mustard ▸ ¼ cup real maple syrup ▸ ½ tsp cracked black pepper ▸ 4 cloves garlic, minced

Preparation:
1. Combine mustard, maple syrup, black pepper, and garlic and pour over chops.
2. Refrigerate for a minimum of 30 minutes.
3. Remove chops from the fridge.

Grilling:
1. Preheat the EGG® to 400°F and place the convEGGtor® inside.
2. Place the chops on the grid and close the dome for 5 minutes.
3. Flip the chops and close the dome for an additional 5 minutes.
4. Close the vents and allow the chops to sit for an additional 3-5 minutes or until the internal temperature reaches 150°F.

PLTS - PORK, LETTUCE AND TOMATO SANDWICHES

You love a BLT, why not a PLT?

Preparation Time: 10 minutes
Cooking Temperature: 400°F
Cooking Time: 5-7 minutes
Serves: 6

Meat	Seasoning	Sandwiches
▸ 6 pork loin chops, cut ½ inch thick	▸ ½ tsp garlic powder ▸ ½ tsp onion powder ▸ ½ tsp poultry seasoning ▸ ½ tsp salt ▸ ¼ tsp pepper	▸ 1 cup shredded lettuce ▸ ½ cup mayonnaise ▸ 2 Tbsp Besto Pesto ▸ 12 slices tomato ▸ 6 sesame seed buns

Preparation:
1. Place each pork chop between two pieces of plastic wrap and pound flat.
2. Combine seasonings and sprinkle both sides of each pork chop liberally.

Grilling:
1. Preheat the EGG® to 400°F.
2. Place the chops on the grid and close the dome for 2 minutes.
3. Flip the chops and replace the dome for 3-5 minutes or until the pork is just cooked through.
4. Remove the chops and set aside.
5. Combine mayonnaise and pesto and spread the buns liberally with the mixture.
6. Top each bun with a pork chop, lettuce, and tomato.

Pork | Chops

SPANAKOPITA STUFFED LOIN CHOPS

Spanakopita is a delicious Greek pastry stuffed with onions, spinach, and feta cheese. These pork chops echo the same flavors, but without the hassle of filo dough.

Preparation Time: 30 minutes
Cooking Temperature: 400°F
Cooking Time: 25-30 minutes
Serves: 6

Meat	Stuffing
▸ 6 boneless loin chops, cut 1 to ¼ inches thick	▸ ½ lb spinach ▸ ¼ lb feta cheese ▸ 1 cup onion, chopped ▸ 2 Tbsp butter ▸ ¼ tsp freshly grated nutmeg ▸ ¼ tsp salt ▸ ¼ tsp pepper

Preparation:

1. In a saute pan, melt butter over medium heat and add onion. Cook until translucent, about 10 minutes. Add spinach and cook until wilted. Season with salt, pepper, and nutmeg. Set aside the mixture to cool.
2. Combine crumbled feta with spinach and onion mixture.
3. Cut a pocket into the side of each pork chop. Stuff with spinach and cheese mixture and secure the chop with a toothpick or butchers twine. Season the outside of each chop with additional salt and pepper.

Grilling:

1. Preheat the EGG® to 400°F with the convEGGtor® in place.
2. Place the chops on the grid and close the dome for 10 minutes.
3. Flip the chops and close for an additional 10 minutes.
4. Close the vents and allow the chops to sit for an additional 5-10 minutes or until the internal temperature reaches 150°F.

TERIYAKI BONE-IN LOIN CHOPS

Teriyaki and pork go together like peas and carrots.

Preparation Time: 30 minutes
Cooking Temperature: 425°F
Cooking Time: 20-22 minutes
Serves: 6

Meat	From This Book	Garnish
▸ 6 bone-in loin chops, cut 1 to 1 ¼ inch thick	▸ 1 cup Teriyaki Marinade, unthickened	▸ 1 pineapple, cut into rings

Preparation:
1. Submerge loin chops in marinade for 30 minutes.

Grilling:
1. Preheat the EGG® to 425°F.
2. Place chops on the grid and close the dome for 10 minutes.
3. Flip the chops and close the dome for an additional 10-12 minutes or until the internal temperature reaches 150°F near the bone.
4. Remove the chops and place the pineapple rings on the grill. Cover with the dome for 1 minutes.
5. Flip pineapple rings and close the dome for an additional 1 minute.
6. Serve chops topped with grilled pineapple.

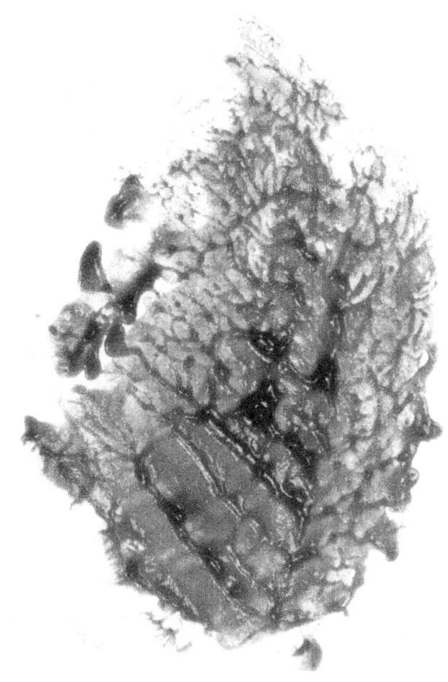

CARIBBEAN ST. LOUIS STYLE RIBS

These sweet and spicy ribs are sure to have you singing reggae.

Preparation Time: 1 hour
Cooking Temperature: 225°F
Cooking Time: 4-5 hours
Serves: 6-8

Meat	From This Book	Wood & Seasoning
▸ 2 racks (about 4 pounds) St. Louis Style Ribs	▸ 2 cups Chipotle Mango Lime Sauce ▸ 1 cup Habanero Rub	▸ 2 cups wood chips, soaked for 30 minutes in water ▸ ½ cup olive oil ▸ ¼ cup lime juice

Preparation:
1. Combine olive oil, lime juice, and Habanero Rub. Set aside.
2. Rinse the spare ribs under cold water and pat-dry with a paper towel.
3. Put them on a cutting board, bone side up.
4. Remove the membrane and the flap of meat running along the entire length of the ribs.
5. After trimming, generously apply rub, olive oil, and lime juice mixture.

Grilling:
1. Let it sit at room temperature while preheating the EGG® to 225°F.
2. Add wood chips, put the convEGGtor® in place, and place the grid on top.
3. Set the ribs on the grid, bone side down.
4. Close the dome and allow the ribs to smoke for 3 hours.
5. Brush the ribs with Chipotle Mango Lime Sauce and close the dome for another hour, or until the internal temperature reaches 185°F.
6. Once done, remove from the smoker and allow to cool for 15 minutes before carving.
7. Serve with more sauce on the side.

Pork | Ribs

CHINESE ST. LOUIS STYLE RIBS

Chinese spare ribs are perennial favorites in American Chinese restaurants. When that craving hits, this recipe does not disappoint.

Preparation Time: 30 minutes
Cooking Temperature: 225°F
Cooking Time: 3-4 hours
Serves: 6-8

Meat	From This Book	Wood & Seasonings
▸ 2 racks St. Louis Style Ribs	▸ 2 cups Chinese Barbecue Sauce (Char Sui) ▸ 1 cup Asian Rub	▸ 2 cups wood chips, soaked for 30 minutes ▸ ¼ cup olive oil

Preparation:

1. Rinse the spare ribs under cold water and pat-dry with a paper towel.
2. Put them on a cutting board, bone side up.
3. Remove the membrane along the entire length of the ribs.
4. After trimming, generously brush with olive oil and apply the rub.

Grilling:

1. Let it sit at room temperature while preheating the EGG® to 225°F.
2. Add wood chips, put the convEGGtor® in place, and place the grid on top.
3. Set the ribs on the grid, bone side down.
4. Close the dome and allow the ribs to smoke for 3 hours.
5. Brush the ribs with Chinese Barbecue Sauce and close the dome for another hour, or until the internal temperature reaches 185°F.
6. Once done, remove from the smoker and allow to cool for 15 minutes before carving.
7. Serve with more sauce on the side.

CLASSIC BARBECUE RIBS

While baby back ribs still rule the day in restaurants, we prefer the meatier St. Louis style rib. This cut stays moist through smoking and gives beginner smokers a chance to make delicious ribs without worrying about them drying out. But if you're jonesing for baby backs, this is the way to go.

Preparation Time: 30 minutes
Cooking Temperature: 225°F
Cooking Time: 2-3 hours
Serves: 4-6

Meat	From This Book	Wood & Seasonings
▸ 2 racks baby back ribs	▸ 2 cups Kansas City Barbecue Sauce ▸ ½ cup Basic BBQ Rub	▸ 2 cups wood chips, soaked in water for 30 minutes ▸ ¼ cup olive oil

Preparation:
1. Rinse the spare ribs under cold water and pat-dry with a paper towel.
2. Brush both sides with olive oil and sprinkle liberally with the Basic BBQ Rub.

Grilling:
1. Let it sit at room temperature while preheating the EGG® to 225°F.
2. Add wood chips, put the convEGGtor® in place, and place the grid on top.
3. Set the ribs on the grid, bone side down.
4. Close the dome and allow the ribs to smoke for 1 hour.
5. Brush the ribs with Kansas City Barbecue Sauce and close the dome for another hour, or until the internal temperature reaches 185°F.
6. Once done, remove from the smoker and allow to cool for 15 minutes before carving.
7. Serve with more sauce on the side.

KOREAN PORK RIBLETS

Riblets, also known as a feather cut, are actually not a part of the rib at all. Instead, this meat is cut from the spine of the pig. Cheaper than ribs and equally delicious, this preparation does not take nearly as long to smoke but yields big flavor.

Preparation Time: 30 minutes
Cooking Temperature: 225°F
Cooking Time: 1 hour
Serves: 6-8

Meat	From This Book	Wood
▸ 4 lbs pork riblets	▸ 3 cups Korean Barbecue Marinade, separated	▸ 2 cups wood chips, soaked in water for 30 minutes

Preparation:
1. Rinse riblets under cold water and pat-dry with a paper towel.
2. Pour 2 cups marinade over pork and let sit for a minimum of 30 minutes.

Grilling:
1. Preheat the EGG® to 225°F.
2. Add wood chips, put the convEGGtor® in place, and place the grid on top.
3. Set the riblets on the grid.
4. Close the dome and allow the ribs to smoke for 30 minutes.
5. Brush the ribs with reserved Korean Barbecue Marinade and close the dome for 30 more minutes, or until the internal temperature reaches 185°F.
6. Once done, remove from the smoker and allow to cool for 15 minutes before carving.
7. Serve with more sauce on the side.

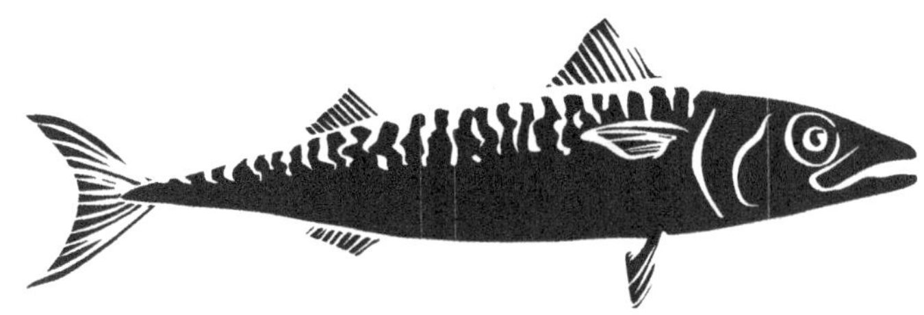

Seafood

Fish, shrimp, lobster, and oysters are ideal foods for the grill. While a grilling basket is ideal for small items, investing in a few metal skewers and a cedar plank will take any seafood you grill to the next level.

FISH	SHELLFISH
Cedar Plank Salmon	Black Pepper Dungeness Crab
Foil Packet Fish Filets	GInger Scallion Scallops
Glazed Salmon Sandwiches with Jicama Slaw	Grilled Lobster Rolls
Greek Seabass	Herb Butter Lobster Tails
Grilled Calamari Salad with Lemon Caper Vinaigrette	Oysters on the Half Shell
Grilled Halibut Tacos with Tomatillo Crema	Perfect Grilled Lobster
Grilled Tilapia Ceviche	Scallops with Pea-sto
Grilled Whole Trout	Shrimp Burgers with Remoulade
Lemon Bed Cod	Shrimp Scampi Kebabs
Swordfish Steaks with Peach Salsa	Thai Shrimp Skewers with Watermelon Salad

FISH

CEDAR PLANK SALMON

A sweet and spicy raspberry sauce is the perfect accompaniment to the flavor of cedar.

Preparation Time: 20 minutes
Cooking Temperature: 350°F
Cooking Time: 25-30 minutes
Serves: 4

Fish	Wood & Seasonings	Sauce
▸ 4 (4-6 oz each) salmon filets	▸ 2 cedar planks, soaked in water for 30 minutes ▸ ½ tsp salt ▸ ¼ tsp black pepper	▸ ½ cup raspberry preserves ▸ 2 Tbsp balsamic vinegar ▸ 1 jalapeño, chopped ▸ 1 clove garlic, minced

Preparation:

1. Season salmon on both sides with salt and pepper.

Grilling:

1. Preheat the EGG® to 350°F.
2. Place the plans on the grid and close the dome for 3 minutes.
3. Flip the planks and place the salmon on the heated side. Close the dome for 20 minutes.
4. Meanwhile, combine preserves, vinegar, jalapeño, and garlic in a small sauce pan and heat over low for 10 minutes, stirring occasionally.
5. Brush the salmon with the sauce and close the dome for another 5 minutes.
6. Serve with additional sauce.

FOIL PACKET FISH FILETS

This recipe can certainly be done with parchment paper if you would like, but foil works for a campfire feel.

Preparation Time: 20 minutes
Cooking Temperature: 375°F
Cooking Time: 12-15 minutes
Serves: 4

Fish	**Packets**
▸ 4 (4 oz each) white fish filets	▸ ½ cup white wine ▸ 4 Tbsp butter ▸ 4 pieces heavy duty foil ▸ 4 sprigs fresh thyme ▸ 4 green onions, cut in thirds ▸ 1 zucchini, julienned ▸ 1 large carrot, julienned ▸ 1 clove garlic, minced

Preparation:
1. On the bottom of each foil sheet, place zucchini, carrot and onion to create a bed.
2. Place one fish filet on each bed of vegetables and top with garlic, thyme, 1 Tbs of butter, salt and pepper to taste.
3. Gather two sides of the foil together and fold down so the foil is almost touching the food.
4. Roll one side of the foil then pour in 2 Tbsp of white wine. Close the remaining side. Repeat

Grilling:
1. Preheat the EGG® to 375°F with the convEGGtor® in place.
2. Place the foil packets on the grid and close the dome for 12-15 minutes or until the fish is cooked through.

GLAZED SALMON SANDWICHES WITH JICAMA SLAW

Crunchy and sweet, jicama is a cross between an apple and a potato and can be found in most grocery stores. Simply peel and julienne it for a tasty alternative to coleslaw.

Preparation Time: 30 minutes
Cooking Temperature:
Cooking Time: 15 minutes
Serves: 4

Fish & Rolls	Glaze	Slaw
▸ 4 (4 oz) salmon filets ▸ 4 soft hoagie rolls	▸ ½ cup orange marmalade ▸ 2 Tbsp soy sauce ▸ 1 Tbsp fresh grated ginger ▸ 1 Tbsp garlic, minced	▸ 2 cups jicama, julienned ▸ ¼ cup shredded carrot ▸ ¼ cup canola or grapeseed oil ▸ 2 Tbsp chopped cilantro ▸ 2 Tbsp freshly squeezed lime juice ▸ 1 tsp sambal or sriracha ▸ 1 tsp sugar

Preparation:

1. In a small saucepan, heat glaze ingredients together for 10 minutes over low heat.
2. In a large bowl, whisk together lime juice, sambal, sugar, cilantro, and oil. Add jicama and carrot and set aside.

Grilling:

1. Preheat the EGG® to 400°F.
2. Place the salmon on the rack and close the dome for 10 minutes.
3. Flip the salmon and brush with the glaze. Cover with the dome for an additional 5 minutes.
4. Flip the salmon once more and brush with the glaze. Cover with the dome for 1 minute and remove from the EGG®.
5. Split soft hoagie rolls in half lengthwise, place salmon on the roll and top with the jicama slaw.

GREEK SEA BASS

Sea Bass is the perfect fish to grill whole but this recipe can be done with any whole fish.

Preparation Time: 10 minutes
Cooking Temperature: 400°F
Cooking Time: 12-15 minutes
Serves: 4

Fish	Seasoning
▸ 2 whole sea bass (approximately 1 pound each), cleaned and gutted	▸ ¼ cup olive oil ▸ 2 Tbsp lemon juice ▸ 2 Tbsp capers ▸ 2 Tbsp parsley, chopped ▸ 1 tsp fresh oregano, chopped ▸ ½ tsp salt ▸ ¼ tsp dried chili flakes ▸ 4 cloves garlic ▸ 1 lemon, thinly sliced

Preparation:
1. Whisk together herbs, lemon juice, capers, olive oil, salt, and chili flakes. Set aside.
2. Season the sea bass with salt and pepper on the inside cavity and place lemon slices inside.

Grilling:
1. Preheat the EGG® to 400°F.
2. Place whole fish on the grid and close the dome for 6 minutes.
3. Gently flip the fish and replace the dome for an additional 6-8 minutes or until the fish is cooked through.
4. Remove the sea bass and drizzle with herb and lemon mixture. Serve more on the side for dressing as the fish is eaten.

GRILLED CALAMARI SALAD WITH LEMON CAPER VINAIGRETTE

Calamari either needs to be cooked for 5 minutes or 1 hour so do not walk away from the grill!

Preparation Time: 30 minutes
Cooking Temperature: 400°F
Cooking Time: 4 minutes
Serves: 6

For the Calamari

- 2 lbs calamari, cleaned, whole tubes and tentacles
- ¼ cup olive oil
- 2 Tbsp mint, roughly chopped
- ½ tsp salt
- ¼ tsp pepper
- 3 cloves garlic, minced
- The juice and zest of 1 lemon

From This Book

- 8 ounces grape tomatoes, cut in half
- 4 ounces Calamata olives, halved
- ½ cup finely chopped red onion
- ½ cup mint leaves
- ⅓ cup olive oil
- 2 Tbsp fresh squeezed lemon juice
- 2 Tbsp white wine vinegar
- 2 Tbsp capers in brine, drained
- 1 Tbsp brown mustard
- 1 (15 ounce) can chickpeas (drained and rinsed)
- 1 cucumber, seeded and roughly chopped

Preparation:

1. In a large bowl, whisk together olive oil, mint, garlic, lemon juice and zest, salt, and pepper. Stir in calamari and set aside for 30 minutes.
2. In a separate large bowl, whisk together mustard, lemon juice, vinegar, and olive oil. Add capers and mint and stir to combine.
3. Stir remaining salad ingredients into the dressing and set aside in the refrigerator.

Grilling:

1. Preheat the EGG® to 400°F.
2. Place the calamari directly on the grid for 2 minutes per side. The calamari will curl, that's okay.
3. Remove the calamari from the grill and set aside until cool enough to handle.
4. Slice the tubes into rings and tentacles in half and add to salad. Serve.

GRILLED HALIBUT TACOS WITH TOMATILLO CREMA

Fish tacos are synonymous with the beach. Escape to Baja California any time with these tasty tacos.

Preparation Time: 30 minutes
Cooking Temperature: 500°F
Cooking Time: 10 minutes
Serves: 4-6

Seafood | Fish

Tacos	Tomatillo Crema
▸ 4 (4 oz each) Halibut filets (or similar white fish) ▸ Salt & Pepper ▸ Corn tortillas ▸ Shredded cabbage ▸ Lime wedges ▸ Pico de Gallo	▸ 1 pound fresh tomatillos, husks removed (about 12 large) ▸ 1 cup heavy cream ▸ ½ cup cilantro leaves ▸ 2 garlic cloves ▸ 2 fresh serrano or jalapeño chiles, stems and tops removed ▸ 1 small onion

Preparation:

1. Preheat the EGG® to 500°F.
2. Place the tomatillos, onion, garlic cloves, and chiles on the grid and close the dome for 5 minutes.
3. Remove the vegetables and lower the temperature to 400°F.
4. In a blender, combine the vegetables with heavy cream and cilantro leaves. Blend until smooth. Chill in the fridge.

Grilling:

1. Season halibut filets with salt and pepper and place directly on the grid.
2. Close the dome for 5 minutes.
3. Gently turn the fish and replace the dome for an additional 5 minutes or until the fish is opaque.
4. Remove the fish from the EGG® and allow to rest 5 minutes.
5. Gently flake apart the fish and serve with tortillas, cabbage, lime wedges, pico de gallo, and the crema.

GRILLED TILAPIA "CEVICHE"

Ceviche is a traditional dish throughout Central and South America. Raw fish is mixed with vegetables and lime juice and allowed to "cook" without heat. The lime juice creates a chemical reaction that results in a texture similar to cooked fish but it takes several hours to prepare. This "quick" version married grilled tilapia with the flavors of ceviche without the hours of passive time.

Preparation Time: 10 minutes
Cooking Temperature: 400°F
Cooking Time: 5-6 minutes
Serves: 4

Seafood | Fish

Fish	Ceviche
▸ 1 lb tilapia filets	▸ ¼ cup chopped fresh parsley ▸ ¼ cup chopped fresh cilantro ▸ ¼ cup freshly squeezed lime juice ▸ 2 Tbsp olive oil ▸ ½ tsp red chile flakes ▸ 5 green onions, minced ▸ 2 tomatoes, diced ▸ 2 stalks celery, sliced ▸ ½ green bell pepper, minced ▸ Salt & pepper to taste

Preparation:
1. Mix lime juice, olive oil, vegetables and herbs together in a large bowl.

Grilling:
1. Preheat the EGG® to 400°F.
2. Season both sides of the tilapia with salt and pepper and place on the grid.
3. Close the dome and cook for 3 minutes.
4. Gently flip the fish and cook for another 2-3 minutes or until the fish is opaque. Set aside.
5. Flake apart the tilapia filets and gently stir into the vegetable mixture to combine.
6. Serve room temperature or chilled.

GRILLED WHOLE TROUT

Trout is one of the most common fish found in fresh waterways throughout the country.

Preparation: 10 minutes
Cooking Temperature: 400°F
Cooking Time: 15-20 minutes
Serves: 2

Fish	Seasonings
▸ 2 whole trout (about 1 lb each), cleaned and gutted	▸ 2 Tbsp olive oil ▸ ½ tsp salt ▸ ¼ tsp pepper ▸ 4 cloves garlic, smashed ▸ ½ sliced lemon ▸ ½ bunch fresh parsley

Preparation:

1. Brush the inside of the cavity and outside of the fish with olive oil and season with salt and pepper.
2. Stuff lemon, garlic, and parsley inside the cavity of each fish.

Grilling:

1. Preheat the EGG® to 400°F.
2. Place the fish directly on the grid and close the dome for 10 minutes.
3. Gently flip the fish and close the dome for an additional 5-10 minutes or until the fish is cooked through.

LEMON BED COD

One of the biggest complaints people have about cooking fish on the grill is that it sticks to the grids. This method not only gently flavors the fish, it also assures the fish won't stick.

Preparation Time: 10 minutes
Cooking Temperature: 400°F
Cooking Time: 15 minutes
Serves: 6

Fish	Seasonings
▸ 6 cod filets	▸ 3 lemons, sliced ¼ inch thick ▸ 1 onion, thinly sliced ▸ Salt & Pepper to taste

Preparation:
1. Place lemon slices directly on the grid so they are shingled one on top of another.
2. Place onion slices on top of the lemon.

Grilling:
1. Preheat the EGG® to 400°F.
2. Season both sides of the cod filets with salt and pepper and place them on top of the onion and lemon beds.
3. Close the dome for 12-15 minutes to allow the lemons to steam the fish.
4. Remove the fish on their lemon beds when the fish is opaque. Serve.

SWORDFISH STEAKS WITH PEACH SALSA

Swordfish is a delightfully oily, meaty fish. If you can find it, it is worth the premium price. Also, be sure to use peaches that are slightly underripe for this salsa so they maintain their form.

Preparation TIme: 30 minutes
Cooking Temperature: 400°F
Cooking Time: 12-15 minutes
Serves: 4

For the Fish	Salsa
▸ 4 swordfish steaks (about 1 inch thick, or 6 ounces) ▸ 1 Tbsp olive oil ▸ Salt & Pepper	▸ ¼ cup finely diced red pell pepper ▸ 1 Tbsp olive oil ▸ ¼ tsp cumin ▸ 2 peaches, slightly underripe, diced ▸ 1 jalapeño, seeded and finely chopped ▸ The juice and zest of 1 lime

Preparation:
1. Combine ingredients for the salsa and set aside.
2. Brush both sides of the swordfish steaks with olive oil and season with salt and pepper.

Grilling:
1. Preheat the EGG® to 400°F.
2. Place the steaks directly on the grid and close the dome for 6 minutes.
3. Gently flip the fish and close the dome for another 6-8 minutes or until the fish is firm.
4. Remove from the grid and serve topped with peach salsa.

BLACK PEPPER DUNGENESS CRAB

While this dish is generally cooked in a wok, the same flavors can be achieved on the EGG®!

Preparation Time: 20 minutes
Cooking Temperature: 500°F
Cooking Time: 10 minutes
Serves: 4

Shellfish	Sauce
▸ 4 lbs Dungeness Crab	▸ 3 Tbsp Hoisin sauce ▸ 3 Tbsp Oyster sauce ▸ 2 Tbsp butter ▸ 2 Tbsp olive oil ▸ 2 Tbsp freshly grated ginger ▸ 2 Tbsp freshly cracked black pepper ▸ 2 Tbsp red chile flakes ▸ 6 garlic cloves, finely chopped ▸ 2 green onions, finely chopped

Preparation:
1. In a small sauce pan, heat butter and olive oil.
2. Add onions, garlic, ginger, pepper, and chile flakes and cook for 1 minute.
3. Add hoisin and oyster sauces and stir to warm. Keep warm over very low heat.

Grilling:
1. Preheat the EGG® to 500°F.
2. Place the crabs on the grid and close the dome for 10 minutes or until the shells turn bright pink.
3. Remove the crabs from the grid and, using heat-proof gloves, quarter the crabs and slightly crack the legs.
4. Stir together half of the crabs and half of the warm sauce. Place on a platter.
5. Continue with the remaining crabs and remaining sauce. Serve.

GINGER SCALLION SCALLOPS

Scallops cook very quickly and have a built in timer for when they are done. If they don't come off of the grid easily to flip, they aren't ready. Give them another minute.

Preparation Time: 10 minutes
Cooking Temperature: 425°F
Cooking Time: 5-7 minutes
Serves: 4

Shellfish	Sauce
▸ 1 lb large sea scallops	▸ ¼ cup chopped green onion ▸ 2 Tbsp fresh orange juice ▸ 2 tsp sesame oil ▸ 1 tsp honey ▸ 1 tsp freshly grated ginger ▸ ½ tsp sriracha

Preparation:

1. Combine onion, orange juice, sesame oil, honey, ginger and sriracha in a shallow dish.
2. Allow the scallops to marinate 3 minutes on each side.

Grilling:

1. Preheat the EGG® to 425°F
2. Place the scallops on the grid and close the dome for 3 minutes.
3. If the scallops turn easily, flip them and close the dome for another 2-4 minutes.

GRILLED LOBSTER ROLLS

Lobster rolls are as common on the Eastern Seaboard as New England Patriots fans. Rather than letting that beautiful lobster flavor leech out into a pot of boiling water, keep it with the meat by cooking the tails on the grill.

Preparation Time: 10 minutes
Cooking Temperature: 500°F
Cooking Time: 10 minutes
Serves: 4-6

Shellfish	**For the Sandwich**
▸ 4 lobster tails	▸ ½ cup diced celery ▸ ¼ cup red onion, finely diced ▸ ¼ cup mayonnaise ▸ ½ tsp Old Bay seasoning ▸ 4-6 split top potato rolls, toasted

Grilling:

1. Preheat the EGG® to 500°F.
2. Place the lobster tails directly on the grid and close the dome for 5 minutes.
3. Flip the lobster tails and close the dome for an additional 5 minutes or until the shells are bright red.

Preparation:

1. Remove the lobster tails and allow them to cool before handling them.
2. Using kitchen shears, split open the lobster shells and remove the meat, taking care to pour any juices into a large bowl.
3. Chop the lobster meat into small pieces and return it to the bowl along with any lobster juices.
4. Add in mayonnaise, red onion, celery, and Old Bay seasoning and stir to combine.
5. Serve on toasted split top potato rolls.

HERB BUTTER LOBSTER TAILS

Think of this like creating little lobster shell boats of flavor.

Preparation Time: 10 minutes
Cooking Temperature: 500°F
Cooking Time: 10 minutes
Serves: 4

Shellfish	From This Book
▸ 4 lobster tails, cut in half	▸ 1 recipe Compound Herb Butter flavored with lemon zest, tarragon, parsley, and garlic

Preparation:

1. Place 1 Tbsp of Compound Herb Butter on top of each lobster tail half.

Grilling:

1. Preheat the EGG® to 500°F.
2. Place the tails directly on the grid and close the dome for 10 minutes.
3. Carefully remove the lobster tails taking care not to spill any of the butter and serve with crusty bread.

OYSTERS ON THE HALF SHELL

This super easy recipe is completely customizable.

Preparation Time: 10 minutes
Cooking Temperature: 425°F
Cooking Time: 7-9 minutes
Serves: 4

Shellfish	Seasonings
▸ 16 whole oysters	▸ ½ cup butter, softened ▸ 2 Tbsp fresh parsley ▸ 2 cloves garlic, minced ▸ The zest of 1 lemon

Preparation:
1. In a small bowl, combine butter, parsley, garlic, and lemon zest. Set aside

Grilling:
1. Preheat the EGG® to 425°F.
2. Place the cleaned oysters, cup side down, directly on the grids and close the dome for 7-9 minutes or until the oysters open up.
3. Remove the top shells and spoon in equal portions of the compound butter. Close the dome for 1 minute more until the butter melts and serve.

PERFECTLY GRILLED LOBSTER

Have a few lobsters laying around? Throw them on the EGG® and serve with a dipping sauce of your choice. We love the Garlic Grill Sauce or Chimichurri.

Preparation Time: 5 minutes
Cooking Temperature: 425°F
Cooking Time: 12-14 minutes
Serves: 4

Ingredients:

- 4 2-lb lobsters

Grilling:

1. Preheat the EGG® to 425°F.
2. Place the lobsters, bottom side down, on the cooking grids.
3. Close the dome for 12-14 minutes or until the shell turns bright red and the protein in the juices that seep from the shell coagulates.
4. Allow to cool slightly before serving with a dipping sauce of your choice.

SCALLOPS WITH PEA-STO

Spring is the perfect season for sea scallops and green peas. This bright sauce is the perfect match for the sweet scallops.

Preparation Time: 10 minutes
Cooking Temperature: 400°F
Cooking Time: 5-7 minutes
Serves: 4

Shellfish	**From This Book**
▸ 1 lb sea scallops ▸ 2 Tbsp olive oil ▸ Salt and Pepper	▸ 1 cup fresh green peas, blanched (you can also use frozen peas that have been thawed) ▸ ½ cup pecorino romano cheese, grated ▸ ¼ cup basil leaves ▸ ¼ cup mint leaves ▸ ¾ tsp salt ▸ ½ tsp pepper ▸ ¼ tsp crushed red chile flakes ▸ Olive oil

Preparation:
1. In a food processor, combine peas, basil, mint, salt, pepper, and chile flakes and process until smooth. Add cheese.
2. Add enough olive oil until the pea-sto becomes a sauce-like consistency (about ½ cup). Set aside.

Grilling:
1. Preheat the EGG® to 400°F.
2. Brush both sides of the scallops with olive oil and season with salt and pepper.
3. Place scallops on the grill and closer the dome for 3 minutes.
4. Gently flip the scallops and lower the dome for an additional 2-4 minutes.
5. Remove the scallops and pour some of the pea-sto on top.
6. Additional pea-sto can be saved in the fridge for 3 days. (It's delicious on pasta!)

SHRIMP BURGERS WITH REMOULADE

Shrimp burgers!?! Yes, shrimp burgers. Don't knock them until you try them.

Preparation TIme: 30 minutes
Cooking Temperature: 500°F
Cooking Time: 10 minutes
Serves: 4

Burgers

- 1 lb raw shrimp, peeled & deveined
- ¾ cup fresh breadcrumbs
- ¼ cup celery, finely diced
- ¼ cup green onion, white and light green parts, chopped
- ¼ cup parsley
- 1 Tbsp Old Bay Seasoning
- 1 Tbsp brown mustard
- The juice and zest of 1 lemon
- Olive Oil for brushing

Remoulade

- ½ cup mayonnaise
- 2 Tbsp dill pickle, finely chopped
- 2 tsp prepared horseradish

Fixings

- 4 hamburger buns
- Shredded lettuce
- Sliced tomato

Preparation:

1. In a food processor, combine burger ingredients, minus the breadcrumbs, and process until smooth. Gently fold in breadcrumbs and form into 4 patties. Refrigerate for 20 minutes.
2. Mix remoulade sauce ingredients and refrigerate.

Grilling:

1. Preheat the EGG® to 500°F.
2. Brush both sides of the burgers with olive oil and place directly on the grids. Cover with the dome for 4 minutes.
3. Turn the burgers and cover for another 3 minutes.
4. Close all of the vents and allow the burgers to sit for another 5 minutes or until the burgers reach an internal temperature of 165°F.
5. Place the burgers on bottom buns and top with a dollop of remoulade, sliced tomato, and shredded lettuce.

SHRIMP SCAMPI KEBABS

Shrimp are classified by a "U" number. This denotes how many shrimp are in a pound. U20 shrimp means there are 20 shrimp per pound while U8 mean there are 8 shrimp per pound.

Preparation Time: 40 minutes
Cooking Temperature: 400°F
Cooking Time: 8-10 minutes
Serves: 4

Shellfish	**Marinade**
▸ 1 lb U20 shrimp, peeled, deveined ▸ 4 wooden skewers, soaked in water for 30 minutes	▸ ¼ cup olive oil ▸ 2 Tbsp parsley, chopped ▸ ½ tsp salt ▸ ¼ tsp pepper ▸ The juice and zest of 1 lemon ▸ 2 cloves garlic, minced

Preparation:

1. In a large glass bowl, combine olive oil, lemon juice, parsley, salt and pepper.
2. Toss shrimp into marinade and set in the fridge for 30 minutes.

Grilling:

1. Preheat the EGG® to 400°F.
2. Thread shrimp evenly onto skewers and place directly on the grids.
3. Close the dome for 5 minutes.
4. Turn skewers and replace the dome for another 3-5 minutes or until the shrimp are opaque.

THAI SHRIMP SKEWERS WITH GRILLED WATERMELON SALAD

Grilling only amplifies the sweetness of watermelon, a necessary trait for the spicy shrimp.

Preparation TIme: 30 minutes
Cooking Temperature: 400°F
Cooking Time: 7-10 minutes
Serves: 4

Shellfish	From This Book	Salad
▸ 1 lb U20 shrimp, peeled and deveined ▸ 4 wooden skewers, soaked in water for 30 minutes	▸ 1 cup Spicy Thai Marinade	▸ ¼ cup olive oil ▸ 2 Tbsp rice wine vinegar ▸ 1 tsp mint leaves, chopped ▸ 1 tsp fish sauce ▸ 1 round slice of watermelon, about 1 inch thick ▸ 1 English cucumber, diced ▸ 1 Fresno chile, sliced ▸ 1 shallot, finely diced

Preparation:

1. Marinate the shrimp in the Spicy Thai Marinade for 20 minutes in the fridge.
2. In a large bowl, Fresno chile, shallot, vinegar, mint, fish sauce, and olive oil.

Grilling:

1. Preheat the EGG® to 400°F.
2. Thread the shrimp onto the skewers and place on the grid. Close the dome for 3 minutes.
3. Flip the skewers and lower the dome for an additional 3 minutes or until the shrimp are opaque.
4. Brush the watermelon on both sides with olive oil and place on the grid for 30 seconds per side.
5. Dice watermelon and cucumber and stir into dressing.
6. Serve a scoop of the salad with a skewer of shrimp on top.

Pizza

Tuscan style pizza in your own backyard. A lofty promise from The Big Green Egg®, but one it easily fulfills.

PIZZA
Buffalo Chicken Pizza
Chicken Bacon Artichoke Pizza
Classic Meat Lovers Pizza
Garlic Clam Pizza
Green Curry Chicken Pizza
Italian Sausage and Pepper Pizza
Marv & Joe Pizza
Mushroom & Caramelized Onion Calzones
Pear, Bacon and Gorgonzola Pizza
Pizza Margarita
Pulled Pork Barbecue Pizza
Shrimp Scampi Pizza
Skirt Steak Fajita Pizza
Thai Chicken Pizza
White Pizza

Pizza

METHOD:

All of the pizza recipes in this section follow the same method. Simply light the natural lump coal, insert the convEGGtor® and add a pizza stone. Let the EGG® come to 500°F and the stone to heat for 10 minutes before cooking. Slide the ready-made pizza onto the stone using a pizza peel, close the dome for 4 minutes and remove.

While the recipes in this section say "Cook according to method", an alternate method can be used. Simply refrain from topping the pizza until the first side has cooked.

ALTERNATE METHOD:

Don't have a convEGGtor® and pizza stone? Never fear. Form pizza dough into a flat shape and place directly on the grill grids once your EGG® reaches 500°F. Close the lid of your EGG® for 2 minutes or until the dough browns on the bottom. Open the lid and flip over the dough, top with desired toppings and shut the lid for an additional 2 minutes. Carefully remove the pizza with a wooden peel, cut, and serve.

Using bread dough in your pizza dough will yield a crisper crust while all-purpose flour will give your crust a chewier texture.

Basic Pizza Dough (Makes 2 14-inch pizzas or 4 7-inch flatbreads)

While grocery stores and pizzerias readily sell balls of dough, making your own pizza dough without kneading is as simple as mixing 3 ingredients and walking away for a little while. Best part, this dough can be made in advance and kept in the refrigerator for up to a week so when the pizza craving hits, you can hit back.

- 1 ½ cup lukewarm water
- ¾ Tbsp yeast
- ¾ Tbsp salt
- 3 ¼ cup bread flour

1. In a medium sized bowl with a lid, mix all of the ingredients until the dough comes together. Do Not Knead.
2. Cover (but do not seal) and set aside the dough in a warm, draft-free place for 1 ½ - 2 hours or until the dough has doubled in size.
3. Cover tightly and refrigerate the dough for 1 hour to allow for easier handling or refrigerate for up to a week and use as desired.

To make moving pizza easier, sprinkle a pizza peel with cornmeal and place formed dough on top. Top your pizza as desired and use the peel to slide the pizza onto the heated stone in your Big Green Egg®. When the pizza is cooked, simply slide the peel under the crust and lift to a waiting cutting board.

Basic Pizza Sauce

Preparation Time: 30 minutes
Yields: 3 cups

- 2 Tbsp olive oil
- 1 tsp basil
- 1 tsp oregano
- 1 can (28 ounces) crushed tomatoes
- 1 small white onion, finely diced
- 1 clove garlic, minced

1. In a medium saucepan, heat olive oil over medium.
2. Saute onion and garlic for 10 minutes or until translucent.
3. Add tomatoes, basil, and oregano and simmer for 10 minutes. Set aside to cool.
4. Can be kept in the fridge for up to 1 week or frozen for up to 3 months.

BUFFALO CHICKEN PIZZA

This recipe combines two bar classics - pizza and Buffalo wings.

Dough	Sauce	Toppings
▸ 1 pizza dough	▸ ¼ cup Franks Buffalo Sauce	▸ 1 cup shredded provolone cheese ▸ ½ cup cooked chicken ▸ ¼ cup sliced celery ▸ ¼ cup crumbled blue cheese

Preparation:

1. Stretch dough to 14" and place on pizza peel.
2. Spread dough with Frank's Buffalo Sauce.
3. Top with provolone and cooked chicken.

Grilling:

1. Cook according to desired method.
2. When pizza comes out, top with sliced celery and crumbled blue cheese.

CHICKEN BACON ARTICHOKE PIZZA

Mmm... bacon

Dough	Sauce	Toppings
▸ 1 pizza dough	▸ 2 Tbsp olive oil ▸ 1 clove garlic, minced ▸ ¼ tsp black pepper	▸ ½ cup shredded mozzarella cheese ▸ ½ cup shredded provolone cheese ▸ ½ cup cooked chicken ▸ ¼ cup marinated artichoke hearts, chopped ▸ 2 Tbsp crumbled bacon

Preparation:

1. Stretch dough to 14" and place on pizza peel.
2. Spread dough with olive oil, garlic, and black pepper.
3. Top with provolone, mozzarella, chicken, artichoke hearts, and bacon.

Grilling:

1. Cook according to desired method.

CLASSIC MEAT LOVERS PIZZA

There's nothing quite like a classic.

Dough	Sauce	Toppings
▸ 1 pizza dough	▸ ¼ cup basic pizza sauce	▸ 1 cup mozzarella cheese ▸ ¼ cup cooked Italian sausage ▸ ¼ cup chopped ham ▸ 12 slices pepperoni ▸ 6 slices salami

Preparation:

1. Stretch pizza dough to 14" and place on a pizza peel.
2. Top with sauce, cheese, and meats.

Grilling:

1. Cook according to desired method.

Pizza

GARLIC CLAM PIZZA

A riff on linguini with clam sauce, this pizza taps into old school Italian American cuisine.

Dough	Sauce	Toppings
▸ 1 pizza dough	▸ 2 Tbsp olive oil ▸ ¼ tsp dried oregano ▸ 3 large garlic cloves, minced ▸ Salt & Pepper	▸ 2 cups baby arugula ▸ ½ cup mozzarella cheese ▸ 2 Tbsp parmesan ▸ 2 Tbsp olive oil ▸ 2 6.5-ounce cans chopped clams, juice drained and reserved ▸ The juice of 1 lemon

Preparation:

1. Stretch pizza dough to 14" and place on a pizza peel.
2. Spread the dough with olive oil and top with chopped garlic, oregano, salt, and pepper.
3. Top with cheeses and clams.

Grilling:

1. Cook according to desired method.
2. When the pizza comes out, top with arugula, lemon juice, some of the reserved clam juice, and olive oil.

GREEN CURRY CHICKEN PIZZA

Trust us. This is a great one. Feel free to use leftover Green Curry Chicken from your Dutch oven for this satisfying pizza.

Dough	Sauce	Toppings
▸ 1 pizza dough	▸ 2 Tbsp Asian fish sauce ▸ 2 Tbsp lime juice ▸ 2 Tbsp cornstarch ▸ 1 ½ Tbsp brown sugar ▸ 2 tsp Thai green curry paste ▸ 1 14-ounce can unsweetened coconut milk ▸ The zest of 2 limes, taken off in strips with a vegetable peeler ▸ 1 inch piece of fresh ginger, peeled and sliced	▸ 1 cup mozzarella cheese ▸ ½ cup cooked chicken ▸ ½ cup cabbage, shredded ▸ ¼ cup carrot, shredded ▸ 1 green onion, sliced

Preparation:

1. In a small sauce pan, combine ¼ cup coconut milk with the Thai green curry paste. Stir to combine.
2. Add remaining coconut milk, lime zest, ginger, fish sauce, and brown sugar and heat over medium for 10 minutes.
3. In a separate bowl, combine cornstarch and lime juice.
4. Remove strips of lime zest and ginger pieces.
5. Add cornstarch and lime juice and stir into sauce until it thickens.
6. Allow the sauce to cool before topping pizza.
7. In a separate bowl, combine cabbage, carrot, green onion, and 1 Tbsp of the sauce. Set aside.
8. Stretch pizza dough to 14" and place on pizza peel.
9. Top with Thai green curry sauce, cheese, and chicken.

Grilling:

1. Cook according to desired method.
2. When the pizza comes out of the EGG®, top with slaw mixture.

Pizza

ITALIAN SAUSAGE AND PEPPER PIZZA

Sausage and pepper sandwiches are favorites at state fairs all over the nation. This is the same idea in pizza form.

Dough	Sauce	Toppings
▸ 1 pizza dough	▸ ¼ cup Basic Pizza Sauce	▸ ½ cup mozzarella cheese ▸ ½ cup provolone cheese ▸ 1 cup cooked Italian sausage ▸ 2 Tbsp olive oil ▸ ½ tsp salt ▸ 1 green bell pepper, sliced ▸ 1 cubanelle pepper, sliced ▸ 1 onion, sliced

Preparation:

1. In a skillet, heat olive oil over medium.
2. Add peppers, onion, and salt and cook until soft, about 10 minutes. Set aside to cool.
3. Stretch pizza dough into a 14" round and place on a pizza peel.
4. Top with basic pizza sauce, cheeses, sausage, and the cooked peppers and onions.

Grilling:

1. Cook according to desired method.

MARV AND JOE PIZZA

Legend has it, two engineering professors at Utah State University invented an open-faced sandwich consisting of a thick slice of homemade bread, garlic butter, tomatoes, and provolone cheese all placed under a broiler. Sounds like a great pizza, right?

Dough	Sauce	Toppings
▸ 1 pizza dough	▸ 2 Tbsp olive oil ▸ ¼ tsp salt ▸ ⅛ tsp black pepper ▸ ⅛ tsp Italian seasoning ▸ 1 clove garlic, minced	▸ 1 cup shredded provolone cheese ▸ ½ tsp red wine vinegar ▸ 10 slices tomato

Pizza

Preparation:
1. Stretch pizza dough into a 14” round.
2. Spread dough with olive oil, salt, pepper, Italian seasoning, and garlic.
3. Top with provolone cheese and sliced tomato.
4. Sprinkle each tomato slice with red wine vinegar and additional salt and pepper.

Grilling:
1. Cook according to desired method.

Pizza

MUSHROOM AND CARAMELIZED ONION CALZONES

Calzones are simply pizza folded over on itself. Stuff them with your favorite fillings!

Dough	Sauce	Filling
▸ 2 pizza dough balls, each cut in half	▸ Basic Pizza Sauce, for dipping	▸ 6 ounces mushrooms, sliced ▸ 1 cup ricotta cheese ▸ ½ cup parmesan, grated ▸ 2 Tbsp olive oil ▸ 2 Tbsp butter ▸ 1 tsp fresh thyme, chopped ▸ ½ tsp salt ▸ ¼ tsp pepper ▸ 2 onions, sliced

Preparation:

1. In a skillet, heat 1 Tbsp olive oil and 1 Tbsp butter over medium heat.
2. Add mushrooms but do not move the pan until mushrooms are brown, about 5 minutes.
3. Stir and continue to cook another 3 minutes. Remove from pan.
4. In the same skillet, add remaining olive oil and butter and sliced onions.
5. Reduce the heat to medium low and allow the onions to cook for 20-25 minutes or until caramelized. Allow the onion to cool.
6. In a bowl, combine ricotta cheese, parmesan, thyme, salt, and pepper.
7. Stretch each pizza dough into a 7 inch round.
8. Place a dollop of the ricotta mixture along with some of the mushrooms and onions on half of the round.
9. Fold the dough over and crimp the edges.
10. Cut 1 vent in the top of the calzone.

Grilling:

1. Prepare the EGG® as you normally would for a pizza.
2. Place each calzone on the stone with the dome closed for 7-9 minutes or until the crust is golden brown.
3. Serve with a side of Basic Pizza Sauce for dipping.

PEAR, BACON & GORGONZOLA PIZZA

This popular salad becomes a pizza!

Dough	Sauce	Toppings
▸ 1 pizza dough	▸ 2 Tbsp olive oil ▸ ¼ tsp salt ▸ ⅛ tsp pepper	▸ 2 cups baby arugula ▸ ¼ cup Gorgonzola, crumbled ▸ 2 Tbsp olive oil ▸ 2 Tbsp crumbled bacon ▸ 1 firm pear, sliced

Preparation:
1. Stretch pizza dough into a 14" round and place on peel.
2. Spread the dough with 2 Tbsp olive oil and sprinkle with salt and pepper.
3. Top with sliced pear, bacon, and Gorgonzola.

Grilling:
1. Cook according to method.
2. When the pizza comes off the EGG®, top with baby arugula drizzled with remaining olive oil.

PIZZA MARGARITA

This classic masterpiece relies on the freshest ingredients for the best flavor.

Dough	Sauce	Toppings
▸ 1 pizza dough	▸ ½ cup Basic Pizza Sauce	▸ 4 ounces fresh mozzarella, sliced ▸ 6 basil leaves, torn

Pizza

Preparation:

1. Stretch pizza dough into a 14" round and place on peel.
2. Spread with Basic Pizza Sauce and top with mozzarella.

Grilling:

1. Cook according to method.
2. Top with torn basil as soon as it comes out of the EGG®.

PULLED PORK BARBECUE PIZZA

This pizza is perfect for leftover smoked pork shoulder, if there is any.

Dough	Sauce	Toppings
▸ 1 pizza dough	▸ 1 cup shredded mozzarella cheese ▸ ½ cup pulled pork ▸ ½ cup sliced red onion	▸ ¼ cup Kansas City Barbecue Sauce

Pizza

Preparation:

1. Stretch pizza dough into a 14" round and place on peel.
2. Spread with Kansas City Barbecue Sauce
3. Top with cheese, pork, and sliced red onion.

Grilling:

1. Cook according to desired method.

SHRIMP SCAMPI PIZZA

Someone once said seafood and cheese don't go together. Well they do in this delicious flavor combination!

Dough	Sauce	Toppings
▸ 1 pizza dough	▸ 1 Tbsp olive oil ▸ 1 Tbsp butter ▸ 1 Tbsp lemon juice ▸ 1 Tbsp fresh parsley ▸ ½ tsp lemon zest ▸ ¼ tsp salt ▸ Pinch of red chile flake ▸ 1 clove garlic, minced	▸ ¼ lb shrimp, peeled, deveined, and cut into small pieces. ▸ ½ cup shredded parmesan cheese

Pizza

Preparation:

1. In a small skillet, heat butter and olive oil.
2. Add shrimp and garlic and saute until the shrimp are opaque.
3. Add lemon zest, lemon juice, parsley, salt, and chile flake. Set aside to cool
4. Stretch pizza dough to 14" round and place on peel.
5. Pour scampi sauce on the dough and spread around.
6. Sprinkle shrimp on top and top with shredded parmesan.

Grilling:

1. Cook according to desired method.

Pizza

SKIRT STEAK FAJITA PIZZA

Tender pieces of skirt steak are accented by spicy pepper jack cheese.

Dough	Toppings
▸ 1 pizza dough	▸ ½ cup pepper jack cheese ▸ ½ cup mozzarella cheese ▸ 2 Tbsp olive oil ▸ 1 tsp Adobo rub ▸ 1 (8 ounce) piece of skirt steak ▸ 1 bell pepper, sliced ▸ 1 onion, sliced ▸ Pico de Gallo

Preparation:

1. Brush skirt steak with olive oil and sprinkle with Adobo rub. Allow to sit for 10 minutes.
2. In a large skillet, heat 1 Tbsp of olive oil over medium high and cook the skirt steak for 2 minutes on each side. Set aside.
3. Reduce heat to medium, add 1 Tbsp olive oil to the skillet and cook bell pepper and onion until translucent. About 10 minutes. Set aside.
4. Slice flank steak across the grain.
5. Stretch pizza dough into 14" round and place on peel.
6. Top with cheeses, steak, and pepper mixture.

Grilling:

1. Cook according to method.
2. When the pizza comes out, sprinkle Pico de Gallo over top.

THAI CHICKEN PIZZA

Sweet and spicy Thai sweet chile sauce gives this pizza an extra zip.

Dough	Sauce	Toppings
▸ 1 pizza dough	▸ ¼ cup Thai sweet chile sauce	▸ 1 cup spinach leaves ▸ 1 cup mozzarella cheese ▸ ½ cup cooked chicken ▸ ½ cup sliced zucchini ▸ ¼ cup finely chopped green onion ▸ ½ tsp crushed red chile flake

Preparation:

1. Stretch dough into 14" round and place on pizza peel.
2. Spread the dough with Thai sweet chile sauce.
3. Top with cheese, spinach, sliced zucchini, chicken, green onion, and chile flake.

Grilling:

1. Cook according to desired method.

WHITE PIZZA

A classic in pizzerias across the country, this creamy, garlicky pie is sure to please the pickiest palate.

Dough	**Sauce**	**Toppings**
▸ 1 pizza dough	▸ 2 Tbsp olive oil ▸ ½ tsp crushed red chile flake (optional) ▸ ¼ tsp salt ▸ ¼ tsp Italian Seasoning ▸ ⅛ tsp pepper ▸ 1 clove garlic, minced	▸ ½ cup mozzarella cheese ▸ ½ cup provolone cheese ▸ ½ cup ricotta cheese

Preparation:

1. Stretch dough into 14" round and place on pizza peel.
2. Spread the dough with olive oil, sprinkle with garlic, and season with salt, pepper, Italian Seasoning and chile flake.
3. Top with mozzarella and provolone and dollop with ricotta cheese.

Grilling:

1. Cook according to desired method.

Pizza

Sides & Salads

For some people, lighting a grill to cook one thing seems like a waste. But when you can use that same outdoor oven to make delicious side dishes and superb salads, the effort (little thought it may be) seems worth it. While your EGG® is heated, give these summery accompaniments a try.

SIDES AND SALADS
Alligator Eggs
Baba Ganoush
Bacon Wrapped Pineapple
Broiled Tomatoes & Parmesan
Cowboy Caviar
Grilled Artichokes
Grilled Cabbage with Champagne Vinaigrette
Grilled Caesar Salad
Grilled Endive Salad
Grilled Lemon Garlic Zucchini
Grilled Onions
Grilled Polenta
Grilled Vegetable Succotash
Mexican Street Corn
Mojito Watermelon
Panzanella
Parmesan Zucchini Spears
Prosciutto and Pear Bruschetta
Smoked Potato Salad
Sweet Potato Fries

Sides & Salads

ALLIGATOR EGGS

This cheesy, spicy appetizer contains neither alligator, nor eggs. Instead, they are named for their shape.

Preparation Time: 15 minutes
Cooking Temperature: 425°F
Cooking Time: 10 minutes
Serves: 6

Fresh Ingredients	From the Pantry
▸ 8 ounces cream cheese, softened ▸ 1 cup sharp cheddar cheese ▸ 12 thin slices bacon	▸ 6 jalapeños

Preparation:
1. Slice jalapeños in half and remove seeds. Set aside.
2. In a small bowl, combine cheddar cheese and cream cheese until mixed.
3. Stuff 2 Tbsp of the cream cheese mixture into each jalapeño half.
4. Wrap each jalapeño half in one strip of bacon, securing with a toothpick.

Grilling:
1. Preheat the EGG® to 425°F.
2. Place the alligator eggs directly on the grid and close the dome for 10 minutes or until the bacon is crisp. Serve immediately.

BABA GANOUSH

This creamy eggplant dip is best served with toasted pita chips and a variety of crunchy veggies for the perfect starter or accompaniment.

Preparation Time: 10 minutes
Cooking Temperature: 425°F
Cooking Time: 6-10 minutes
Serves: 8

Fresh Ingredients	**From the Pantry**
▸ 2 Tbsp fresh parsley	▸ 2 Tbsp olive oil
▸ 1 eggplant, sliced into ½ inch rounds	▸ 2 Tbsp tahini
▸ 1 clove garlic	▸ Salt & Pepper
▸ The juice and zest of 1 lemon	

Grilling:
1. Brush both sides of each eggplant slice with olive oil and season with salt and pepper.
2. Place on a 425°F EGG® and close the dome for 3-5 minutes.
3. Flip the eggplant and close the dome for another 3-5 minutes.

Assembly:
1. Peel the eggplant skins away from the flesh and discard.
2. In a food processor, combine eggplant, tahini, parsley, garlic, lemon zest and lemon juice and puree until smooth.
3. Taste for seasoning and add salt and pepper accordingly.
4. Serve at room temperature with pita chips, pretzels, or raw vegetables.

BACON WRAPPED PINEAPPLE

Grilling brings out the sweetness in fruit, especially when it is wrapped in bacon.

Preparation Time: 10 minutes
Cooking Temperature: 425°F
Cooking Time: 10 minutes
Serves: 6

From this Book	Other Ingredients
▸ 1 cup Classic Texas Barbecue Sauce (or your favorite sauce)	▸ 1 lb bacon, cut into 4 inch strips ▸ 1 pineapple cut into 2 inch cubes

Preparation:

1. Wrap each pineapple piece with a 4 inch strip of bacon and secure with a toothpick.

Grilling:

1. Place on the grid of a 425°F EGG® and close the dome for 8 minutes or until the bacon is crispy.
2. Brush each pineapple chunk with barbecue sauce and close the dome for another 2 minutes.
3. Serve warm with additional barbecue sauce for dipping.

BROILED TOMATOES AND PARMESAN

A steakhouse favorite, this take on a classic is best when cooked over a very hot EGG®.

Preparation Time: 10 minutes
Cooking Temperature: 500°F
Cooking Time: 5 minutes
Serves: 4

Fresh Ingredients	From the Pantry
▸ ¼ cup parmesan, shredded ▸ 4 roma tomatoes	▸ 1 Tbsp olive oil ▸ 1 tsp red wine vinegar ▸ Salt & Pepper

Preparation:

1. Cut each tomato in half, lengthwise, and brush with olive oil.

Grilling:

1. Place in a 500°F EGG® and lower the dome for 2 minutes.
2. Turn the tomatoes, season with vinegar, salt, and pepper and top with parmesan cheese.
3. Lower the dome for an additional 2 minutes or until the cheese melts. Serve warm.

COWBOY CAVIAR

This dish is a cross between a bean salad and a salsa. Enjoy it on its own or with tortilla chips.

Preparation Time: 10 minutes
Cooking Temperature: 425°F
Cooking Time: 10 minutes
Serves: 8

Fresh Ingredients	From the Pantry
▸ 2 ears fresh corn on the cob ▸ 1 large tomato, finely diced ▸ 1 bell pepper, finely diced ▸ 1 jalapeño, very finely chopped	▸ ¼ cup bottled Italian salad dressing (or make your own) ▸ 2 cans black beans, drained and rinsed ▸ 1 can pinto beans, drained and rinsed

Grilling:

1. Place shucked and cleaned ears of corn on a 425°F EGG® and close the dome for 5 minutes.
2. Turn the corn and close the dome for another 5 minutes before removing and setting aside.

Assembly:

1. Carefully cut the corn off the cob and place it in a large bow.
2. Add remaining ingredients and toss to combine.

GRILLED ARTICHOKES

The trick to great grilled artichokes is steaming them until they are almost cooked and finishing them on the grill.

Preparation Time: 1 hour, 10 minutes
Cooking Temperature: 425°F
Cooking Time: 5-7 minutes
Serves: 4-6

For the Artichokes	Dipping Sauce
▸ 4 large artichokes ▸ 2 Tbsp olive oil ▸ 1 lemon ▸ Salt and pepper	▸ ½ cup mayonnaise ▸ 2 Tbsp lemon juice ▸ 2 Tbsp basil pesto (Try our Besto Pesto!) ▸ ½ tsp sriracha

Sides & Salads

Preparation:

1. Trim artichokes of their fibrous ends and thorny leaves.
2. Quarter the artichokes and remove the thistle in the middle.
3. Rub all cut ends with half of a lemon to prevent browning.
4. In a large steamer, cook artichokes 45 minutes or until just fork tender.
5. Brush each artichoke with olive oil and season with salt and pepper.

Grilling:

1. Place on a 425°F EGG® and close the dome for 3 minutes.
2. Turn the artichokes and close the dome for another 2-4 minutes.
3. Serve with dipping sauce.

GRILLED CABBAGE WITH CHAMPAGNE VINAIGRETTE

Cabbage is the unsung hero of the green vegetable family. Sweet when cooked, these cabbage "steaks" make a great vegetarian option to your meal.

Preparation Time: 10 minutes
Cooking Temperature: 425°F
Cooking Time: 10 minutes
Serves: 6-8

For the Cabbage	For the Dressing
▸ 1 head cabbage ▸ 2 Tbsp olive oil ▸ Salt and Pepper	▸ ½ cup olive oil ▸ ¼ cup Champagne vinegar ▸ 2 Tbsp capers in brine, drained ▸ 1 Tbsp Dijon mustard ▸ 1 shallot, finely chopped

Preparation:

1. Cut the cabbage into ½ inch "steaks" from top to root.
2. Brush each side with olive oil and season with salt and pepper.

Grilling:

1. Place on a 425°F EGG® and close the lid for 5 minutes.
2. Meanwhile, in a small bowl, combine shallot, mustard, capers, and vinegar.
3. While whisking, stream in olive oil until dressing emulsifies.
4. Flip cabbage steaks and cook on the other side for an additional 5 minutes with the dome closed.
5. Remove cabbage from the grill to a platter and pour dressing over top. Serve warm.

GRILLED CAESAR SALAD

Grilling smoking the romaine lettuce adds a little something special to an ordinary Caesar salad. And skip the store bought croutons, homemade are so much better.

Preparation Time: 10 minutes
Cooking Temperature: 400°F
Cooking Time: 1 minute
Serves: 6

Salad	Dressing	Croutons
▸ 2 Tbsp shredded Parmesan cheese ▸ 1 Tbsp olive oil ▸ ¼ tsp salt ▸ 2 heads romaine lettuce, split lengthwise	▸ 1 cup grated Parmesan cheese ▸ 2 Tbsp Dijon mustard ▸ 3 garlic cloves ▸ 3 anchovy fillets ▸ 2 lemons, juiced ▸ Extra-virgin olive oil ▸ Kosher salt	▸ 2 Tbsp olive oil ▸ 4 slices day old Italian bread, cubed ▸ Kosher Salt & Black Pepper to taste

Preparation:

1. In a blender or food processor, combine dressing ingredients, minus olive oil and salt.
2. Gradually stream in olive oil until the dressing reaches your desired consistency.
3. Taste and season with salt, if necessary.

Grilling:

1. Preheat the EGG® to 400°F.
2. Toss bread cubes with olive oil, a pinch of salt and a pinch of black pepper and place on a small sheet tray.
3. Place the bread in the EGG® for 8-10 minutes or until golden brown.
4. Brush cut side of the romaine halves with olive oil and season with salt and pepper.
5. Grill 1 minute over direct heat.
6. Cut the romaine into bite size pieces.
7. Toss lettuce with dressing, croutons, and shredded Parmesan Serve immediately.

GRILLED ENDIVE SALAD

Bitter, sweet and crunchy, this salad hits all the right notes.

Preparation Time: 10 minutes
Cooking Temperature: 425°F
Cooking Time: 2 minutes
Serves: 6

Salad	Dressing
▸ 2 cups frisee ▸ ½ cup pecan halves ▸ ¼ cup dried cranberries ▸ ¼ cup crumbled bacon ▸ 2 heads endive ▸ 1 bunch spinach, cleaned and stems removed	▸ 1/4 cup olive oil ▸ 2 Tbsp Dijon Mustard ▸ 1 Tbsp honey ▸ 1 shallot, finely minced ▸ The juice of 1 lemon ▸ Kosher salt and fresh cracked pepper to taste

Preparation:

1. In a large bowl, combine dressing ingredients. Set aside.

Grilling:

1. Split endive down the middle, lengthwise and place on a 425°F EGG® for 2 minutes.
2. Remove the endive and slice into half rounds.
3. Toss shredded frisee, sliced endive, spinach, pecans, and cranberries in the dressing and serve immediately.

GRILLED LEMON GARLIC ZUCCHINI

When zucchini is plentiful in the garden, this recipe will jazz up the beginner's plant. The secret to crispy zucchini is a very hot EGG®.

Preparation Time: 10 minutes
Cooking Temperature: 500°F
Cooking Time: 5 minutes
Serves: 6-8

Vegetable	For the Topping
▸ 4 zucchini, sliced lengthwise into ½ inch slices	▸ ¼ cup butter, softened ▸ 2 tsp parsley, chopped ▸ 3 cloves garlic, minced ▸ The zest and juice of 1 lemon

Sides & Salads

Preparation:

1. In a small dish, combine butter, parsley, garlic, lemon zest, and lemon juice.
2. Liberally brush each zucchini slice with the butter mixture.

Grilling:

1. Place the zucchini on a 500°F EGG® and close the dome for 3 minutes.
2. Flip the zucchini and recover with the dome for an additional 2 minutes.
3. Drizzle remaining butter on top of zucchini as it comes off the grill. Serve warm.

GRILLED ONIONS

Onions as a side dish? Yes. These caramelized beauties are the perfect accompaniment to any meaty dish that is cooking low and slow.

Preparation Time: 10 minutes
Cooking Temperature: 225°F
Cooking Time: 1 hour
Serves: 4

Vegetable	Other Ingredients
▸ 4 large sweet onions (we like Vidalias)	▸ 4 Tbsp butter ▸ 1 tsp salt ▸ ½ tsp pepper

Preparation:

1. Remove the stem end of each onion and peel the skin away.
2. With a melon baller, remove 1 inch of the core of the onion being careful not to disturb the root end.
3. Place 1 Tbsp of butter, ¼ tsp salt, and ⅛ tsp pepper into each onion.

Grilling:

1. Wrap the onions in aluminum foil and place on a 225°F EGG® for 1 hour with the dome closed.
2. Unwrap the onions and serve warm.

GRILLED POLENTA

Grilled polenta makes the perfect accompaniment to our Dutch Oven Bolognese.

Preparation Time: 2 hours
Cooking Temperature: 400°F
Cooking Time: 5 minutes
Serves: 8

Fresh Ingredients	From the Pantry
▸ 3 cups water	▸ 1 ½ cups quick cooking polenta
▸ ¾ cup parmesan cheese, grated	▸ 2 tsp salt
▸ 2 Tbsp butter	▸ 1 tsp pepper
▸ 1 tsp fresh thyme, chopped	▸ Olive oil for brushing

Preparation:

1. In a large pot, bring water to a boil with the salt.
2. Slowly whisk in polenta and season with pepper.
3. Continue to whisk until polenta becomes firm.
4. Stir in parmesan and thyme.
5. Pour polenta into a buttered 10 inch springform pan and refrigerate for 1 ½ - 2 hours or until the polenta is firm.
6. Remove the polenta from the springform pan and slice into 8 pieces.

Grilling:

1. Brush both sides with olive oil and place on a 400°F EGG®.
2. Close the dome and cook for 2 minutes.
3. Turn the polenta, close the dome and continue to cook for another 2 minutes. Serve warm.

Sides & Salads

GRILLED VEGETABLE SUCCOTASH

Succotash is traditionally made from corn and lima beans with other vegetables and seasonings. Ours is kicked up a few notches with jalapeño and chopped tomato for an extra flair.

Preparation Time: 20 minutes
Cooking Temperature: 500°F
Cooking Time: 10 minutes
Serves: 6-8

Vegetables

- 3 ears corn, shucked and cleaned
- 1 (9 ounces) package baby lima beans, thawed and rinsed
- 1 large tomato, diced
- 1 zucchini, cut lengthwise into ½ inch thick slices
- 1 jalapeño
- Additional olive oil for brushing

Dressing

- ⅓ cup olive oil
- ½ tsp salt
- ½ tsp pepper
- ¼ tsp cumin
- The juice of 2 limes

Grilling:

1. Brush the corn and zucchini on all sides with olive oil.
2. Place the corn on a 500°F EGG® and lower the dome for 5 minutes.
3. Turn the corn, place the zucchini on the EGG®, and lower the dome for an additional 5 minutes.
4. Remove the corn, turn the zucchini and cook for 1 minute more.

Assembly:

1. Remove the corn from the cob and dice the cooked zucchini.
2. In a large bowl, combine dressing ingredients.
3. Add lima beans, corn, zucchini, tomato, and jalapeño to the bowl and stir to combine.
4. Serve at room temperature.

MEXICAN STREET CORN

There is nothing like corn on the cob straight off the grill. Except when it's slathered in mayonnaise, coated in cotija cheese, and spritzed with lime.

Preparation Time: 30 minutes
Cooking Temperature: 450°F
Cooking Time: 10 minutes
Serves: 6

Fresh Ingredients	**From the Pantry**
▸ 6 ears corn ▸ ½ cup cotija cheese ▸ 1 Tbsp chili powder	▸ 1 cup mayonnaise ▸ 1 lime, cut into wedges

Preparation:

1. Pull back the husk of the corn and thoroughly remove the silk from each ear of corn.
2. Soak the corn in water for 20 minutes before cooking.
3. Peel back the husks to reveal the corn.

Grilling:

1. Place the cobs on a 450°F EGG®.
2. Close the dome for 5 minutes, turn the corn, and close the dome for an additional 5 minutes.
3. Remove the corn from the EGG®. Spread with mayonnaise, sprinkle with chili powder, and coat with cotija cheese.
4. Serve with lime wedges.

MOJITO WATERMELON

Of course, you could grill the watermelon in this dish, but the smoky grilled limes are really the star of the show. Better make extra for the mojitos.

Preparation Time: 10 minutes
Cooking Temperature: 500°F
Cooking Time: 5 minutes
Serves: 8

Fresh Ingredients	From the Pantry
‣ 2 slices watermelon, 1 inch thick ‣ 1 lime, halved ‣ 2 Tbsp mint, julienned	‣ 1 tsp honey ‣ ½ tsp salt

Grilling:

1. Place the lime halves, cut side down, on a 500°F EGG® for 5 minutes.

Assembly:

1. Cut the watermelon slices into 8 pie-shaped pieces.
2. Squeeze grilled limes over watermelon.
3. Sprinkle the watermelon with salt, drizzle with honey, and top with mint.

PANZANELLA

Panzanella, a traditional Italian bread salad, is usually made from day-old bread and ripe tomatoes. Here, we add a grilled twist.

Preparation Time: 10 minutes
Cooking Temperature: 425°F
Cooking Time: 5 minutes
Serves: 6-8

Salad

- ½ cup basil leaves
- 3 Tbsp capers
- 2 large tomatoes, cut into 1 inch cubes
- 1 baguette, cut into 1 inch slices
- 1 yellow pepper, cut into 1 inch pieces
- 1 English cucumber, cut into 1 inch pieces
- ½ red onion, thinly sliced
- Olive oil
- Salt and Pepper

Dressing

- 2 Tbsp Dijon mustard
- ¼ cup Champagne vinegar
- ½ cup olive oil
- ¼ tsp salt
- ¼ tsp pepper
- 2 cloves garlic, finely minced

Grilling:

1. Brush the baguette slices with olive oil and place them on a 425°F EGG®.
2. Close the dome for 2 minutes, turn the bread, and close the dome for another 2-3 minutes or until the bread is golden brown.

Assembly:

1. Cut the toasted bread into 1 inch cubes and set aside.
2. In the bottom of a large bowl, combine dressing ingredients.
3. Add bread cubes, cucumber, tomato, bell pepper, and sliced onion and stir to combine.
4. Set aside at room temperature for 20 minutes before serving.

PARMESAN ZUCCHINI SPEARS

These crispy, salty french fry alternatives are the perfect side dish to throw on the grill once your burger has finished cooking.

Preparation Time: 10 minutes
Cooking Temperature: 500°F
Cooking Time: 10 minutes
Serves: 4

Fresh Ingredients	From the Pantry
▸ 4 zucchini, cut in half, then cut into quarters lengthwise ▸ ½ cup parmesan, grated	▸ 1 tsp Italian seasoning ▸ ½ tsp garlic powder ▸ Salt and Pepper to taste ▸ Olive oil for brushing

Preparation:

1. Brush each zucchini spear with olive oil and season with salt and pepper.
2. In a small bowl, combine Italian seasoning, garlic powder, and parmesan.
3. Place zucchini spears on a small sheet tray and sprinkle the parmesan over each spear.

Grilling:

1. Place the sheet tray on the grid of a 500°F EGG®.
2. Close the dome and cook for 10 minutes or until the parmesan is golden brown. Serve warm.

PROSCIUTTO AND PEAR BRUSCHETTA

Everyone is starving and the pork shoulder is resting. What do you do? Break out this amazing little appetizer.

Preparation Time: 10 minutes
Cooking Temperature: 325°F
Cooking Time: 5 minutes
Serves: 6-8

Fresh Ingredients	From the Pantry
▸ 4 oz prosciutto ▸ 4 oz shaved parmesan cheese ▸ 1 cup baby arugula ▸ 1 baguette, sliced ½ inch thick ▸ 1 pear, sliced thin	▸ 2 Tbsp olive oil ▸ 2 Tbsp high quality balsamic vinegar

Grilling:

1. Brush each baguette slice with olive oil and place on a 325°F EGG® with the dome closed for 5 minutes.

Assembly:

1. Remove bread slices and top each with prosciutto, pear slices, parmesan, and baby arugula.
2. Drizzle a few drops of balsamic vinegar over each bruschetta and serve.

SMOKED POTATO SALAD

This traditional potato salad is amped up with a little smoked potato. The trick is to let the potatoes with your meat and allow them to cool completely before assembling.

Preparation Time: 10 minutes
Cooking Temperature: 225°F
Cooking Time: 2 hours
Serves: 8

Salad	Dressing
▸ 4 large baking potatoes ▸ 4 large eggs, hard boiled and finely chopped ▸ 2 green onions, finely chopped ▸ 2 large dill pickles, finely chopped ▸ 1 rib celery, finely diced	▸ ½ cup mayonnaise ▸ The juice of 1 lemon ▸ ½ tsp black pepper ▸ ½ tsp celery seed ▸ ½ tsp dried dill

Preparation:
1. Scrub the potatoes.

Grilling:
1. Place the potatoes alongside meat that is smoking at 225°F.

Assembly:
1. When the potatoes are fork tender, chill in the refrigerator for 30 minutes.
2. Peel and cut potatoes into small cubes.
3. In a large bowl, combine dressing ingredients.
4. Add potatoes, eggs, green onion, pickle, and celery to the dressing and gently toss.

SWEET POTATO FRIES

Tired of the same old french fries? Give these thick-cut sweet and garlicky bad boys a try.

Preparation Time: 10 minutes
Cooking Temperature: 425°F
Cooking Time: 25 minutes
Serves: 4

Fresh Ingredients	From the Pantry
▸ 1 tsp fresh thyme, chopped ▸ 4 large sweet potatoes ▸ 4 cloves garlic, minced	▸ ¼ cup olive oil ▸ Salt and Pepper

Preparation:
1. In a large pot, cover sweet potatoes with cold water and add 2 tsp salt.
2. Bring the water to a boil and cook until the potatoes are soft, but firm, about 15 minutes.
3. In a small sauce pan, heat 2 Tbsp of the olive oil, garlic, and thyme until fragrant.
4. Cut each sweet potato in half, lengthwise, then in 3 or 4 spears.
5. Brush each spear on cut sides with olive oil, season with salt and pepper.

Grilling:
1. Place the potatoes on a 425°F EGG® and close the dome for 3 minutes.
2. Turn the potatoes and close the dome for an additional 3 minutes or until the sweet potatoes have finished cooking through.
3. Remove the fries and toss with the garlic and thyme oil before serving.

Desserts

A delicious dinner just isn't complete without a little something sweet at the end. From simple to decadent, these desserts are sure to please your grill-crazy crowd.

DESSERTS
Apple Pizza
Banana Boats
Chocolate Chip Cookie Peanut Butter Cup S'Mores
Fresh Peach Crisp
Grilled Pineapple Sundaes
Grilled Plums with Honey & Ricotta
Grilled Sopapillas
Grilled Watermelon with Honey Yogurt
Nutella & Strawberry Pizza
Orange Scented Vanilla Cake
Peaches & Pound Cake
S'Mores Pizza
Tin Foil Desserts
Triple Berry Crostata
Whole Apples With Caramel Sauce

Desserts

APPLE PIZZA

Once you discover how delicious fruit pizza is, you won't end a pizza meal without one.

Preparation Time: 5 minutes
Cooking Temperature: 500°F
Cooking Time: 5 minutes
Serves: 8

Dough	Sauce	Toppings
▸ 1 pizza dough	▸ 1 cup apple pie filling	▸ ¼ cup vanilla cake mix ▸ 2 Tbsp melted butter ▸ Vanilla Ice Cream

Preparation:
1. Stretch pizza dough into a 14" round and place on a pizza peel.
2. In a small bowl, combine cake mix and melted butter until it forms a crumbly texture.
3. Spread apple pie filling over pizza dough and top with crumb mixture.

Grilling:
1. Bake on a pizza stone in a 500°F EGG® for 5 minutes.
2. Slice and serve with vanilla frosting.

BANANA BOATS

This campfire favorite is all grown up on the grill.

Preparation Time: 10 minutes
Cooking Temperature: 400°F
Cooking Time: 10 minutes
Serves: 4

Fresh Ingredients	From the Pantry
▸ 4 green bananas	▸ Chocolate chips ▸ Miniature marshmallows ▸ Peanut butter chips ▸ Crushed cookies

Preparation:

1. Split a banana lengthwise from end to end leaving the peel intact on the opposite side.
2. Top with desired toppings.
3. Wrap the banana in heavy duty aluminum foil.

Grilling:

1. Place the bananas on a 400°F EGG® and close the dome for 10 minutes
2. Unwrap and serve topped with vanilla ice cream, whipped cream, or by themselves

CHOCOLATE CHIP COOKIE PEANUT BUTTER CUP S'MORES

As if s'mores weren't decadent enough, give these a try to satisfy your sweet tooth.

Preparation Time: 5 minutes
Cooking Temperature: 225°F
Cooking Time: 5 minutes
Serves: 4

- 8 chocolate chip cookies
- 4 peanut butter cup candies
- 4 marshmallows

Grilling:

1. On the grid of a 225°F EGG®, place one cookie, flat side up, with one peanut butter cup candy and one marshmallow on top.
2. Close the dome for 5 minutes or until the marshmallow begins to puff.

Assembly:

1. Close the s'more with the other chocolate chip cookie and get ready for the sugar rush.

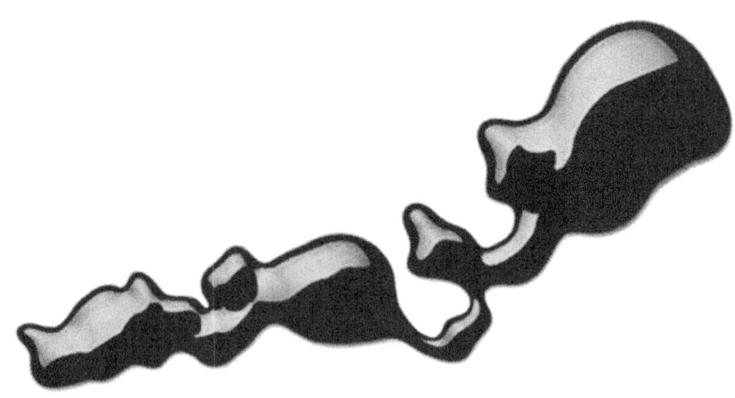

FRESH PEACH CRISP

This short cut to a peach crisp is perfect for a quick summer dessert.

Preparation Time:10 minutes
Cooking Temperature: 400°F
Cooking Time: 5 minutes
Serves: 4

Fresh Ingredients	From the Pantry
▸ 2 peaches, halved with pits removed ▸ Vanilla Ice Cream	▸ 1 cup good quality granola

Grilling:
1. Place the peach halves, cut side down, on a 400°F EGG® and cover with the dome for 5 minutes.

Assembly:
1. Remove the peaches and place them, cut side up, in a bowl. Top with vanilla ice cream and granola.

Desserts

GRILLED PINEAPPLE SUNDAES

Grilled pineapple is delicious by itself. It's even more delicious with vanilla ice cream and toasted coconut.

Preparation Time: 5 minutes
Cooking Temperature: 400°F
Cooking Time: 5 minutes
Serves: 4

Fresh Ingredients	From the Pantry
▸ 4 fresh pineapple spears ▸ Vanilla Ice Cream	▸ Jarred Caramel Sauce ▸ Toasted Coconut

Grilling:

1. Place pineapple spears on a 400°F EGG® and close the dome for 2 minutes.
2. Turn the pineapple and close the dome for another 2 minutes.
3. Turn the pineapple once more and close the dome for another minute.

Assembly:

1. Serve pineapple topped with ice cream, caramel sauce, and toasted coconut.

GRILLED PLUMS WITH HONEY AND RICOTTA

Stone fruit and the EGG® go hand in hand. Add something creamy and something sweet and you have the perfect dessert!

Preparation Time: 10 minutes
Cooking Temperature: 400°F
Cooking Time: 5 minutes
Serves: 4

Fresh Ingredients	From the Pantry
▸ 4 plums, cut in half and pitted ▸ ½ cup whole milk ricotta cheese	▸ 2 Tbsp honey ▸ ¼ tsp cracked black pepper

Grilling:

1. Place the plums, cut side down on a 400°F EGG®.
2. Close the dome for 5 minutes.

Assembly:

1. Serve the plums, cut side up, with a dollop of ricotta, a drizzle of honey, and a sprinkling of cracked black pepper.

GRILLED SOPAPILLAS

This sweet treat is so simple, but so delicious. Traditionally made by frying dough, this baked version is easy to make at the end of a pizza dinner.

Preparation Time: 5 minutes
Cooking Temperature: 500°F
Cooking Time: 18 minutes
Serves: 6

Fresh Ingredients	From the Pantry
▸ 1 pizza dough, divided into 6 pieces ▸ 3 Tbsp melted butter	▸ ¼ cup sugar ▸ 1 Tbsp cinnamon

Instructions:

1. Stretch dough into round shape.
2. Place the dough directly on the pizza stone in a 500°F EGG®.
3. Brush with melted butter and top with cinnamon sugar.
4. Close the dome for 3 minutes, then remove.
5. Repeat with remaining dough.

GRILLED WATERMELON WITH HONEY YOGURT

Grilling brings out the sweetness in the watermelon.

Preparation Time: 10 minutes
Cooking Temperature: 400°F
Cooking Time: 4 minutes
Serves: 4

Fresh Ingredients	From the Pantry
▸ 1 round of watermelon, 1 inch thick ▸ ½ cup Greek-style yogurt	▸ 1 Tbsp honey ▸ ¼ tsp vanilla

Grilling:

1. Place the watermelon on a 400°F EGG® with the dome down for 1 minute.
2. Turn the watermelon and lower the dome for an additional minute.

Assembly:

1. Cut the watermelon in quarters and place each on a small plate.
2. In a small bowl, combine yogurt, honey, and vanilla and spoon equal amounts over the watermelon. Serve.

NUTELLA AND STRAWBERRY PIZZA

Nutella is a chocolate and hazelnut spread that is particularly popular in Italy. It can easily be found in the US in major grocery stores.

Preparation Time: 10 minutes
Cooking Temperature: 500°F
Cooking Time: 5 minutes
Serves: 8

Dough	Toppings
▸ 1 pizza dough	▸ ½ lb sliced strawberries ▸ ¼ cup Nutella

Preparation:

1. Stretch the pizza dough into a 14 inch round and place it on a pizza peel.
2. Spread the dough with the Nutella and top with strawberries.

Grilling:

1. Slide the pizza onto the prepared stone in a 500°F EGG® and cook for 5 minutes.
2. Remove from the stone with a pizza peel and slice into 8 pieces.

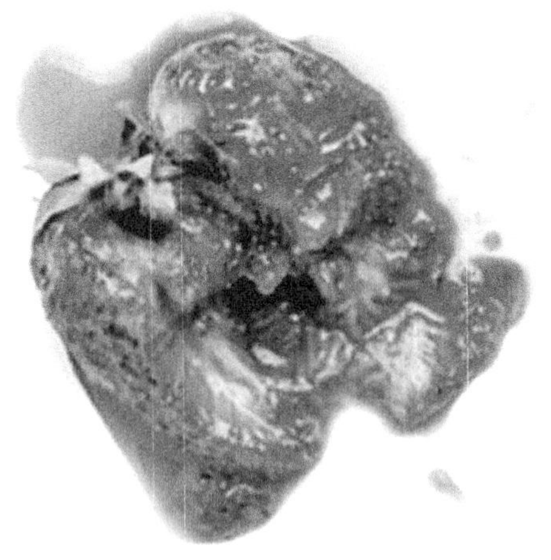

ORANGE SCENTED VANILLA CAKE

Who would have thought to use oranges as cupcake liners?

Preparation Time: 20 minutes
Cooking Temperature: 350°F
Cooking Time: 30 minutes
Serves: 12

Fresh Ingredients	From the Pantry
▸ 12 oranges ▸ ½ stick of butter	▸ 1 vanilla cake mix, prepared according to package instructions ▸ ½ lb of powdered sugar

Preparation:

1. Cut the tops off of the oranges and, using a spoon, scoop out the insides of the orange. Eat the insides of the orange while you wait for the cake to cook.
2. Pour ⅓ of a cup of batter into each orange, replace the top and wrap with heavy duty aluminum foil.
3. In a separate bowl, combine butter, powdered sugar, and 2 Tbsp orange juice.
4. When cakes are ready, drizzle some of the glaze over top of each cake and serve inside the orange.

Grilling:

1. Place the oranges on a 350°F EGG® for 30 minutes or until the cake is done.

Desserts

PEACHES AND POUND CAKE

What could be better than peaches and cream? Peaches and cream and pound cake, of course!

Preparation Time: 10 minutes
Cooking Temperature: 400°F
Cooking Time: 5 minutes
Serves: 6

Fresh Ingredients	From the Pantry
▸ ½ cup heavy whipping cream ▸ 2 Tbsp sour cream ▸ 3 peaches, halved and pitted	▸ 1 store-bought pound cake, cut into 6 slices

Grilling:

1. Place the peaches, cut side down, on a 400°F EGG®.
2. Place the pound cake slices alongside the peaches and close the dome for 2 minutes.
3. Flip the pound cake, and close the dome for an additional 2-3 minutes.

Assembly:

1. In a stand mixer, whip the whipping cream until stiff peaks form. Fold in the sour cream to combine.
2. Place a slice of pound cake on a plate, top with a peach half, and a dollop of the cream.

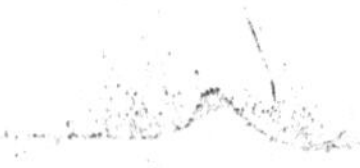

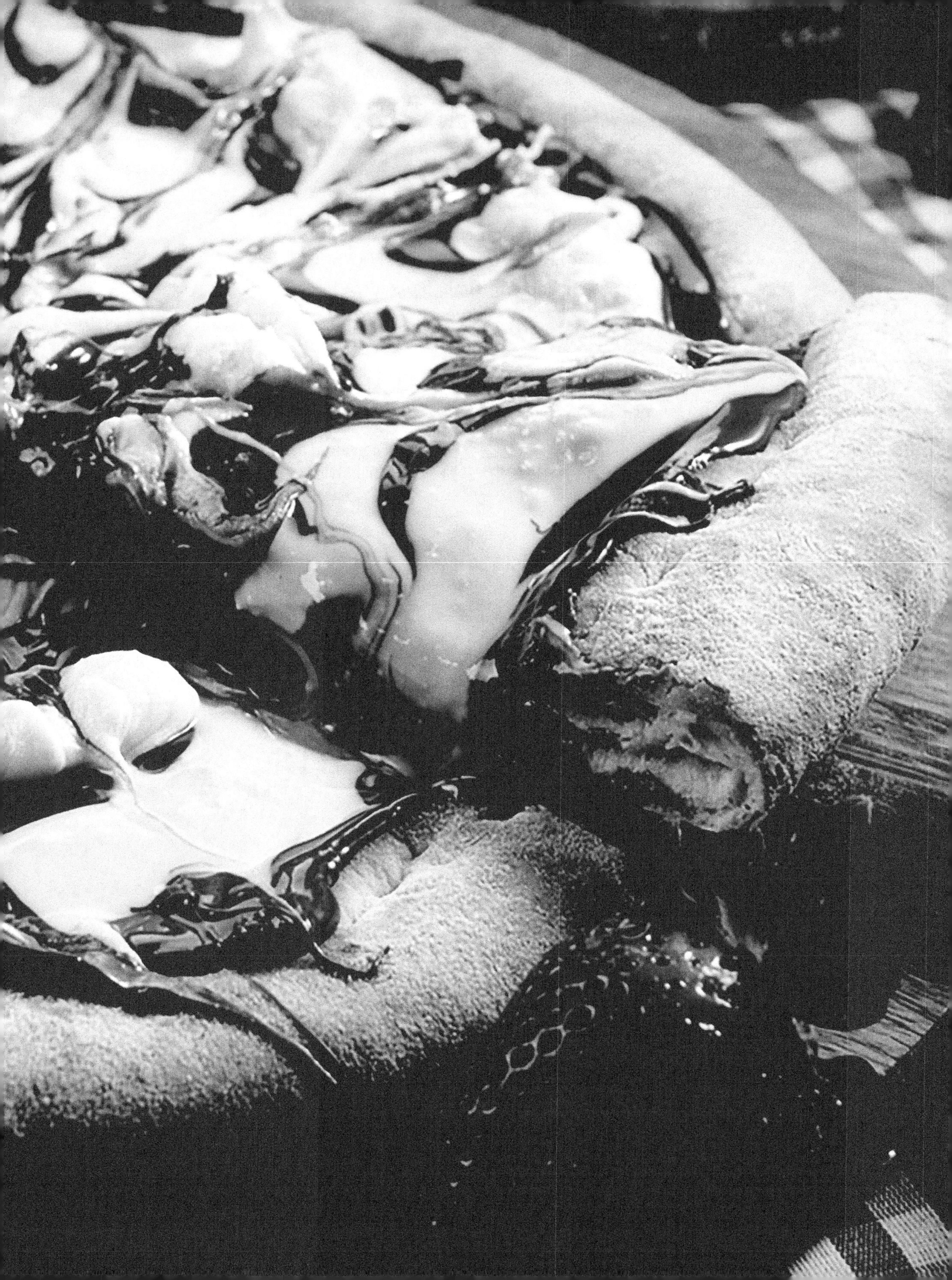

S'MORES PIZZA

Before you put the pizza stone away, give this treat a try!

Preparation Time: 10 minutes
Cooking Temperature: 500°F
Cooking Time: 5 minutes
Serves: 8

Dough	Toppings
▸ 1 pizza dough	▸ ½ cup semi-sweet chocolate chips ▸ ½ cup miniature marshmallows ▸ ¼ cup slightly crushed graham crackers

Preparation:

1. Stretch dough to a 14" round and place on a pizza peel.
2. Sprinkle dough with chocolate chips, miniature marshmallows, and graham cracker crumbs.

Grilling:

1. Slide the pizza onto the prepared stone at 500°F.
2. Cook for 5 minutes, remove from the stone, slice, and serve.

TINFOIL DESSERTS

The best part about this dessert is that there are no rules.

Preparation Time: 10 minutes
Cooking Temperature: 350°F
Cooking Time: 10 minutes
Serves: 4-6

Preparation:

1. In a square piece of foil, choose from a variety of fruit, granola, nuts, cookies, cake, and chocolate chips to form a personalized ideal dessert packet.

Grilling:

1. Fold foil around the contents and cook on a 350°F EGG® for 10 minutes.
2. Unwrap the creations and serve with vanilla ice cream or cold whipped cream.

TRIPLE BERRY CROSTATA

Think of this as a free-form pie. While you can certainly buy a pie crust, making one from scratch is easy.

Preparation Time: 30 minutes
Cooking Temperature: 350°F
Cooking Time: 40-50 minutes
Serves: 8

Crust	Filling
▸ 1 ½ cups all-purpose flour ▸ 11 Tbsp butter, cut into ½ inch cubes ▸ 3 Tbsp whole milk ▸ 2 tsp sugar ▸ 1 large egg yolk	▸ 2 cups frozen triple berry blend ▸ ¼ cup sugar ▸ 2 Tbsp cornstarch

Preparation:

1. In a food processor, combine flour and butter and pulse until pea-sized cubes of butter can be seen throughout the flour.
2. Add sugar, egg yolk, and milk and pulse until the dough comes together.
3. Form the dough into a circle, cover tightly with plastic wrap, and refrigerate 20 minutes.
4. Roll the dough into a large round and place on a pizza peel covered in cornmeal.
5. In a bowl, combine fruit, sugar, and cornstarch and pile into the center of the dough.
6. Beginning on one side, fold the dough ⅓ of the way over the fruit, repeating until a free-form tart is formed.

Grilling:

1. Preheat the EGG® to 350°F with the convEGGtor® in place for pizza and the stone on top.
2. Slide the crostata onto the pizza stone and close the dome for 40-55 minutes or until the crust is golden brown.
3. Remove the crostata from the EGG® and allow to cool slightly before slicing and serving.

Desserts

WHOLE APPLES WITH CARAMEL SAUCE

What better way to end a slow smoked meal than with slow roasted apples?

Preparation Time: 10 minutes
Cooking Temperature: 225°F
Cooking Time: 1 hour
Serves: 4

Fruit	Caramel Sauce
▸ 4 Jonathan Apples	▸ 1 cup packed dark brown sugar ▸ ½ cup half and half ▸ 4 Tbsp butter ▸ 1 tsp vanilla extract

Preparation:

1. In a medium saucepan, whisk together the brown sugar, butter, and half and half until melted.
2. Continue whisking 5-7 minutes until the caramel begins to thicken.
3. Add vanilla and set aside to cool before storing in a jar in the fridge.
4. Using a melon baller, scoop the core from the apple.
5. Wrap each apple in aluminum foil.

Grilling:

1. Place on a 225°F EGG® for 1 hour.
2. Remove apples from the EGG®, serve topped with caramel sauce.

Getting the Most From Your Big Green Egg®

The best part of the Big Green Egg® is the versatility. Its superior temperature control offers something no other charcoal grill can - versatility.

- The EGG® is ideal for finishing casseroles on a hot summer day. Not only do they come to temperature faster than your oven, you won't heat up the house!
- Want to bake but don't want to turn on the oven? With the convEGGtor® and stoneware cookie sheets, baking pans, and muffin pans, the EGG® can go from grill to convection oven with a few pieces of equipment.
- With the convEGGtor® and a Dutch Oven not only can you create delicious casseroles, stews, and braised dishes, you can also bake bread, cakes, and decadent desserts..

DUTCH OVEN BUYING GUIDE

Cast iron Dutch Ovens have been around for centuries. Originally favored for their durability and versatility, today they are used for a variety of outdoor cooking applications as well as indoor cooking. Their superior heat retention make them ideal for cooking low and slow while using minimal amounts of fuel. With a variety of sizes on the market, it is possible to cook casseroles, stews, soups, and even loaves of bread right inside your EGG®.

It may seem like a simple purchase, but buying a Dutch Oven is actually an investment.

- **Material:** A Dutch Oven should be made of cast iron in order to maintain a constant temperature. It can be enamel coated to make it non-reactive to acidic foods, but does not necessarily have to be.
- **Weight:** A Dutch Oven should be heavy with thick walls and a thick bottom. The handles should be easy to hold when the pot is filled and hot. Any knobs should be heat resistant and easy to grab.
- **Price:** Dutch Ovens vary in price from $50 for a simple cast iron pot to $300 for a high-end, enamel coated version. Does the $300 version cook better than the $50 version? Not really. Once you master Dutch Oven cooking, having a simple low-end cast iron model will serve you well as you cook in situations outside of your Big Green Egg®, like over campfires and with charcoal briquettes. If you are looking to cook more in your standard oven and stovetop with your Dutch Oven, an enamel coated model will work to your advantage.
- **Size:** Dutch Oven sizes range from 8" with a 2 quart capacity to 17" with a 30 quart capacity. Some things to consider are, the number of people you generally cook for and the size of your Big Green Egg®. If you generally cook for 4-6 people, a 6 quart Dutch Oven will offer plenty of versatility without breaking the bank or taking up valuable kitchen space. It will also comfortably fit inside the Big Green Egg® with the dome down.

- **Feet:** Several traditional cast iron Dutch ovens on the market have feet on the bottom of them. These are designed to allow airflow to the hot charcoal that normally sits under the pot, without having to set the pot directly on the coals. This feature is extremely handy if you plan on using your Dutch oven camping in a firepit situation, but completely unnecessary for The Big Green Egg®. In fact, it will likely annoy you to have it if you plan on using your Dutch oven on The Big Green Egg®. Go ahead and skip the feet.

BEGINNERS GUIDE TO USING A DUTCH OVEN

Seasoning a Dutch Oven

The process of preparing a Dutch Oven for cooking is called "seasoning". This process, where thin coats of oil are burned into the cast iron, creates a non-stick surface while preventing the oil from turning rancid after long periods of rest.

While most cast iron models come "pre-seasoned", the process bears repeating before use.

1. Lightly spray the inside, and outside of your Dutch Oven and lid with vegetable oil cooking spray.
2. Lightly rub the oil into the cast iron with a paper towel.
3. Place the Dutch Oven and lid in a 400°F oven for 20-30 minutes and allow it to cool completely.
4. Repeat the process.

Using a Dutch Oven

You can use a Dutch Oven as you would any other pot or pan. Because of the heavy nature of cast iron and the tight fitting lid, Dutch Ovens are ideal for slow braises and soups. However, if you plan on cooking acidic foods, such as tomato sauce, you will want to either use an enamel coated Dutch Oven or a Dutch Oven liner. These foil or parchment liners are ideal for cooking sticky or reactive foods and minimizing clean up.

Cleaning a Dutch Oven

Never, ever, ever use soap on a non-coated Dutch Oven. That seems counter-intuitive since soap kills bacteria. But bear in mind, heat also kills bacteria.

1. Use a non-soap steel wool pad to scrub out any food particles.
2. Rinse thoroughly with hot water.
3. Allow the Dutch Oven to air dry.
4. Spray the Dutch Oven with vegetable oil cooking spray.
5. Lightly rub the oil into the cast iron with a paper towel.
6. Place the Dutch Oven and lid in a 400°F oven for 20-30 minutes and allow it to cool completely.
7. Store the Dutch Oven in a cool, dry place.

Storing a Dutch Oven

If you are planning on not using your Dutch Oven for a time, it is essential that you place it in a cool, dry place. When cast iron becomes wet, it will eventually rust. While it is possible to get rid of the rust on a Dutch Oven, the process is gruelling and easy to prevent.

Place a dry paper towel in the bottom of the Dutch Oven and leave the lid slightly ajar. Store the Dutch Oven in a cool, dry place on a lower cabinet of the kitchen.

Now that you are an expert on this essential piece of equipment, you are ready to begin using it in the Big Green Egg®.

Dutch Oven Recipes

Many of these Dutch Oven recipes call for heating the Dutch oven on the EGG® at a high temperature then lowering the temperature to finish the dish. If you would prefer, feel free to set the EGG® for the final cooking temperature and begin the recipe by placing the Dutch oven on the stove to begin the browning or cooking process. The pot would then be transferred to the EGG® to finish cooking.

Note: These recipes are based on a 12″ Dutch oven. Please make adjustments to cooking times accordingly.

CHICKEN

Braised Chicken Thighs With Mushrooms
Chicken all'Arrabbiata
Chicken Cacciatore
Green Chile Chicken Chili
Green Curry Chicken
Rotisserie Chicken
Sweet and Sour Chicken

BRAISED CHICKEN THIGHS WITH MUSHROOMS

Chicken thighs are king when it comes to braising. This meaty, savory dish only needs crusty bread and a light salad to complete the meal.

Preparation Time: 20 minutes
Cooking Temperature: 500°F then 350°F
Cooking Time: 1 hour
Serves: 4

Fresh Ingredients

- 2 lbs chicken thighs, bone in and skin on
- 1 lb mushrooms, thinly sliced
- 1 cup finely chopped onion
- 1 Tbsp butter
- 1 Tbsp fresh thyme, chopped

From the Pantry

- ½ cup white wine
- ½ cup chicken broth
- ¼ cup flour
- 2 Tbsp olive oil
- Salt and Pepper

On the Grill:

1. Lightly dredge each chicken thigh in flour and season with salt and pepper.
2. Preheat the EGG® to 500°F.
3. Place the Dutch oven directly on the grid and allow the pot to heat for 5-7 minutes.
4. Pour olive oil into the oven and add chicken thighs, being careful not to crowd the pan.
5. Brown the chicken thighs in batches until they are golden brown on all sides. Remove from the Dutch oven and set aside.
6. To the pan, add butter and mushrooms, but do not stir for 2-3 minutes or until the mushrooms begin to brown.
7. Add onions and cook until softened.
8. Return the chicken to the pot and add wine, chicken, broth, and thyme.
9. Cover the Dutch oven, reduce the heat of The EGG® to 350°F and close the dome.
10. Allow the chicken to cook 30-40 minutes or until the internal temperature reaches 170°F. Serve warm.

CHICKEN ALL'ARRABBIATA

The phrase "all'Arrabbiata" means "in an angry way" in Italian. This spicy dish will leave you anything but angry.

Preparation Time: 20 minutes
Cooking Temperature: 500°F then 350°F
Cooking Time: 1 hour
Serves: 6

Fresh Ingredients	From the Pantry
▸ 6 leg quarters, cut into drumsticks and thighs ▸ 6 cloves garlic, diced ▸ 1 small poblano pepper, finely diced ▸ 1 large yellow pepper, diced ▸ 1 large onion, diced	▸ 1 cup dry white wine ▸ 3 Tbsp olive oil ▸ 2 Tbsp red wine vinegar ▸ 1 Tbsp tomato paste ▸ 1 ½ tsp crushed red chile flake ▸ 1 28-ounce can crushed tomatoes ▸ 1 bay leaf

On the Grill:
1. Preheat The EGG® to 500°F with the Dutch oven on the grid.
2. Season chicken on all sides with salt and pepper.
3. Place oil and chicken pieces in the Dutch oven. Brown on all sides.
4. Remove chicken and pour off all but 2 Tbsp of the remaining oil.
5. Add onion, garlic, crushed red chile flake and cook until softened.
6. Add the bell pepper and poblano pepper and cook until softened.
7. Stir in tomato paste and cook for 1-2 minutes or until the tomato paste begins to darken.
8. Add wine and cook for 2 minutes, scraping the bottom of the Dutch oven.
9. Add tomatoes, vinegar, and chicken back into the pot.
10. Cover, reduce the heat to 400°F, and close the dome for 35 minutes.
11. Remove the bay leaf and serve.

CHICKEN CACCIATORE

Chicken Cacciatore is the less angry cousin of all'Arrabbiata.

Preparation Time: 10 minutes
Cooking Temperature: 500°F then 350°F
Cooking Time: 40 minutes
Serves: 4-6

Fresh Ingredients

- 4 lbs chicken thighs, bone in and skin on
- ¼ cup freshly chopped basil
- 3 cloves garlic, minced
- 1 bell pepper, sliced
- 1 onion, sliced

From the Pantry

- ¾ cup dry white wine
- ¾ cup chicken stock
- ½ cup flour
- 3 Tbsp olive oil
- 3 Tbsp capers
- 1 ½ tsp dried oregano
- 1 (28 ounce) can diced tomatoes with juice
- Salt and Pepper

On the Grill:

1. Preheat the EGG® to 500°F with the Dutch oven on the grid.
2. Season each chicken piece with salt and pepper and lightly dredge in flour.
3. Place olive oil in the Dutch oven and brown chicken pieces on all sides. Work in batches and set chicken aside.
4. Drain all but 2 Tbsp of the fat in the Dutch oven and add onion, garlic, and bell pepper and cook until soft.
5. Add chicken back into the pot and add wine and chicken stock, scraping the bottom of the Dutch oven.
6. Add tomatoes, oregano and capers, stir and cover.
7. Reduce the heat in the EGG® to 400°F and lower the dome for 35 minutes.
8. Garnish with fresh basil and serve.

GREEN CHILE CHICKEN CHILI

Not only is the dish fun to say, it feeds a crowd on the cheap.

Preparation Time: 10 minutes
Cooking Temperature: 500°F then 350°F
Cooking Time: 45 minutes - 1 hour
Serves: 8

Fresh Ingredients

- 2 lbs ground chicken
- 1 cup chopped onion
- 1 Tbsp garlic, minced

From the Pantry

- 1 quart chicken stock
- 2 Tbsp olive oil
- 1 Tbsp ground cumin
- 1 Tbsp dried oregano
- 4 cans (14.5 ounce) Great Northern Beans, drained and rinsed
- 2 cans (4 ounce) chopped green chiles
- Salt & Pepper

On the Grill:

1. Preheat The EGG® to 500°F with the Dutch oven on the grid.
2. Add oil, onion, and garlic to the pot and cook until soft.
3. Add ground chicken, salt and pepper to taste, and cook until brown.
4. Add cumin and oregano and cook for 1 minute.
5. Add chicken stock and green chiles.
6. Reduce the heat in the EGG® to 350°F
7. Cover the Dutch oven and lower the dome for 40-50 minutes. Serve hot with shredded cheese and lime wedges.

GREEN CURRY CHICKEN

This sweet and spicy dish puts a new spin on the old "chicken and rice". Serve over jasmine rice with lime wedges.

Preparation Time: 20 minutes
Cooking Temperature: 500°F then 350°F
Cooking Time: 40 minutes
Serves: 4

Fresh Ingredients

- 2 lbs boneless skinless chicken breast, cut into 1 inch cubes
- 1 Tbsp garlic, minced
- 1 Tbsp ginger, grated
- 2 green onions, chopped

From the Pantry

- 2 cups unsweetened coconut milk
- 2 Tbsp canola oil
- 2 Tbsp soy sauce
- 2 Tbsp cornstarch
- 2 Tbsp Thai green curry paste
- 2 Tbsp brown sugar
- 1 Tbsp fish sauce

On the Grill:

1. Preheat the EGG® to 500°F with the Dutch oven on the grid.
2. Dredge chicken breast pieces in soy sauce, then corn starch.
3. Place oil and chicken in the heated Dutch oven and brown. Work in batches, being careful not to overcrowd the pan.
4. Add garlic, ginger, and green onion and stir until fragrant.
5. Add Thai green curry paste, fish sauce, coconut milk, and sugar and stir to combine.
6. Lower the temperature in the EGG® to 350°F.
7. Cover the Dutch oven and the dome and simmer for 25-30 minutes.
8. Serve over jasmine rice with lime wedges and whole cilantro leaves.

ROTISSERIE CHICKEN

While a bit of a misnomer, the Dutch oven becomes a miniature roaster in this easy, one-pot dinner.

Preparation Time: 2-8 hours
Cooking Temperature: 425°F
Cooking Time: 1-1 ½ hours
Serves: 6

Meat	Brine	Vegetables
▸ 1 (4-5 lb) whole chicken, gizzards and giblets removed	▸ 2 quarts warm water ▸ ¼ cup kosher salt ▸ ¼ cup brown sugar ▸ 2 Tbsp whole peppercorns ▸ 1 lemon, halved	▸ 2 lbs small waxy potatoes, cut in half (we like Yukon golds) ▸ 1 lbs carrots, cut into 2 inch chunks ▸ ¼ cup butter, softened ▸ 1 onion, cut into wedges ▸ 2 sprigs fresh thyme ▸ 4 whole cloves garlic

Preparation:

1. Combine brine ingredients until the salt and sugar dissolve and add enough ice to bring the brine to room temperature.
2. Submerge the chicken into the brine and allow to chill in the refrigerator for a minimum of 2 hours and up to overnight.
3. Remove the chicken from the brine and pat dry.
4. In the bottom of a cold Dutch oven, place the vegetables and top with the chicken, breast side up.
5. Gently lift the skin away from the meat and rub butter beneath the skin.

Grilling:

1. Preheat the EGG® to 425°F.
2. Cover the Dutch oven and place on the EGG®. Lower the dome for 1-1 ½ hours or until the internal temperature of the meatiest part of the thigh registers 160°F
3. Remove the Dutch oven from the EGG® and allow it to sit for an additional 10 minutes before removing the lid.
4. Remove the chicken, place the vegetables on a platter or in a bowl. Carve the chicken and serve.

SWEET AND SOUR CHICKEN

This recipe can be made with boneless, skinless chicken breasts if you prefer.

Preparation Time: 10 minutes
Cooking Temperature: 375°F
Cooking Time: 45 minutes
Serves: 6

Fresh Ingredients	From the Pantry
▸ 3 lbs boneless, skinless chicken thighs	▸ 1 cup apricot preserves ▸ 1 cup Russian salad dressing ▸ ¼ cup pineapple juice ▸ 1 envelope onion soup mix

Preparation:

1. Place a Dutch oven liner in the bottom of a cold Dutch oven.
2. Arrange the chicken pieces over the bottom of the pot.
3. In a separate bowl, combine preserves, dressing, juice, and soup mix.
4. Pour the sauce over the chicken thighs and cover with the lid.

Grilling:

1. Preheat the EGG® to 375°F.
2. Place the Dutch oven on the EGG® grid and close the dome for 45 minutes.
3. Remove the Dutch oven carefully from the EGG® and serve over cooked rice.

BEEF

Beef Bourguignonne
Bolognese
Chili
Pot Roast
Short Ribs & Polenta
Sloppy Joes
Taco Soup

BEEF BOURGUIGNONNE

Tough cuts of beef turn tender as they are slow simmered in red wine sauce. The only difference between this version and the original? It's cooked outdoors!

Preparation Time: 30 minutes
Cooking Temperature: 450°F then 250°F
Cooking Time: 1 hour, 15 minutes
Serves: 6

Fresh Ingredients	From the Pantry
▸ 2 ½ lbs beef chuck roast, cut into 1 inch cubes	▸ 2 cups beef broth
▸ 1 lb carrots, cut into 1 inch chunks	▸ ½ cup sherry
▸ 1 lb fresh mushrooms, thickly sliced	▸ ¼ cup flour
▸ 8 oz bacon, diced	▸ 2 Tbsp olive oil
▸ 1 tsp fresh thyme	▸ 1 Tbsp tomato paste
▸ 2 cloves garlic, minced	▸ 1 bottle dry red wine
▸ 1 onion, sliced	▸ Salt & Pepper

On the Grill:

1. Preheat the EGG® to 450°F.
2. Place bacon in a cold Dutch oven and place on the grid with the dome closed for 10 minutes or until the bacon is crisp.
3. Drain the bacon on paper towels.
4. Pat the pieces of chuck roast with paper towels to dry and season with salt and pepper.
5. In the hot bacon fat, begin browning the chuck roast in batches, setting each browned back aside.
6. Drain all fat but 2 Tbsp from the Dutch oven, but reserve it.
7. Add mushrooms and do not move for 5 minutes until they begin to brown. Remove and set aside.
8. Add 2 Tbsp olive oil to the Dutch oven along with 2 Tbsp of the reserved fat, the carrots, and the sliced onions. Cook until they begin to soften, about 5 minutes.
9. Add tomato paste and cook 1 minute more.
10. Add flour to the pot and cook for 2 minutes.
11. Add back the beef, bacon, and mushrooms and pour in red wine and beef broth.
12. Add thyme and season with salt and pepper.
13. Cover the Dutch oven, reduce the heat in the EGG® to 250°F, and lower the dome for 1 hour.
14. Serve the Beef Bourguignon with crusty bread.

Dutch Oven Recipes | Beef

BOLOGNESE

A riff on traditional bolognese, this meat sauce is ideal for short-cut pasta like rigatoni.

Preparation Time: 20 minutes
Cooking Temperature: 300°F
Cooking Time: 1 ½ hours
Serves: 6

Fresh Ingredients	From the Pantry
▸ 2 lbs ground beef	▸ 2 cups chicken broth
▸ 4 oz bacon, diced	▸ 1 cup red wine
▸ 1 cup milk	▸ ¼ cup tomato paste
▸ 2 cloves garlic	▸ 1 tsp Italian seasoning
▸ 1 stalk celery	
▸ 1 carrot	
▸ 1 small onion	

Preparation:

1. In the bowl of a food processor, combine celery, carrot, onion, and garlic and pulse until finely chopped.

Grilling:

1. Preheat the EGG® to 300°F.
2. Place the bacon in a cold Dutch oven and begin heating on the stove over medium heat.
3. Cook the bacon until it is crisp and the fat is rendered.
4. Remove all but 2 Tbsp of the fat.
5. Add ground beef and cook until brown.
6. Add chopped vegetables and cook for 5 minutes.
7. Add tomato paste and cook for an additional 2 minutes.
8. Add milk and stir. Allow the liquid to evaporate until the milk solids are left behind.
9. Add wine, chicken broth, and Italian seasoning.
10. Cover the Dutch oven and transfer it to the EGG®. Allow the sauce to cook for 1 hour before serving over pasta.

CHILI

Chili is like barbecue sauce. Everyone has their favorite recipe, and no one wants to share it. Ours uses masa harina as a thickening agent. This versatile corn flour is ideal for making tortillas and tamales and can be found in the Latin foods aisle of every grocery store in the country.

Preparation Time: 20 minutes
Cooking Temperature: 500°F then 300°F
Cooking Time: 2 hours
Serves: 6

Fresh Ingredients

- 4 lbs of beef chuck roast, trimmed of fat and cut into 1 ½ inch cubes
- 4 oz bacon, cut into ¼ inch pieces
- 4 cloves garlic, minced
- 2 jalapeños, cored, seeded, and diced
- 1 large onion, diced

From the Pantry

- 4 cups low sodium beef broth
- 2 cups water
- 2 cups dark beer
- 1 cup crushed tomatoes
- ¼ cup ancho chili powder
- ¼ cup masa harina
- 2 Tbsp ground cumin
- 1 Tbsp chipotle chili powder
- 1 Tbsp brown sugar
- 2 tsp salt
- 2 tsp dried oregano
- 2 tsp unsweetened cocoa powder
- 1 tsp ground coriander
- ¼ tsp cinnamon
- Salt and Pepper

On the Grill:

1. Preheat the EGG® to 500°F.
2. Place the bacon in the bottom of a cold Dutch oven and place the pot in the EGG® with the dome closed for 10 minutes, or until the bacon is crispy.
3. Remove the bacon from the pot and set aside.
4. Season the beef chunks with salt and pepper and begin browning them in the bacon fat. Work in batches taking care not to crowd the pan. Set aside.
5. Add the spices to the remaining fat and stir for 1 minute until fragrant.
6. Add onion, jalapeño, and garlic to the pan and cook until soft, 5 minutes.
7. Add back bacon and beef and pour in beer, water, and beef broth.
8. Reduce the heat in the EGG® to 300°F.
9. Cover the Dutch oven and lower the dome for 1 hour.
10. Remove the lid of the Dutch oven and stir in the masa harina until the chili begins to thicken.
11. Serve with cheese, sour cream, lime wedges, and fresh cilantro.

POT ROAST

This comfort classic can't be beat on a cool evening.

Preparation Time: 20 minutes
Cooking Temperature: 300°F
Cooking Time: 3-4 hours
Serves: 6

Fresh Ingredients	From the Pantry
▸ 1 4-pound chuck roast, trimmed of excess fat	▸ 2 cups beef broth
▸ 1 lb carrots, cut into 2 inch chunks	▸ ¼ cup flour
▸ 1 lb crimini mushrooms, cleaned	▸ 2 Tbsp olive oil
▸ 1 onion, cut into wedges	▸ 1 Tbsp flour
▸ 1 Tbsp butter	▸ Salt and Pepper
▸ 2 sprigs fresh thyme	
▸ 1 sprig fresh rosemary	

Preparation:

1. On top of a stove, heat a Dutch oven.
2. Season both sides of the roast with salt and pepper and lightly dredge it with flour.
3. Add oil to the Dutch oven and brown the roast on all sides.
4. Add carrots, mushrooms, onion wedges, and enough beef broth to come ⅔ of the way up the sides of the roast.
5. Nestle thyme and rosemary into the broth.

Grilling:

1. Preheat the EGG® to 300°F
2. Cover the Dutch oven and transfer to the EGG®.
3. Lower the dome for 3-4 hours or until the roast is tender.
4. Remove the roast and vegetables and set aside.
5. In a small bowl, combine 1 Tbsp flour and 1 Tbsp melted butter.
6. Place the Dutch oven back on the stove over medium heat.
7. Stir in the butter and flour mixture, whisking until the sauce thickens slightly.
8. Serve meat and vegetables with the gravy on the side.

SHORT RIBS & POLENTA

Short ribs are an affordable cut, and when slow cooked yield a finger-licking delicious result.

Preparation Time: 20 minutes
Cooking Temperature: 325°F
Cooking Time: 3 hours, 20 minutes
Serves: 4

For the Short Ribs

- 8 beef short ribs
- 6 slices bacon, diced
- 3 carrots, diced
- 2 cloves garlic, minced
- 1 onion, diced
- 4 cups beef broth
- ½ cup red wine
- ¼ cup flour
- 1 Tbsp tomato paste
- ½ tsp ground fennel
- 2 sprigs fresh thyme
- 2 sprigs fresh rosemary
- Salt and Pepper

For the Polenta

- 4 cups water
- 4 cups milk
- 2 cups polenta
- ½ cup sour cream
- ½ cup parmesan cheese, grated
- 3 Tbsp butter
- 2 tsp salt

Preparation:

1. Season the short ribs with salt and pepper and lightly dredge in the flour.
2. Place the bacon in a cold Dutch oven over medium heat on the stove top.
3. Remove the bacon when it becomes crispy and set aside.
4. Working in batches, brown the short ribs on all sides. Set aside.
5. Remove all but 2 Tbsp of the fat.
6. Add carrots, onion, and garlic and cook until soft.
7. Add tomato paste and cook for 2 minutes.
8. Add red wine and scrape the bottom of the Dutch oven for 1 minute.
9. Add back bacon and beef, stir in fennel, thyme, and rosemary.
10. When there is 40 minutes left, bring the water, butter, and milk for the polenta to a simmer in a large sauce pan.
11. Add the salt and polenta to the water mixture and whisk constantly for 3-4 minutes.
12. Simmer partially covered for 45 minutes, stirring every 10 minutes.
13. Add sour cream and parmesan to the polenta and stir. Keep the polenta covered until you are ready to serve.

Grilling:

1. Preheat the EGG® to 325°F.
2. Cover the Dutch oven and transfer to the EGG®.
3. Close the dome for 2 ½ hours.
4. When the ribs have been in the EGG® for 2 ½ hours, close all the vents and allow the Dutch oven to sit inside the EGG® for another 20 minutes.
5. Remove the Dutch oven from the EGG®, remove stems from the herbs, and skim any fat that has come to the surface.
6. Serve two short ribs on a bed of creamy polenta.

SLOPPY JOES

These aren't your Mama's sloppy joes! Then again, maybe they are.

Preparation Time: 10 minutes
Cooking Temperature: 400°F
Cooking Time: 30-40 minutes
Serves: 4

Fresh Ingredients

- 1 lb ground beef
- ¼ cup onion, finely chopped
- ¼ cup bell pepper, finely chopped
- 1 clove garlic, finely chopped

From the Pantry

- ½ cup tomato sauce
- ¼ cup ketchup
- 2 Tbsp brown sugar
- 1 Tbsp brown mustard
- Salt & Pepper

On the Grill:

1. Preheat the EGG® to 400°F with the Dutch oven on the grid.
2. Place all ingredients in the Dutch oven and stir.
3. Cover the Dutch oven and lower the dome for 30-40 minutes or until the beef is cooked through.
4. Serve on hamburger buns.

TACO SOUP

This satisfying soup is easy to throw together on a weeknight when you have a million things going on. It only gets better the longer it sits.

Preparation Time: 10 minutes
Cooking Temperature: 350°F
Cooking Time: 1 hour
Serves: 8

Fresh Ingredients

- 1 lb ground beef

From the Pantry

- 4 cups chicken broth
- ½ cup chopped onion
- 1 Tbsp garlic, minced
- 1 Tbsp chili powder
- 1 Tbsp smoked paprika
- 1 tsp ground cumin
- 2 cans pinto beans, rinsed and drained
- 1 can black beans, rinsed and drained
- 1 can corn, drained
- Salt & Pepper

Preparation:

1. Place ingredients in a cold Dutch oven and stir.

Grilling:

1. Preheat the EGG® to 350°F.
2. Place the Dutch oven on the grid of the EGG® and lower the dome for 1 hour.
3. Soup is done when the ground beef is cooked through.
4. Serve with shredded cheese, cut up avocado, shredded cabbage and tortilla chips.

PORK & SEAFOOD

Barbecue Spare Ribs
Cioppino
Clam Bake
Dutch Oven Pork Roast
Shrimp Boil
Smothered Pork Chops
Steamed Mussels

BARBECUE SPARE RIBS

This delicious alternative to smoking is perfect for a "forget about it" dinner.

Preparation Time: 20 minutes
Cooking Temperature: 350°F
Cooking Time: 2 hours
Serves: 6-8

Meat	From This Book	Other Ingredients
▸ 4 lbs boneless country style ribs	▸ ¼ cup Basic Barbecue Rub	▸ 2 cups your favorite barbecue sauce (We like our Kansas City Barbecue Sauce) ▸ 2 Tbsp olive oil

Preparation:
1. Liberally season the country style ribs with the rub. Set aside.

Grilling:
1. Heat the EGG® to 350°F.
2. Heat the Dutch oven on the stove with 2 Tbsp of olive oil.
3. Brown each seasoned rib on all sides. Set aside.
4. Add ribs back into the pot along with barbecue sauce.
5. Cover the Dutch oven and place on the EGG®.
6. Lower the dome for 2 hours.
7. Remove the Dutch oven from the EGG® and serve.

CIOPPINO (CHIP-EE-NO)

While its name certainly sounds Italian, this dish actually has its roots on the Central Coast of California. Invented by local fishermen, each would "chip in" part of their catch for a communal stew with a garlic and tomato broth. Today, this dish is still popular from the Bay Area to Big Sur and varies with the catch of the day.

Preparation: 20 minutes
Cooking Temperature: 350°F
Cooking Time: 50 minutes
Serves: 6-8

Fresh Ingredients	From the Pantry
▸ 1 ½ lbs halibut, or other firm fish, cut into 2 inch chunks	▸ 5 cups chicken or fish stock
▸ 1 lb clams, scrubbed	▸ 1 ½ cups dry white wine
▸ 1 lb mussels, scrubbed and debearded	▸ ¼ cup tomato paste
▸ 1 lb shrimp, peeled and deveined	▸ 3 Tbsp olive oil
▸ 4 cloves garlic, minced	▸ 1 tsp crushed red chile flakes
▸ 1 large fennel bulb, thinly sliced	▸ 1 (28 ounce) can diced tomatoes
▸ 1 onion, thinly sliced	

On the Grill:

1. Preheat the EGG® to 350°F with the Dutch oven on the grid.
2. Heat the oil in the Dutch oven and add fennel, onion, and garlic and cook until translucent.
3. Stir in tomato paste and chili flake and cook for 1 minute.
4. Add diced tomatoes with their juice, wine, and stock and cover with the lid.
5. Lower the dome for 30 minutes.
6. Remove the lid of the Dutch oven and add the clams and mussels.
7. Replace the lid and lower the dome for 5 minutes.
8. Remove the lid of the Dutch oven and add the shrimp and fish and gently stir.
9. Replace the lid and lower the dome for 5 minutes.
10. When the fish is cooked through, the shrimp are pink, and the mussels and clams are open, the stew is done.
11. Serve immediately with crusty sourdough bread.

CLAM BAKE

Clam bakes were so popular in the 60's, there is a whole Elvis movie about them. This easy one-pot dish is perfect for sharing with friends.

Preparation Time: 20 minutes
Cooking Temperature: 350°F
Cooking Time: 30 minutes
Serves: 6-8

Fresh Ingredients	From the Pantry
▸ 2 lbs mussels, scrubbed and debearded ▸ 1 ½ lbs kielbasa sausage, sliced into 1 inch chunks ▸ 1 ½ lbs small potatoes (we like red potatoes) ▸ 2 large onions, roughly chopped ▸ 2 dozen littleneck clams, scrubbed ▸ 2 dozen steamer clams, scrubbed	▸ 2 cups dry white wine ▸ 2 Tbsp olive oil ▸ 1 Tbsp salt ▸ ½ Tbsp black pepper

On the Grill:

1. Preheat the EGG® to 350°F with the Dutch oven on the grid.
2. Add olive oil and onion to the pot and cook until soft, about 5 minutes.
3. Add ingredients in layers in the following order:
    a. Kielbasa
    b. Potatoes
    c. Clams
    d. Mussels
4. Pour in the white wine and cover.
5. Lower the dome for 15-20 minutes or until the potatoes are cooked through and the shellfish have opened up.
6. Ladle out the sausage, potatoes, and seafood and strain the broth, taking care not to get any sand from the clams.
7. Serve on sheets of parchment paper with broth in small bowls for dipping and sipping.

If you have never tried parsnips before, they look like a white carrot and taste like a cross between a carrot and horseradish. When they are braised they become sweet, a perfect alternative to plain carrots.

DUTCH OVEN PORK ROAST

One pot meals are never a bad thing.

Preparation Time: 20 minutes
Cooking Temperature: 425°F
Cooking Time: 1 hour 15 minutes
Serves: 6

Fresh Ingredients	From the Pantry
▸ 1 3-4 lb boneless pork loin roast ▸ 2 lbs small potatoes (we like reds or Yukon golds) ▸ 1 lb parsnips, peeled and cut into 1 inch chunks ▸ 1 Tbsp fresh thyme ▸ Salt and Pepper	▸ ¼ cup brown mustard ▸ 2 Tbsp Worcestershire sauce ▸ 2 Tbsp olive oil

Preparation:

1. In a cold Dutch oven, toss vegetables with olive oil and a sprinkling of salt and pepper.
2. In a small bowl, combine mustard, Worcestershire, and thyme. Paint all over the loin roast.
3. Place the roast on top of the vegetables.

Grilling:

1. Preheat the EGG® to 425°F.
2. Cover the Dutch oven and place on the waiting EGG®.
3. Lower the dome for 1 hour to 1 hour and 15 minutes or until the internal temperature of the roast reaches 155°F
4. Remove the Dutch oven from the EGG®, remove the pork and set aside to rest for 20 minutes before carving. Recover the Dutch oven to keep the vegetables warm in the meantime.
5. Serve warm.

SHRIMP BOIL

Down south, crawfish boils are the way people celebrate cool spring days. Because crawfish are more difficult to find outside of the Deep South, shrimp can easily take their place.

Preparation Time: 15 minutes
Cooking Temperature: 450°F
Cooking Time: 35-40 minutes
Serves: 4

Fresh Ingredients	**From the Pantry**
▸ 1 ½ lbs "easy peel" shrimp (this means the shrimp have been deveined, but the shells are still on) ▸ 1 lb baby red potatoes ▸ 2 Tbsp butter ▸ 8 cloves garlic ▸ 6 sprigs fresh thyme ▸ 4 ears of corn, husked and snapped in half ▸ 2 lemons, halved	▸ ½ cup Old Bay seasoning ▸ Hot sauce and lemon wedges for garnish

On the Grill:

1. Preheat the EGG® to 450°F with the Dutch oven on the grid.
2. Fill the Dutch oven with 4 quarts of water, lemons, thyme, garlic, and Old Bay seasoning and bring to a rolling boil with the lid on and the dome closed, about 20 minutes.
3. Lift the dome, remove the lid, and add potatoes.
4. Replace the lid and dome and cook for 10 minutes or until the potatoes are tender.
5. Add shrimp and corn and replace the lid and dome for an additional 5-7 minutes or until the shrimp are pink.
6. Transfer the shrimp and vegetables to a large bowl with a slotted spoon and toss with butter.
7. Serve with lemon wedges and hot sauce.

SMOTHERED PORK CHOPS

There is nothing like a thick pork chop smothered in gravy. In this case, bone-in loin chops keep the meat moist while it slowly braises.

Preparation Time: 15 minutes
Cooking Temperature: 400°F
Cooking Time: 30-40 minutes
Serves: 4

Fresh Ingredients	From the Pantry
▸ 4 bone-in pork chops, cut 1 inch thick ▸ ¾ cup buttermilk ▸ 1 medium onion, sliced	▸ 2 cups chicken broth ▸ ½ cup flour ▸ ¼ cup canola or peanut oil ▸ 1 Tbsp hot sauce ▸ 1 Tbsp garlic powder ▸ 1 Tbsp onion powder ▸ 1 Tbsp paprika ▸ 1 tsp salt ▸ 1 tsp black pepper

Preparation:

1. Season the flour with garlic powder, onion powder, paprika, salt and pepper.
2. Pat the pork chops dry and dredge in the seasoned flour on all sides, shaking off the excess.

Grilling:

1. Preheat the EGG® to 400°F with the Dutch oven on the grid.
2. Heat the oil in the Dutch oven until shimmering.
3. Add pork chops and cook until brown on both sides, about 5-7 minutes on each side.
4. Remove the pork chops and add 2 Tbsp of the seasoned flour to the oil in the bottom of the Dutch oven. Stir until the roux becomes the consistency of wet sand.
5. Add chicken broth and stir until thickened.
6. Add buttermilk and stir.
7. Return the pork chops to the sauce, cover, and lower the dome for 15-20 minutes.
8. Serve warm over mashed potatoes.

STEAMED MUSSELS

There is nothing like a bowl of steamed mussels and a crusty baguette to make the heart happy.

Preparation Time: 40 minutes
Cooking Temperature: 400°F
Cooking Time: 20 minutes
Serves: 4

Fresh Ingredients	From the Pantry
▸ 4 pounds mussels	▸ ½ cup dry white wine
▸ ½ cup fresh, diced tomato	▸ 2 Tbsp olive oil
▸ ¼ cup parsley, chopped	
▸ 2 Tbsp butter	
▸ 4 sprigs fresh thyme	
▸ 2 cloves garlic, sliced	
▸ 1 shallot, sliced	
▸ 1 lemon, juiced	

Preparation:

1. Clean the mussels by brushing with a vegetable brush and removing the beards. If any of the mussels are open, gently tap them on the counter. If they do not close, discard them.

Grilling:

1. Preheat the EGG® to 400°F with the Dutch oven on the grid.
2. Heat olive oil in the pot and saute the garlic, thyme, and shallot until soft.
3. Add mussels and toss.
4. Add wine and lemon juice and cover the Dutch oven and the dome for 15 minutes.
5. Remove the dome, uncover the Dutch oven, and add tomato and parsley.
6. Recover the Dutch oven and replace the dome for 2 more minutes.
7. Serve with crusty bread.

CASSEROLES

Breakfast Casserole
Arroz con Pollo
Chicken Enchilada Bake
Ham, Potato, and Broccoli Casserole
Lasagna
Paella
Ratatouille

BREAKFAST CASSEROLE

This hearty breakfast is perfect for feeding a crowd.

Preparation Time: 10 minutes
Cooking Temperature: 350°F
Cooking Time: 35-40 minutes
Serves: 6-8

Fresh Ingredients	From the Pantry
▸ 1 lb bulk pork breakfast sausage ▸ 1 (16 oz) bag of frozen O'Brien style hash browns ▸ 1 dozen eggs, beaten ▸ ¼ cup grated onion	▸ ¼ tsp black pepper ▸ Hot sauce for garnish

On the Grill:

1. Preheat the EGG® to 350°F with the Dutch oven on the grid.
2. Brown sausage with onion in the Dutch oven.
3. Add hash browns and stir to combine.
4. Add eggs and cover.
5. Lower the dome for 15 minutes or until the eggs are just cooked through.
6. Serve the casserole with hot sauce for garnish.

ARROZ CON POLLO

Literally translated, this dish is "chicken and rice". But it is so much more than that. Saffron threads give the rice a yellow color while it absorbs all of the flavors from the chicken. If you can't find saffron, annatto seeds, widely available in Latin markets, will do the trick.

Preparation Time: 20 minutes
Cooking Temperature: 400°F
Cooking Time: 1 hour
Serves: 6-8

For The Chicken

- 1 large chicken, cut into 8 pieces
- 2 Tbsp olive oil
- 2 Tbsp lime juice
- 1 tsp salt
- 1 tsp dried oregano
- 1 tsp ground cumin
- 1/2 tsp freshly ground white pepper

For The Rice

- 1 lb Arborio rice
- 3 cups water
- 1 ½ cup chicken stock
- 1 cup dry white wine
- ¼ cup frozen peas, thawed, for garnish
- 2 Tbsp olive oil
- 1 Tbsp tomato paste
- ½ tsp annatto seeds, or ¼ tsp saffron threads
- 3 cloves garlic, minced
- 1 small onion, finely chopped
- 1 small red bell pepper, cored, seeded and finely chopped
- 1 small tomato, seeded and diced
- Salt and freshly ground black pepper, to taste

Preparation:

1. Wash the chicken and pat dry with paper towels.
2. Mix the oregano, cumin, white pepper, salt and lime juice in a casserole dish. Add the chicken, turning the pieces to cover with the mixture. Let marinate at least 15 minutes.

Grilling:

1. Preheat the EGG® to 400°F with the Dutch oven on the grid.
2. Add olive oil and brown the pieces of chicken on all sides.
3. Remove the chicken and drain all but 2 Tbsp of the fat.
4. Add the onion, bell pepper and garlic to the oil, cook until soft.
5. Add the tomato paste and cook for 1 minute more.
6. Return the chicken to the pan.
7. Add the water, wine, chicken stock, saffron, and season with salt and pepper.

NOTE: If you are using annatto seeds, combine the seed with ¼ cup of the chicken stock in a small saucepan and simmer for 5 minutes. Strain the seeds out and discard. Add the broth to the rice.

8. Cover with the lid and lower the dome for 30 minutes.
9. Thoroughly wash the rice until the water runs clear.
10. Add rice to the chicken mixture, cover, and lower the dome for 20 more minutes or until the rice is cooked.
11. Garnish with green peas and serve.

CHICKEN ENCHILADA BAKE

This easy version of chicken enchiladas is a great way to turn leftover chicken into a whole new meal.

Preparation Time: 10 minutes
Cooking Temperature: 375°F
Cooking Time: 35-40 minutes
Serves: 6-8

Fresh Ingredients	From the Pantry
‣ 2 cups cooked chicken, shredded ‣ 2 cups frozen corn, thawed ‣ 2 cups shredded cheddar cheese	‣ 10 flour tortillas, cut in half ‣ 1 can (15 ounce) black beans, drained and rinsed ‣ 1 can (28 ounce) mild enchilada sauce ‣ 1 tsp chili powder ‣ 1 tsp cumin ‣ 1 tsp garlic powder ‣ 1 tsp smoked paprika

Preparation:

1. Season the chicken with the chili powder, cumin, garlic powder, and smoked paprika.
2. Line the Dutch oven with a liner.
3. In the bottom of the Dutch oven, spread ½ cup enchilada sauce.
4. Top with a layer of tortillas, chicken, corn, black beans, and more enchilada sauce. Repeat.
5. Top the whole casserole with shredded cheese and cover.

Grilling:

1. Preheat the EGG® to 375°F.
2. Place the Dutch oven on the grid of the EGG® and close the dome for 35-40 minutes or until the casserole is hot and bubbly.

HAM, POTATO, AND BROCCOLI CASSEROLE

This one-pot meal is ideal for leftover ham and comes together in a flash!

Preparation Time: 10 minutes
Cooking Temperature: 375°F
Cooking Time: 40 minutes
Serves: 6-8

Fresh Ingredients	From the Pantry
▸ 1 ½ cups cooked ham, cubed ▸ 1 ½ cups milk ▸ 1 cup grated cheddar cheese ▸ 1 (16 oz) package frozen O'Brien style hash browns ▸ 1 (16 oz) package frozen chopped broccoli	▸ ¼ cup mayonnaise ▸ 1 (10.75 oz) can cream of mushroom soup

Preparation:

1. Combine all ingredients, minus the cheese, in a large bowl and pour into a Dutch oven lined with a Dutch oven liner. Cover.

Grilling:

1. Preheat the EGG® to 375°F.
2. Place the Dutch oven on the grid and lower the dome.
3. Cook for 40 minutes.
4. Top the casserole with cheese and recover until the cheese melts. Serve hot.

LASAGNA

Lasagna in a Dutch oven? Of course! Just be sure to use a Dutch oven liner if you don't want to scrub it out of the pot for days afterward. By the way, of course you could make everything from scratch, but why not take a little help from the store for a weeknight supper?

Preparation Time: 30 minutes
Cooking Temperature: 350°F
Cooking Time: 1 hour, 15 minutes
Serves: 12

Fresh Ingredients

- 2 cups ricotta cheese
- 1 cup mozzarella cheese
- ½ cup grated parmesan cheese
- 1 egg

From the Pantry

- 1 tsp Italian seasoning
- 2 jars (24 oz) marinara sauce or 1 recipe Bolognese sauce
- 1 package no-boil lasagna noodles

Preparation:

1. In a medium sized bowl, combine ricotta, parmesan, Italian seasoning, and egg.
2. In a lined Dutch oven, pour 1 cup marinara sauce into the bottom of the pot. Layer noodles, ricotta mixture, and sauce in repeating layers ending with sauce.

Grilling:

1. Preheat the EGG® to 350°F.
2. Cover the Dutch oven and place it in the EGG® for 1 hour.
3. Remove from the EGG®, uncover, and top with mozzarella cheese.
4. Recover the Dutch oven and allow the lasagna to sit for 5 more minutes before uncovering.
5. Allow the lasagna to rest for 10 minutes before serving.

PAELLA

Traditional Spanish Paella has rabbit, small clams, and chorizo in it. Cubans use lobster, shrimp, and chicken. This version is a combination of the two but the protein is really a matter of taste.
Paella is a traditional Spanish rice dish made in a large, shallow pan over an open flame. A Dutch oven is the perfect vehicle for this delicious dish.

Preparation Time: 30 minutes
Cooking Temperature: 400°F
Cooking Time: 1 hour
Serves: 6-8

Fresh Ingredients	From the Pantry
▸ 2 lbs boneless, skinless chicken thighs	▸ 1 quart chicken stock
▸ 1 lb bulk chorizo	▸ 2 cups Arborio rice
▸ 1 lb shrimp, peeled and deveined	▸ 2 Tbsp olive oil
▸ 3 cloves garlic, minced	▸ 1 Tbsp smoked paprika
▸ 2 lemons, zested	▸ 1 tsp dried oregano
▸ 1 onion, chopped	▸ ½ tsp salt
▸ 1 bell pepper, chopped	▸ ¼ tsp crushed red chile flakes

Preparation:
1. In a large bowl, combine olive oil, paprika, oregano, salt, and chile flakes
2. Add chicken thighs and stir to combine. Refrigerate while assembling the rest of the ingredients.

Grilling:
1. Preheat the EGG® to 400°F with the Dutch oven on the grid.
2. Add chorizo into the Dutch oven and cook until browned. Drain all but 2 Tbsp of the fat.
3. Add chicken to the chorizo and brown on both sides.
4. Add onion and bell pepper and cook until vegetables begin to soften.
5. Add rice and garlic and cook for 3 minutes, until the rice begins to toast.
6. Add chicken stock, cover, and lower the dome for 25-30 minutes or until the rice is cooked through.
7. Remove the lid and allow the rice to toast for an additional 5 minutes. Serve.

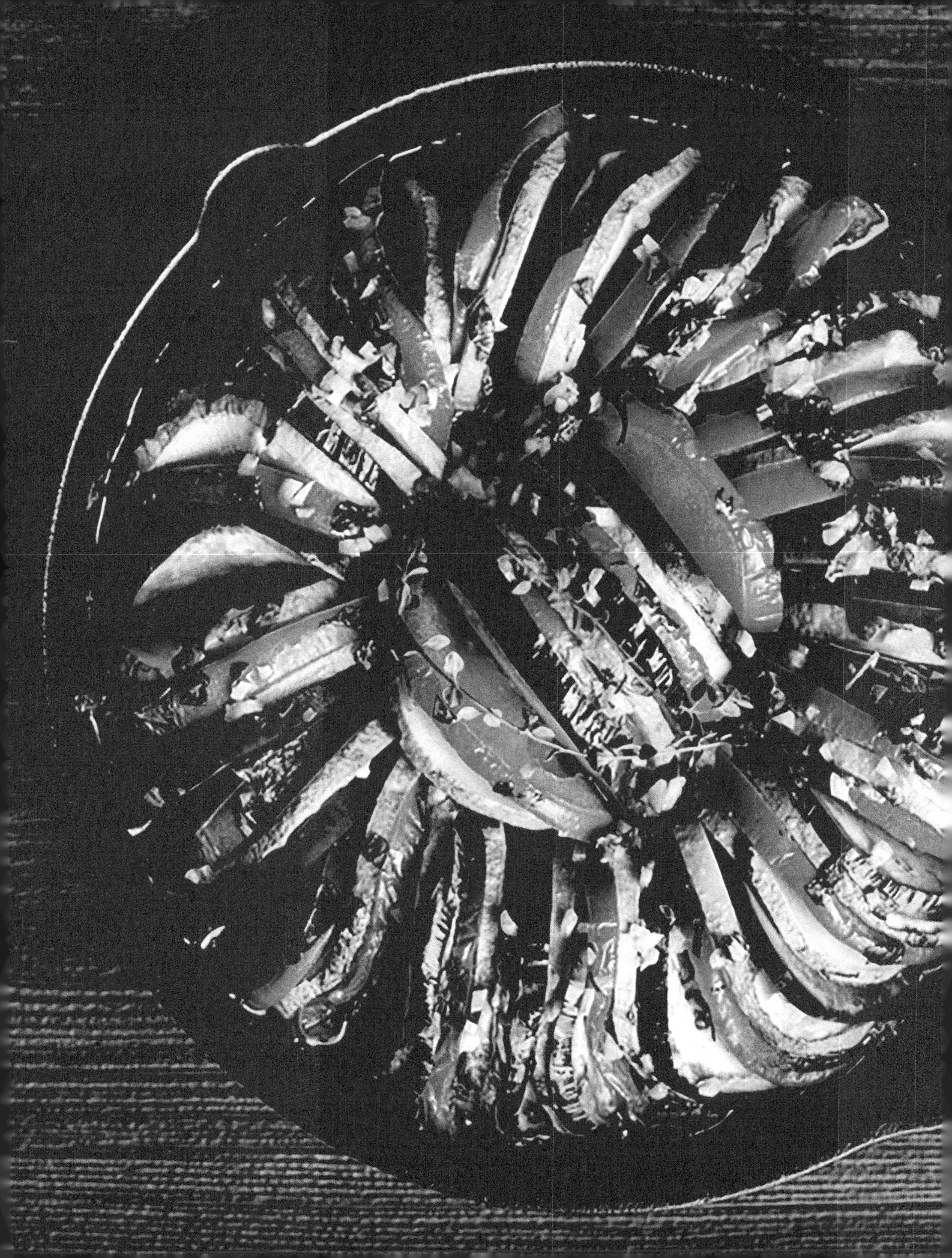

RATATOUILLE

No, it's not a movie about a rat. This French dish is ideal for the end of summer vegetables that come pouring out of the garden.

Preparation Time: 20 minutes
Cooking Temperature: 350°F
Cooking Time: 30 minutes
Serves: 4-6

Fresh Ingredients

- ½ cup fresh, shredded basil
- 2 cloves garlic, minced
- 2 large tomatoes, chopped
- 1 red bell pepper, chopped
- 1 large eggplant, peeled and cut into ½ inch cubes
- 1 onion, sliced thin

From the Pantry

- ¼ cup olive oil
- ¼ tsp dried oregano
- ¼ tsp dried thyme
- ¼ tsp fennel seeds
- ¾ tsp salt

On the Grill:

1. Preheat the EGG® to 350°F with the Dutch oven on the grid.
2. Add olive oil to the pot and toast oregano, thyme, and fennel for 1 minute.
3. Add onion and cook for 5 minutes or until the onion is soft.
4. Add remaining vegetables, cover, and lower the dome for 20-25 minutes.
5. Serve topped with basil.

SIDES

Burnt End Baked Beans
Cowboy Potatoes
Creamed Corn
Mac & Cheese
Potato, Squash, and Tomato Gratin
Sweet Potato Bake
Thanksgiving Stuffing

BURNT END BAKED BEANS

The end pieces of a smoked brisket are generally known as "burnt ends". This is a bit of a misnomer since they aren't actually burnt. Instead, they are full of smoky, meaty goodness - the perfect addition to baked beans.

Preparation Time: 30 minutes
Cooking Temperature: 350°F
Cooking Time: 30 minutes
Serves: 6-8

Fresh Ingredients

- 8 oz bacon, finely diced
- 2 cups "burnt ends" from smoked brisket, finely chopped
- ½ cup onion, minced
- 2 cloves garlic, minced

From the Pantry

- 1 cup favorite barbecue sauce (we like the Classic Texas Barbecue Sauce)
- 1 cup chicken broth
- ¼ cup brown sugar
- 2 Tbsp ketchup
- 1 Tbsp brown mustard
- 2 (15 oz) cans pinto beans, drained and rinsed

On the Grill:

1. Preheat the EGG® to 350°F with the Dutch oven on the grid.
2. Add the bacon to the Dutch oven and cook until crisp.
3. Add onion and garlic and cook 1 minute more.
4. Add remaining ingredients, stir to combine.
5. Cover and lower the dome for 1 hour. Serve hot.

COWBOY POTATOES

These potatoes are a surefire way to please a crowd.

Preparation Time: 20 minutes
Cooking Temperature: 375°F
Cooking Time: 1 hour
Serves: 6-8

Fresh Ingredients	From the Pantry
▸ 2 lbs Russet potatoes, very thinly sliced	▸ 1 tsp salt
▸ ½ lb bacon, diced	▸ ½ tsp pepper
▸ 2 cups cheddar cheese	
▸ 1 onion, thinly sliced	

On the Grill:

1. Preheat the EGG® to 375°F with the Dutch oven on the grid.
2. Add bacon and cook until crisp.
3. Add onion and cook for 3 minutes until it begins to soften.
4. Add sliced potatoes and gently stir to coat the potatoes in the bacon fat. Season with salt and pepper
5. Cover the Dutch oven and lower the dome for 40 minutes or until the potatoes are soft.
6. Remove the cover and top with cheese. Replace the cover and allow the Dutch oven to sit off the heat for another 2-3 minutes until the cheese is melted.

Dutch Oven Recipes | Sides

CREAMED CORN

Creamed corn is delicious on its own, but this uses sriracha and lime to make your taste buds wake up and take notice.

Preparation Time: 20 minutes
Cooking Temperature: 350°F
Cooking Time: 30 minutes
Serves: 6-8

Fresh Ingredients	From the Pantry
▸ 1 cup heavy cream	▸ 1 tsp sriracha
▸ ¼ cup parmesan cheese	▸ 1 tsp salt
▸ 2 (10 oz) packages of frozen sweet corn	▸ ½ tsp pepper
▸ 1 lime, zested and juiced	

Preparation:

1. Combine all ingredients, minus the lime juice in the Dutch oven.

Grilling:

1. Preheat the EGG® to 350°F.
2. Cover and close the dome for 30 minutes.
3. Add lime juice and serve.

MAC AND CHEESE

Using smoked cheese makes this mac and cheese extra special.

Preparation Time: 10 minutes
Cooking Temperature: 350°F
Cooking Time: 1 hour
Serves: 6-8

Fresh Ingredients	From the Pantry
▸ 1 lb smoked cheddar cheese, shredded, divided	▸ ½ lb elbow macaroni
▸ ¼ cup butter	▸ ¾ cup evaporated milk
▸ 2 eggs	▸ ¼ cup Panko breadcrumbs
	▸ 1 tsp salt
	▸ ¾ tsp dry mustard

Preparation:
1. In a large pot of boiling, salted water cook the macaroni according to package directions and drain.
2. In a separate bowl, whisk together the eggs, milk, hot sauce, salt, pepper, and mustard.

Grilling:
1. Preheat the EGG® to 350°F with the Dutch oven on the grid.
2. Melt the butter in the Dutch oven and place macaroni in the pot. Toss to coat.
3. Stir the egg and milk mixture into the pasta and add half of the cheese.
4. Continuously stir the mac and cheese for 3 minutes or until creamy.
5. Top with remaining cheese and Panko breadcrumbs.
6. Cover the Dutch oven, lower the dome, and cook for 20-25 minutes.
7. Serve immediately.

POTATO, SQUASH, AND TOMATO GRATIN

When tomatoes and squash are coming out your ears, put them to work in this delicious side dish.

Preparation Time: 20 minutes
Cooking Temperature: 375°F
Cooking Time: 35 minutes
Serves: 8-10

Fresh Ingredients	From the Pantry
▸ 1 lb Yukon gold potatoes, sliced ¼ inch thick	▸ ¼ cup olive oil, divided
▸ 1 lb yellow squash, sliced ¼ inch thick	▸ 2 Tbsp garlic, minced
▸ ½ cup shredded parmesan cheese	▸ 1 tsp salt
▸ 5 tomatoes, sliced ¼ inch thick	▸ ½ tsp pepper

Preparation:
1. Line the bottom of the Dutch oven with 2 Tbsp olive oil.
2. Layer potatoes on the bottom, topped with squash, and topped with tomatoes.
3. Season the tomatoes with salt, pepper, half of the garlic, and half of the parmesan cheese.
4. Repeat with remaining potatoes, squash, and tomatoes.
5. Season with salt, pepper, and remaining garlic.
6. Drizzle with remaining 2 Tbsp of olive oil and top with remaining parmesan cheese.

Grilling:
1. Preheat the EGG® to 375°F.
2. Place the Dutch oven, uncovered, into the EGG® and close the dome for 30-35 minutes or until the potatoes are cooked through.

SWEET POTATO BAKE

This sweet side dish is so yummy, you'll want to eat it for dessert!

Preparation Time: 40 minutes
Cooking Temperature: 400°F
Cooking Time: 20 minutes
Serves: 6-8

Sweet Potatoes	Topping
▸ 3 cups cooked and mashed sweet potatoes, cooled ▸ ½ cup butter, melted ▸ ½ cup sugar ▸ ½ cup milk ▸ 1 tsp vanilla extract ▸ ½ tsp salt ▸ 3 eggs, beaten	▸ 1 cup brown sugar ▸ ½ cup self-rising flour ▸ 1 cup chopped pecans ▸ 4 Tbsp butter at room temperature

Preparation:

1. Line the Dutch oven with a liner.
2. In a large bowl, combine souffle ingredients. Pour into the prepared Dutch oven.
3. In a separate small bowl, combine brown sugar, self-rising flour, chopped pecans, and room temperature butter until a crumbly mixture forms.
4. Sprinkle the crumb mixture over the sweet potato mixture.

Grilling:

1. Preheat the EGG® to 400°F.
2. Place the Dutch oven, uncovered, into the EGG® for 20-25 minutes or until the top is golden brown.

THANKSGIVING STUFFING

This delicious stuffing isn't just for Thanksgiving anymore.

Preparation Time: 20 minutes
Cooking Temperature: 375°F
Cooking Time: 45 minutes
Serves: 8-10

Fresh Ingredients	From the Pantry
▸ 8 ounces bulk breakfast sausage ▸ 4 cups cornbread, crumbled ▸ 4 cups sourdough bread, cut in cubes ▸ ½ cup onion, diced ▸ ½ cup celery, diced ▸ ½ cup Granny Smith apple, diced ▸ 4 Tbsp butter, softened	▸ 2 cups chicken broth ▸ 1 tsp poultry seasoning

On The Grill:

1. Preheat the EGG® to 375°F with the Dutch oven on the grid.
2. Cook breakfast sausage in the Dutch oven until brown.
3. Add onion and celery and cook until soft, about 5 minutes.
4. Add apple and cook an additional 2 minutes.
5. Stir in crumbled cornbread and sourdough bread cubes.
6. Pour chicken broth over mixture and season with poultry seasoning.
7. Dot the top of the stuffing with butter, cover, and lower the dome.
8. Cook the stuffing for 30 minutes. Serve warm.

DESSERTS

3 Ingredient Fruit Cobbler
Apple Cake
Bread Pudding
Brownies
Caramel Cinnamon Rolls
Death by Chocolate
Lemon Poppy Seed Cake
Peach Dutch Baby
Peanut Butter Bacon Bars
Upside Down Triple Berry Pie

3 INGREDIENT FRUIT COBBLER

This fruit cobbler couldn't be easier to throw together at the last minute. You probably already have the ingredients on hand. We like to use a combination of peaches and cherries, but you can use any canned fruit.

Preparation Time: 10 minutes
Cooking Temperature: 350°F
Cooking Time: 30 minutes
Serves: 8-10

Fresh Ingredients	From the Pantry
▸ 1 stick butter, sliced	▸ 2 (29 oz) cans fruit, drained but reserving ½ cup of the liquid ▸ 1 yellow cake mix

Preparation:
1. Line the Dutch oven with a liner
2. Pour fruit into the bottom of the Dutch oven with ½ cup of reserved liquid
3. Sprinkle the top with cake mix
4. Dot the top with butter.

Grilling:
1. Preheat the EGG® to 350°F.
2. Cover the Dutch oven and place on the grid of the EGG®.
3. Lower the dome for 30 minutes.
4. Allow the cobbler to sit for 10 minutes off the heat before serving.

TIP: Did you know a 12 ounce can of soda can perfectly replace the eggs, oil, and water for a cake mix?

APPLE CAKE

This delicious cake is the perfect end to a delightful fall meal

Preparation Time: 20 minutes
Cooking Temperature: 350°F
Cooking Time: 1 hour
Serves: 12

- 2 (21 oz) cans apple pie filling
- 1 (14 oz) jar caramel ice cream topping
- 1 box yellow cake mix, prepared according to package directions and mixed with 2 tsp cinnamon

Preparation:

1. Prepare cake according to package directions.
2. Line a Dutch oven with a liner.
3. Pour pie filling into the bottom of the Dutch oven.
4. Top with caramel ice cream topping.
5. Top with prepared cake mix.

Grilling:

1. Preheat the EGG® to 350°F.
2. Cover the Dutch oven and place on the grid of the EGG®.
3. Lower the dome and cook for 1 hour.
4. Serve warm with whipped cream or ice cream.

BREAD PUDDING

What could be better than warm bread pudding?

Preparation Time: 40 minutes
Cooking Temperature: 350°F
Cooking Time: 1 hour
Serves: 8-10

Fresh Ingredients	From the Pantry
▸ 1 ½ cups milk ▸ 10 eggs ▸ 1 loaf French bread, cut into 1 ½ inch cubes	▸ 1 ½ cups sugar ▸ 1 cup raisins (optional) ▸ 2 Tbsp vanilla ▸ 2 tsp cinnamon ▸ ½ tsp nutmeg ▸ ¼ tsp salt

Preparation:
1. Line the Dutch oven with a liner.
2. Place bread cubes and raisins into the Dutch oven.
3. In a large bowl, combine eggs, milk, sugar, vanilla, cinnamon, nutmeg, and salt.
4. Pour the mixture over the bread and raisins.
5. Allow the bread mixture to sit for 30 minutes.

Grilling:
1. Preheat the EGG® to 350°F.
2. Cover the Dutch oven, place it on the grid, and lower the dome for 1 hour.
3. Serve the bread pudding with vanilla ice cream or whipped cream.

BROWNIES

This recipe can easily be made with a boxed brownie mix, we just thought we'd give you the real deal.

Preparation Time: 10 minutes
Cooking Temperature: 350°F
Cooking Time: 25-30 minutes
Serves: 6

Brownie Batter	**Topping**
▸ 1 ½ cup flour ▸ 1 cup white sugar ▸ 1 cup brown sugar ▸ ¾ cup cocoa powder ▸ ½ cup butter, melted ▸ ¼ cup vegetable oil ▸ 2 tsp vanilla ▸ 1 tsp baking powder ▸ ½ tsp salt ▸ 4 eggs	▸ ½ cup chocolate chips ▸ ½ chip marshmallows

Preparation:
1. In a large bowl, combine butter, oil and sugars.
2. Add eggs, one at a time, stirring in between.
3. Add vanilla and stir.
4. Sift together cocoa powder, baking powder, and flour.
5. Add to the butter and egg mixture and stir until just combined.

Grilling:
1. Preheat the EGG® to 350°F.
2. Line the Dutch oven with a liner.
3. Pour the batter into the liner.
4. Cover the Dutch oven, place on the grid, and lower the dome for 25-30 minutes or until a toothpick inserted into the middle comes out clean.
5. Remove the lid, top the brownies with chocolate chips and marshmallows and replace the lid for 5 minutes until the toppings are melted.

CARAMEL CINNAMON ROLLS

Taking a little help from the frozen food section, these cinnamon rolls come apart in bite-sized pieces, perfect for popping.

Preparation Time: 20 minutes
Cooking Temperature: 350°F
Cooking Time: 30 minutes
Serves: 4

Fresh Ingredients	From the Pantry
▸ 18 frozen cinnamon rolls, thawed (you can also used canned cinnamon rolls)	▸ ½ cup brown sugar ▸ ½ cup graham cracker crumbs ▸ ½ cup caramel ice cream topping ▸ 1 tsp cinnamon

Preparation:

1. Line the Dutch oven with a liner.
2. Cut each cinnamon roll into 4 pieces and arrange them around the bottom of the Dutch oven.
3. In a separate bowl, combine brown sugar, graham cracker crumbs, and cinnamon.
4. Sprinkle some of the mixture over the layer of cinnamon rolls. Repeat.

Grilling:

1. Preheat the EGG® to 350°F.
2. Cover the Dutch oven and place it on the grid of the EGG®.
3. Lower the dome for 25-30 minutes or until the cinnamon rolls are golden brown.
4. Drizzle caramel ice cream topping over the warm rolls and serve.

DEATH BY CHOCOLATE

This strange recipe yields the best molten chocolate cake you have ever had. Just be sure to use a Dutch oven liner.

Preparation Time: 10 minutes
Cooking Temperature: 350°F
Cooking Time: 1 hour
Serves: 8-10

For the Cake	Toppings
▸ 1 chocolate cake mix, prepared according to package directions	▸ 2 cups chocolate chips ▸ 1 cup brown sugar ▸ 1 ½ cups water ▸ ½ cup cocoa powder ▸ 1 (10 oz) bag miniature marshmallows

Preparation:

1. Prepare cake mix according to package instructions.
2. Line the Dutch oven with a liner.
3. In a medium bowl, combine water, brown sugar, and cocoa powder.
4. Pour the mixture into the bottom of the Dutch oven.
5. Top with miniature marshmallows
6. Pour prepared cake mix on top.
7. Top with chocolate chips.

Grilling:

1. Preheat the EGG® to 350°F.
2. Place the lid on the Dutch oven and set on the grid of the EGG®.
3. Close the dome for 1 hour.
4. Remove the Dutch oven from the EGG®, uncover, and serve warm.

LEMON POPPY SEED CAKE

Doctoring up a boring old cake mix is as easy as adding a few extra ingredients.

Preparation Time: 10 minutes
Cooking Temperature: 350°F
Cooking Time: 30-45 minutes
Serves: 10-12

Cake	**Glaze**
▶ 1 tsp poppy seeds ▶ 2 lemons, zested and juiced ▶ 1 vanilla cake mix prepared according to package directions, substituting melted butter for oil and buttermilk for water	▶ 1 lb powdered sugar ▶ 4 ounces cream cheese ▶ 1 stick butter, softened ▶ ½ tsp vanilla ▶ ½ tsp lemon extract ▶ The juice and zest of 1 lemon

Preparation:

1. Prepare cake mix according to package directions, substituting melted butter for the oil and buttermilk for the water.
2. Add the lemon zest, lemon juice, and poppy seeds.
3. Line the Dutch oven with a liner.
4. Pour prepare cake mix into the liner and cover.

Grilling:

1. Preheat the EGG® to 350°F.
2. Place the Dutch oven on the grid and lower the dome for 30-40 minutes or until a toothpick inserted into the center comes out clean.
3. Meanwhile, combine glaze ingredients, adding milk to thin out the glaze if necessary.
4. Remove the cake from the EGG® and set aside to cool for 10 minutes before pouring glaze over the cake.
5. Serve warm.

PEACH DUTCH BABY

This impressive fruit pancake puffs while it cooks and deflates as it cools.

Preparation Time: 20 minutes
Cooking Temperature: 425°F
Cooking Time: 20-25 minutes
Serves: 8

Fresh Ingredients	From the Pantry
▸ 8 oz frozen peaches, thawed (or 3 ripe peaches, peeled and sliced) ▸ 1 cup whole milk ▸ 4 eggs	▸ 1 cup flour ▸ ¼ cup sugar ▸ ¼ cup butter ▸ 1 tsp vanilla ▸ 1 tsp cinnamon ▸ ½ tsp salt

Preparation:

1. In a blender, combine milk, flour, sugar, vanilla, cinnamon, salt, and eggs until smooth.

Grilling:

1. Preheat the EGG® to 425°F.
2. Place the Dutch oven on the grid of the EGG® and melt the butter.
3. Line the bottom of the pot with peaches and pour over milk and egg mixture.
4. Close the dome for 20 minutes or until the top of the Dutch Baby is golden brown.
5. Serve with a sprinkling of powdered sugar.

PEANUT BUTTER BACON BARS

Just when you think you have had enough bacon, we go and do something like this.

Preparation Time: 10 minutes
Cooking Temperature: 350°F
Cooking Time: 25 minutes
Serves: 8-10

For The Bar	**Toppings**
▸ 1 package peanut butter cookie mix ▸ ½ cup chopped peanuts ▸ ½ cup bacon, cooked and crumbled ▸ ⅓ cup vegetable oil ▸ 1 egg	▸ 1 cup semi-sweet chocolate chips ▸ ½ cup bacon, cooked and crumbled

Preparation:

1. Combine cookie mix, vegetable oil, egg, bacon, and peanuts and press into a lined Dutch oven.

Grilling:

1. Preheat the EGG® to 350°F.
2. Cover the Dutch oven and place on the grid.
3. Lower the dome for 25 minutes.
4. Remove the lid and top with chocolate chips.
5. Replace the cover for 5 minutes until the chocolate chips are melted.
6. Spread the chocolate over the bars to coat them evenly.
7. Top with remaining bacon.
8. Allow the bars to cool before cutting.

UPSIDE DOWN TRIPLE BERRY PIE

Cooking a pie with the crust on top always ensures it will remain flaky and delicious.

Preparation Time: 10 minutes
Cooking Temperature: 425°F
Cooking Time: 35 minutes
Serves: 8

Fresh Ingredients	From the Pantry
▸ 6 cups frozen triple berry mix ▸ 2 Tbsp lemon juice ▸ 1 refrigerated pie crust	▸ 1 cup sugar, divided ▸ 4 Tbsp cornstarch

Preparation:

1. Place a liner in the Dutch oven.
2. In a separate bowl, combine frozen berries with ¾ cup sugar, cornstarch, and lemon juice.
3. Pour berries into the bottom of the lined Dutch oven.
4. Unroll pie crust and place on top of berry mixture.
5. Cut 4 vent holes into the crust.
6. Sprinkle remaining sugar over the pie crust.

Grilling:

1. Preheat the EGG® to 425°F.
2. Cover the Dutch oven and place on the grid.
3. Lower the dome for 35 minutes or until the crust is golden and the berry mixture has thickened.
4. Cut the crust as you would any pie.
5. Serve a piece of crust topped with ice cream and a scoop of the thickened berry mixture.

BREAD & BISCUITS

3 Ingredient, No Knead Bread
Best Banana Bread
Buttermilk Biscuits
Honey Whole Wheat Bread
Sweet Zucchini Cornbread

4 INGREDIENT, NO KNEAD BREAD

This simple recipe yields perfect bread, every time. Keep the dough in your fridge for up to 3 days and have fresh bread anytime.

Preparation Time: 2 hours
Cooking Temperature: 425°F
Cooking Time: 30 minutes
Yields: 4 loaves

- 3 cups warm water
- 1 ½ Tbsp yeast
- 1 ½ Tbsp salt
- 6 ½ cups bread flour

Preparation:

1. In a 4 quart ice cream container, mix all ingredients until they come together. DO NOT KNEAD.
2. Cover, but do not seal the container and allow it to sit in a warm, dry place until it doubles in size, about 30 minutes.
3. Seal the container and place in the fridge for 1 hour.
4. Place a sheet of parchment paper in the bottom of the Dutch oven.
5. Pinch off ¼ of the dough and form into a ball.
6. Place the ball on the parchment paper and allow it to rest while the EGG® heats.

Grilling:

1. Preheat the EGG® to 425°F.
2. Score the top of the dough ball with an "X".
3. Cover the Dutch oven and place it on the grid of the EGG®.
4. Lower the Dome for 30 minutes.
5. Remove the bread from the Dutch oven and allow it to cool before slicing.

BEST BANANA BREAD

Have brown bananas? Don't throw them away. Use them in this super moist, not-too-sweet banana bread.

Preparation Time: 10 minutes
Cooking Temperature: 350°F
Cooking Time: 30-40 minutes
Serves: 6-8

Fresh Ingredients	From the Pantry
▸ 1 cup plain yogurt	▸ 2 cups flour
▸ ¼ cup butter	▸ ⅔ cup sugar
▸ 3 very ripe bananas, peeled	▸ ¾ tsp salt
▸ 2 eggs	▸ ½ tsp vanilla extract
	▸ ½ tsp baking soda
	▸ ¼ tsp baking powder

Preparation:

1. In a blender, combine bananas, yogurt, sugar, butter, vanilla, and eggs until smooth.
2. In a large bowl, sift together flour, salt, baking powder, and baking soda.
3. Gradually add the wet ingredients into the dry ingredients and gently stir to combine. DO NOT OVER MIX.
4. Line a Dutch oven with a liner.
5. Pour batter into the Dutch oven and cover.

Grilling:

1. Preheat the EGG® to 350°F and place the Dutch oven on the grid.
2. Lower the dome for 30 minutes or until a toothpick inserted into the center comes out clean.

BUTTERMILK BISCUITS

Once you realize how easy it is to make tall, fluffy biscuits, you'll never buy them in a can again.

Preparation Time: 10 minutes
Cooking Temperature: 425°F
Cooking Time: 12-15 minutes
Yields: 12 biscuits

Fresh Ingredients	From the Pantry
▸ ¾ cup buttermilk ▸ ½ cup butter, cut into ½ inch cubes	▸ 3 cups flour ▸ 1 ½ tsp baking powder ▸ ½ tsp salt

Preparation:

1. In the bowl of a food processor, combine flour, baking powder, salt and butter and pulse until the butter is the size of small peas.
2. With the food processor going, stream in buttermilk until the dough just comes together.
3. Turn out on a floured surface.
4. Pat the dough to ½ inch thickness and fold in half.
5. Pat the dough to ½ inch thickness and fold in half again.
6. Pat the dough a third time to ½ inch thickness.
7. Using a pizza cutter, cut the dough into 12 square biscuits.
8. Place a sheet of parchment in the bottom of the Dutch oven.
9. Place biscuits on the bottom of the Dutch oven, being careful that they do not touch. (You may have to do this in two batches.)

Grilling:

1. Preheat the EGG® to 425°F.
2. Cover the Dutch oven with the lid and place on the grid.
3. Lower the dome for 12-15 minutes.
4. Biscuits are done when they are golden brown. Serve with butter, honey, or jam.

HONEY WHOLE WHEAT BREAD

This delicious bread is the perfect alternative to boring sandwich slices.

Preparation Time: 2 hours
Cooking Temperature: 425°F
Cooking Time: 30 minutes
Yields: 2 loaves

Fresh Ingredients	From the Pantry
▸ 1 ½ cup water	▸ 2 ¼ c bread flour ▸ ¾ cup whole wheat flour ▸ 2 Tbsp honey ▸ 1 ½ tsp salt ▸ 1 ½ tsp yeast

Preparation:

1. In a large bowl with a lid, combine water and honey until the honey is dissolved.
2. In a separate bowl, combine flours, salt, and yeast.
3. Stir the dry ingredients into the wet ingredients until well combined. DO NOT KNEAD.
4. Allow the dough to sit in a warm, dry place until it doubles in size, about 30 minutes.
5. Refrigerate the dough for 1 hour or up to 3 days.
6. Remove the dough from the fridge and form half into a round loaf.
7. Place a sheet of parchment paper in the bottom of the Dutch oven and place the loaf on top.

Grilling:

1. Preheat the EGG® to 425°F.
2. Score the top of the loaf with an "X", cover, and place the Dutch oven on the grid.
3. Lower the dome for 30 minutes.
4. Carefully remove the loaf from the Dutch oven and allow it to cool before slicing.

A PERSONAL INVITATION TO JOIN THE FIRESIDE PIT

Hi BBQ Friend,

Thank you for checking out my book. I think you'll love it.

I'm very grateful to have wonderful readers who support us, so I'm going to extend to you an invitation to join my exclusive club—**the Fireside Pit.**

This is a brand new oer I created to see whether folks would be interested in seeing more great products from me. It will be like a reside chat by the barbecue pit.

Once in a while, you will receive promotional offers on top-of-the-line products that either I sell or ones from companies I personally trust.

Membership is always free, even if you decide to leave and come back later.

What do Fireside Pit Members get?

1. Get recipes, secrets and techniques straight from the pros right to your inbox
2. Get printable BBQ information guides and charts
3. Incredible offers on popular bbq and kitchen products like the one featured below

Sign Up At fpclub.smokeandgrillmeat.com

Made in the USA
Middletown, DE
05 December 2023